SERGEI AKSAKOV
and Russian Pastoral

Studies of the Russian Institute  Columbia University

SERGEI AKSAKOV
and Russian
Pastoral

Andrew R. Durkin

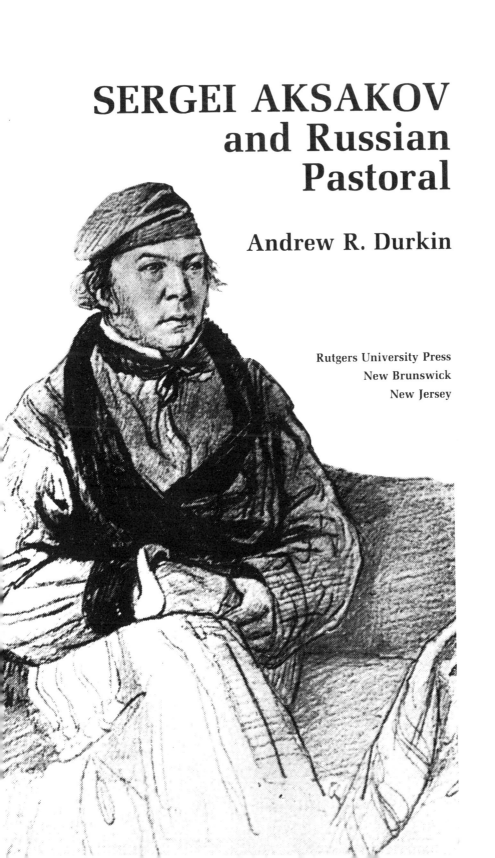

Rutgers University Press
New Brunswick
New Jersey

To my parents

The Russian Institute of Columbia University
sponsors the *Studies of the Russian Institute*
in the belief that their publication contrib-
utes to scholarly research and public understanding. In this way the Institute, while
not necessarily endorsing their conclusions,
is pleased to make available the results of
some of the research conducted under its
auspices. A list of the *Studies of the Russian
Institute* appears at the back of the book.

Title-page illustration: S. T. Aksakov, part of a sketch
by E. A. Dmitriev-Mamonov (ca. 1840)

Library of Congress Cataloging in Publication Data

Durkin, Andrew R., 1945–
Sergei Aksakov and Russian pastoral.

Bibliography: p.
Includes index.
1. Aksakov, S. T. (Sergeï Timofeevich), 1791–1859—
Criticism and interpretation. I. Title.
PG3321.A5Z64   891.73′3   81–23384
ISBN 0–8135–0954–8   AACR2

Contents

Acknowledgments

I owe debts of gratitude to many people who in substantial ways have aided me at various stages of the growth of this study. The late Professor Rufus W. Mathewson, Jr., professor of Russian literature at Columbia University, enthusiastically encouraged my initial work on Aksakov. Professor William E. Harkins, as director of a dissertation on Aksakov, offered many suggestions that greatly clarified both my ideas and their expression. Professor Robert A. Maguire, also of Columbia, offered much-appreciated concern and advice during the lengthy metamorphosis of dissertation into monograph. Lynn Solotaroff of the Russian Institute, Columbia University, greatly facilitated many practical matters for an inexperienced author. The merits of this study I owe in large part to these people; its shortcomings are my own, but would certainly be greater without their interest and assistance.

Support by several institutions must also be acknowledged. The International Research and Exchange Board (IREX) made possible a year of research and study in the Soviet Union. The Russian Institute of Columbia University provided a year of uninterrupted work on the topic while it was still in the dissertation stage. Both the American Council of Learned Societies and the Office of Research and Graduate Development of Indiana University awarded grant-in-aid at crucial junctures. I would also like to thank the editors of *Ulbandus Review* for permission to use material which appeared, in a somewhat different form, in my article "Pastoral in Aksakov: The Transformation of Poetry," in the fall 1979 issue of *Ulbandus Review*, in memory of Professor Mathewson.

I would also like to thank colleagues, students, and friends at Indiana University; in particular, Professors C. H. van Schooneveld, William B. Edgerton, Michael Holquist, Eva Kagan-Kans, and Felix J. Oinas for their concern for a younger colleague; Marilyn Nelson for meticulous typing of sections of the manuscript; Maria G. Carlson, Henry R. Cooper, Jr., Constance Link, B.R. Nagle, Cecil W. Wooten, and Hugh M. Lee for their interest and friendship.

Finally, my sincerest gratitude to my parents, to whom this book is dedicated, for their unfailing trust.

A Note on Transliterations, Translations, and Abbreviations

I have used the Library of Congress system of transliteration of the Cyrillic alphabet, with some simplifications, as the most reasonable compromise between the absolute precision desired by the specialist and the accessibility necessary for the non-specialist. Thus I have omitted the apostrophe as an indication of the Russian soft sign in a few frequently occuring names (thus Gogol rather than Gogol'). In the case of some well-known names, I have used the form in general use in English (Herzen rather than Gertsen), while adhering to the LC version when it seemed as unproblematic for the general reader as other common renderings (thus Dostoevskii and Tolstoi rather than Dostoevsky or Tolstoy). Translations from the Russian are my own unless otherwise indicated.

The following abbreviations are used for the principal archival repositories in the Soviet Union for unpublished letters, manuscripts, and other Aksakov material.

TsGALI   Central Government Archive of Literature and Art, Moscow (Tsentral'nyi gosudarstvennyi arkhiv literatury i iskusstva)

PD   Institute of Russian Literature and Art, Pushkin House, Leningrad (Institut russkoi literatury i iskusstva, Pushkinskii dom)

LL   Manuscript Division of the Lenin Library, Moscow (Rukopisnyi otdel, Biblioteka imeni Lenina)

Introduction

Outside Russia, Sergei Timofeevich Aksakov (1791–1859) is less well known than some of his contemporaries in Russian prose. Yet he ranks with Ivan Turgenev, Ivan Goncharov, Fedor Dostoevskii, and Lev Tolstoi as a major figure in the Age of Realism, that extraordinary outpouring of fiction in Russia that lasted from the 1840s to the 1880s. Within this period, Turgenev's *Fathers and Sons* (1862) divides the works of the forties and fifties—more intimate in form and theme—from the novels of the sixties and seventies, with their sweeping social and philosophical concerns. Both biographically and artistically, Aksakov belongs entirely to the earlier phase and in certain respects is its most representative figure. In his day, his works were not only highly esteemed by critics and other writers but also extremely popular with the Russian reading public. He once commented to M. P. Pogodin, editor of the *Muscovite (Moskvitianin)*, the journal in which much of his writing appeared, that readers would seek out a work of his, regardless of where the journal placed it. This was no empty boast on Aksakov's part but an accurate assessment of his standing with his audience. The first edition of *Family Chronicle* in 1856 was followed by a second, expanded edition within a year, and his first book, *Notes on Fishing* (1846), went through several editions in Aksakov's lifetime, indicating an appeal far greater than its title would suggest.

Nor has this popularity proved to be ephemeral. Writing in the 1890s, the historian of Russian culture Pavel Miliukov pointed out that *Family Chronicle* had become firmly entrenched in literature courses and formed an inseparable part of everyone's childhood memories, a situation that has changed little for Russian readers today. Despite a virtual ban on publication of Aksakov's works in the early decades of the Soviet period, both scholarly and popular editions of his major works have appeared intermittently since the death of Stalin, attesting to a continued demand for those works, although the official attitude toward their author is still rather hesitant.

The perennial appeal of Aksakov's works for Russian readers at first seems surprising, considering that they deemphasize such traditional features of fiction, at least of the novel, as elaborate plot, complex characterization, and narrative continuity. In fact, judged by criteria derived from and applicable to the novel, Aksakov's works seem archaic or even rudimentary. Gauged by other standards, however, his "deficiencies" are more likely to become merits. For his works belong not so much to the tradition of the novel as to that of pastoral prose—the nineteenth century's continuation and modification of the themes and, in part, the methods of pastoral verse. Aksakov himself admitted to an inability to invent, to create pure fiction; consequently, virtually all his works draw directly on his own experience. Such an overt link with personal biography, however carefully selected and shaped that biography may be, is one of the hallmarks of pastoral, in both prose and verse, particularly in the nineteenth and twentieth centuries. As pastoral prose, Aksakov's works appeal on two levels: aesthetically, through the intimate, subtle, and poetic quality of the prose; and psychologically, through the evocation of an idyllically remote, natural, and simplified world which is yet familiar and which seems just beyond the horizon of a present grown oppressive in its complexity, modernity, and artificiality. Furthermore, like most modern pastoral writing, Aksakov's is concrete and localized, situated within the world of Russian nature, which Aksakov's art transforms into a source of aesthetic value.

Although one can find pastoral elements in many authors of the period, such as Nikolai Gogol, Goncharov, and Tolstoi, Aksakov was the first Russian writer whose works were almost exclusively pastoral. The relationship between man and nature, the tension between nature and society, which are often alluded to in the fiction of Turgenev, Tolstoi, Goncharov, and others, become the most significant themes in Aksakov's. He thus explores fully a component of the Russian literary imagination that informs much of nineteenth-century Russian fiction. Indeed, the pastoral tradition he helped inaugurate in Russia remains a viable mode down to the present, with echoes in writers as disparate as Anton Chekhov, Boris Pasternak, and Vladimir Nabokov.

In the course of this study, the expression of Aksakov's pastoral vision in individual works—its specific qualities, development, and the means by which it is created—will be explored in greater detail. But for now it might be well to consider how Aksakov has fared with the critics and scholars. If his popularity with readers has been considerable and enduring, it also has been direct, virtually unmediated by Russian critics. Indeed, comments on Aksakov by Russian and Soviet critics and scholars have been rather meager and often mediocre as well. The public's immediate acceptance of and continued interest in Aksakov's works, as well as its tendency sometimes to relegate them to children's reading, partly account for this dearth of criticism. Aksakov's works immediately became part of the accepted canon, so there was no need (at least with respect to Russian readers) to rescue them from undeserved obscurity, nor, conversely, to cast them from an unmerited pedestal. Nevertheless, although literary criticism in Russia has, since the mid-nineteenth century, itself been a flourishing and often highly creative intellectual enterprise, we might infer that its relative lack of interest in Aksakov stems from a failure to perceive him correctly. Criticism has considered him either a memorist or, more rarely, a creator of fiction, rather than an author of pastoral.

In fairness to the critics, one should point out that as a writer Aksakov presents a number of anomalous features, not the least of which is his literary biography itself. In an age that valued literary precocity as a sign of creative genius, and had such examples of early literary success as Mikhail Lermontov, Gogol, Tolstoi, and Dostoevskii, Aksakov's late-blooming talent seems not only idiosyncratic but a willful breach of literary-biographical etiquette. In his early years, which were concerned primarily with family and a modest career, Aksakov exhibited (and this continued well into middle age) only a dilettante's interest in literature and theater. Even in these he usually aligned himself with the most conservative literary camp. Partly because we lack evidence, we can only make conjectures as to how Aksakov developed from an adherent of rather conservative literary views into a talent that felt itself at home in the new, realistic prose literature of the forties and fifties. For whatever reasons, he emerged as a mature, accomplished, and prolific author only in the last fifteen years of his life.

More important than the problems raised by the fact of Aksakov's late development are those that criticism has created for itself by failing to appreciate fully the pastoral nature of Aksakov's art. To a great extent the interpretation of Aksakov's works in Russia and the Soviet Union has remained within the boundaries established by the earliest commentary on him. Both major critical camps of the day, the utilitarian and the aesthetic, sought to claim Aksakov's works during the debates that raged in the major Russian journals in the 1850s over the social value of art. The utilitarian position on Aksakov, which was promulgated by the fiery radical critic N. A. Dobroliubov, has remained the dominant interpretation to the present; this view in general stresses the importance of art as a source of knowledge that prompts political or social action. As read by Dobroliubov, Aksakov's works, being basically memoiristic in form, afforded an unwittingly accurate picture of serfdom and its contradictions in the past and, by implication, in the present. Thus, whatever Aksakov's purpose, Dobroliubov believed his works could further the struggle against the status quo by exposing the errors of the old ways. In Dobroliubov's attempt to make Aksakov, who had close personal ties with the Slavophiles, a radical *malgré lui*, one senses a desire to make political capital of the popularity Aksakov had achieved with his pictures of the gentry of the past. Dobroliubov focused on certain incidents, such as the tyrannical Kurolesov's mistreatment of his serfs in chapter 2 of *Family Chronicle*, or young Sergei's inability to comprehend social relations under serfdom in the early chapters of *Years of Childhood*. Despite evidence to the contrary, such passages, few in number and often considered out of context, have been central to recurrent efforts by critics of a "progressive" bent to "save" Aksakov. For instance, the Kurolesov chapter was issued as a separate brochure in the early 1920s; together with similar passages it figures prominently in the Soviet treatment of Aksakov. Apart from historical illustrations or social messages, the problem of value in Aksakov—of the permanent significance of art—is not broached in such criticism.

Opposed to Dobroliubov's point of view was that of Pavel Annenkov and other aesthetic critics who, in seeking to dissociate art entirely from any direct social purpose or concern, emphasized the tranquility and contemplative quality of Aksakov's world. While such critics rightly pointed out both Aksakov's striking use of realistic detail and his impartiality toward his characters, their categorization of his works as epic in quality, while assuring Aksakov permanent relevance, seems somewhat less tenable. Rather than being a direct reaction to the texts, the aesthetic critics' allusion to epic probably reflects the tendency of the time to search for a continuation of the epic in modern prose works, as Aksakov's own son Konstantin had done with regard to Gogol's *Dead Souls* when it appeared in 1842. An analogue to Aksakov's prose works can indeed be found in classical verse, but the analogue is pastoral, not epic. Identification with traditional epic fails to account for the emotional and psychological appeal of Aksakov's works or to locate that appeal in the author's personal, even intimate, rendering of experience. Of the commentaries offered by Aksakov's contemporaries, only an obituary notice by his friend, the Slavophile philosopher A. S. Khomiakov, dwelt on this point. Khomiakov's brief tribute, though less well known or influential than Dobroliubov's or Annenkov's discussions, remains one of the most perceptive early statements on Aksakov. The early Aksakov criticism, in which his works often become obscured by abstractions and polemics, has probably done more to shape the views of critics than to determine the response of readers, either in the nineteenth century or subsequently.

The criticism that appeared in later decades was not extensive and often tended to follow paths laid out by the critics of the 1850s. In the late nineteenth and early twentieth centuries, Aksakov, along with other nineteenth-century writers such as Aleksandr Pushkin and Gogol, became the object of study by academic historians of culture such as V. P. Ostrogorskii and V. I. Shenrok. Curators of the cultural tradition rather than literary critics, they advanced no new interpretations of Aksakov, but did publish important biographical material, including Aksakov's correspondence with Gogol and with Turgenev. The only serious attempt at this time to arrive at an understanding of Aksakov was made by Pavel Miliukov, who sought to define his place within Russian cultural history. Miliukov's objections to overemphasizing Aksakov's links with Gogol and with Slavophilism are still pertinent, though Miliukov says little about Aksakov's works specifically as literature.

The historical and biographical approach of the critics at the turn of the century was followed by criticism rooted in the new literary movements that swept Russia before and after the Revolution (Symbolism, Acmeism, and Futurism, with its critical ally, Formalism). Interested in various ways in the philosophical and formal elements of literature, particularly of verse, adherents of these critical schools found little of interest in Aksakov, whose works must have seemed to them the embodiment of the nineteenth-century realist prose tradition they had rejected.

After the imposition of a single, official critical approach in the 1930s, Soviet interpretation of Aksakov has stayed well within the limits set by Dobroliubov, whose views have been accepted as normative and definitive. The only substantial study of Aksakov, S. I. Mashinskii's biography-cum-criticism, which first appeared in 1961, draws on Dobroliubov for its ideological underpinnings whenever questions of interpretation or value arise, while using the historical-biographical approach of the late nineteenth century in its treatment of Aksakov's life, primarily in its public aspect. Little sense of Aksakov as an artist or as a person emerges. Reading such criticism, one feels that its purpose is not so much to enhance our understanding of Aksakov and his work as to save the appearances. It seeks to reclaim for official orthodoxy classic works of Russian literature by an author whose political sympathies and idyllic pictures of gentry life should exclude him from the approved pantheon. Such social or political criticism fails to touch the heart of the matter. Aksakov appeals to the modern reader, Soviet or otherwise, through his ability to suggest a world of value apart from social reality, apart from historical contingency—a world of timeless meaning available to people in the modern world through the twin sources of nature and personal memory.

In sum, despite his unquestioned place in the development of Russian Realism and his continued and deserved popularity with readers, Aksakov has resisted criticism. While this fact is partly attributable to the limitations of his critics and their approaches, part of the problem (if it can be termed one) lies with Aksakov himself. His techniques are never obvious or overt, his themes never stridently announced. His effects are contextual, cumulative, and essentially poetic, in this respect not unlike those of Chekhov, who also has fared ill at the hands of the critics. The effectiveness of Aksakov's text depends in large measure on the reader himself, who is offered not so much a challenge to the intellect as a subtle invitation to the senses and emotions. The reader Aksakov addresses is not the adherent of a critical school, but a collaborator in the creative unfolding of experience.

The present study seeks to elucidate, as far as possible, the manner in which that experience is conveyed, the techniques by which Aksakov captivates his readers. In a certain sense, it is an attempt to account for my own fascination with his works. For that reason I have used a rather eclectic approach, since it allows for a fuller understanding of the works themselves. I have begun by treating the problem of Aksakov's literary biography: why an obscure Russian gentleman, bureaucrat, and paterfamilias should, in his last decades, have produced such powerful works. After briefly surveying his early works in verse and his first venture into original prose, I discuss his major works in roughly chronological order, which fortuitously provides a thematic order: the works of the 1840s on hunting, the "historical" works that culminated in *Family Chronicle*, and finally the writings on childhood, particularly *Years of Childhood*, where Aksakov's emotional intensity and artistic mastery reached their peak. I have also devoted attention to some of Aksakov's lesser-known works, partly to spark new interest in them and partly because I am convinced that his famous trilogy (*Family Chronicle, Years of Childhood,* and *Reminiscences*) requires the context of his entire creative output for full understanding.

Aksakov's works reveal certain basic preoccupations with the themes of nature, the past, and childhood, which are common both to the Russian literary tradition and to modern consciousness. From our vantage point in the late twentieth century, a time with its own self-conscious pastoralism and radical nostalgia, we may be able to appreciate more fully Aksakov's formulation and exploration of these themes. Readers of this study should approach it not as an exhaustive analysis of the works of a significant Russian writer, but as a guide to a first or fuller reading of Sergei Timofeevich Aksakov and to a fuller awareness of the modern pastoral myth he helped to form.

1

A Russian Life

Sergei Timofeevich Aksakov has, in a sense, preempted attempts at biography.[1] He himself has in his own writings provided extensive information, most of it available from no other source, on certain aspects of his life, especially his younger years. The copiousness of his information is somewhat offset by his own reticence regarding his later years; those few of his works pertaining to them focus more on his acquaintances, notably Gogol, than on himself. Other sources such as letters only partially fill the gaps. Most surviving letters date from the last fifteen years of Aksakov's life, when he was in semiretirement and often in ill health.[2] This was also the period of greatest literary creativity for Aksakov, so his letters often contain comments of interest to the critic of his works. Their yield is somewhat less for the biographer. In the extensive memoir literature that records the intellectual ferment of the 1840s and 1850s in Russia, Sergei Timofeevich, a man of

1. Aksakov treats his childhood and student years in *Years of Childhood of Young Bagrov* (*Detskie gody Bagrova-vnuka*) and *Reminiscences* (*Vospominaniia*). He treats episodes in his later years in various works, including "Memoir of A. S. Shishkov" ("Vospominanie ob A. S. Shishkove"), "Acquaintance with Derzhavin" ("Znakomstvo s Derzhavinym"), *Literary and Theatrical Memoirs* (*Literaturnye i teatral'nye vospominaniia*), and several shorter works. All of these are in the basic modern edition of *Sobranie sochinenii* in four volumes (Moscow: GIKhL, 1955–1956). There are also several biographies of Aksakov in Russian; these include A. S. Arkhangel'skii, "S. T. Aksakov: Detstvo i studenchestvo" and V. I. Shenrok, "S. T. Aksakov i ego sem'ia." The most recent and most extensive treatment is S. M. Mashinskii, *S. T. Aksakov: Zhizn' i tvorchestvo*, in two editions. References to S. I. Mashinskii's work will be to the second, expanded edition.

2. Aksakov's correspondence with his son Ivan is contained in part in footnotes to vols. 1 and 2 of *I. S. Aksakov v ego pis'makh*. His letters to Gogol are contained in Aksakov's *History of My Acquaintance with Gogol* (*Istoriia moego znakomstva s Gogolem*), in vol. 3 of *Sobranie sochinenii*. Aksakov's letters to Turgenev as well as those of his sons to Turgenev can be found in L. N. Maikov, ed., "Pis'ma S. T., K. S., i I. S. Aksakovykh k I. S. Turgenevu."

the generation prior to the one that now dominated the drawing-room debates of thinking Moscow, appears briefly, as the father of two important Slavophiles and as a host of social gatherings of the Moscow elite. On the basis of the information we do possess, Aksakov's life emerges as uneventful, even placid, with few sudden changes or moments of high drama. A sketch of Aksakov's life thus must skirt several dangers; repetition of Aksakov's own works, which depict his background and early life with a fullness and richness that still captivate readers, is just as undesirable as the inflation of a quiet life and its minutiae into something it was not. Since this study focuses primarily on Aksakov's works, I will here consider his life briefly, devoting most attention to certain topics, such as his family or his relations with the Slavophiles, that his own works do not treat in any detail but that are important both for his life and his works. Finally I will speculate (all that is possible, given the scanty evidence) on a possible reason for Aksakov's emergence as a major writer so late in life.

Sergei Timofeevich Aksakov was born 20 September 1791 (old style)[3] in Ufa, the administrative center of Orenburg Province in the southern Urals, a rather remote area in the eighteenth century. His father, Timofei Stepanovich Aksakov, held the post of procurator of the provincial court (zemskii sud). The Aksakov family, though neither prominent nor particularly cultured, proudly claimed a noble pedigree of considerable antiquity.[4] Sergei's mother, Maria Nikolaevna, née Zubova, was from a rather different social background. Her father was a prominent official in Ufa, but one who had risen on merit through the bureaucracy, with no claim to traditional nobility; his father, Aksakov's great-grandfather, had been a Cossack. According to Sergei Timofeevich, his mother's intelligence and savoir-faire considerably surpassed his father's, and both her lowly origins and relative sophistication gave rise to considerable hostility toward her on the part of her husband's family, who were pro-

3. All Russian dates prior to the Revolution are old style, that is, according to the Julian calendar. In the eighteenth century, dates are eleven days behind those of the Gregorian calendar; in the nineteenth century they are twelve days behind.
4. The name Aksakov itself was only some two hundred and fifty years old, deriving from Oksak ("lame" in Tartar). In the fifteenth century, when many Tartars were espousing Russian allegiance and their names were becoming Russian surnames, the nickname was adopted by a member of the princely Veniaminov (or Veliaminov) family, which traced its origins back to a Norwegian prince who settled in Kiev in 1027.

vincial but wary of any diminution of their claim to status based on heredity. Although Aksakov's portrait of his mother may be idealized, she seems to have been very much an intelligent, forceful, relatively well-educated, and beautiful woman. Her awareness of a wider horizon was communicated to her son at an early age and ultimately prevented him from becoming a provincial nonentity in the mold of his paternal forebears.

Aksakov spent his earliest years in Ufa and at Novoe Aksakovo (New Aksakovo), also known simply as Aksakovo, the estate his paternal grandfather had carved out for himself on the Buguruslan River some 240 versts (about 160 miles) from Ufa. According to his memoirs, Aksakov's childhood was marked by several episodes of serious illness, and while recuperating he developed an early inclination for omnivorous reading; under his father's tutelage, he also became passionately devoted to angling and hunting in all its forms. Thus the seeds both of Aksakov's love of nature and his love of literature were planted quite early.

After some elementary instruction by his parents, Sergei entered the gymnasium at Kazan in January 1801. Such early and radical separation of the young male gentry from their families for purposes of schooling was the norm in eighteenth-century Russia, but he soon fell ill, primarily as a result of the emotional shock of separation from his mother, and withdrew till the spring of 1802.[5] The Kazan gymnasium was partially reorganized as a university in 1804 (making it the second oldest Russian university, after Moscow's, founded in 1755), so Aksakov remained there for three more years. As Aksakov himself freely admitted, his education could hardly be termed deep or thorough even for its day, taking place as it did in a provincial institution in the process of reorganization; his son Ivan states that his father was "not only not learned, but did not even possess an adequate level of education."[6]

---

5. There seems to be some confusion on Aksakov's part on this matter in his *Reminiscences* (1856); according to Mashinskii, drawing on documents in Kazan, Aksakov in fact returned to the gymnasium in the spring of 1802, not the fall of 1801, as he states. See Aksakov, *Vospominaniia*, in *Sobranie sochinenii*, 2:470–471 and Mashinskii, *S. T. Aksakov*, 2d ed., p. 18. The change may in part be for artistic reasons.

6. Ivan Aksakov, "Ocherk semeinogo byta Aksakovykh," in *I. S. Aksakov v ego pis'makh*, 1:13. Ivan Aksakov began this sketch as part of a projected biography of his late brother Konstantin, but never completed more than a few pages on the Aksakovs' home life.

Although he was apparently an interested and enthusiastic student, little of the specifics of his formal education seems to have had a lasting effect on Aksakov. More important were the social aspects of his schooling and what would today be classified as extracurricular activities. Despite its distance from the centers of Russian literary culture, the literary battles of the capitals were followed closely by both faculty and students at Kazan. Aksakov's teachers were opposed to the vogue for Sentimentalism, as propagated in Russia by Nikolai Karamzin and his followers, and favored more traditional and civic-minded forms of literary expression. After a brief flirtation with the subjective sentiment and delicate style of the Karamzinians (some verse by Aksakov in this manner survives in a student journal from Kazan),[7] Aksakov was "set on the proper path" by his teacher of Slavonic grammar, N. M. Ibragimov.[8] The proper path emphasized decorum, avoidance of subjective indulgence of feeling, and the lofty diction of the odes of Mikhail Lomonosov. The encounter with Karamzinism and the turning away from it are not without some relevance, albeit remote, to Aksakov's late works. Despite his delicately vague and sentimental style, Karamzin was the first Russian writer to focus on the individual and subjective, particularly as revealed in the receptive psyche's reaction to nature. While Aksakov, drawing in part on his formal education, was a lifelong foe of the mellifluously vague, his emphasis on the individual's aesthetic response to nature and his interest, particularly in *Years of Childhood,* in the realm of subjective experience echo Karamzin, who first introduced such themes into Russian literature. One of the first treatments of childhood as an "Arcadia of life" in Russian literature can be found in Karamzin's story of 1803, "A Knight of Our Time" ("Rytsar' nashego vremeni").

The influence of Admiral A. S. Shishkov's opposing literary school was stronger at Kazan, and was reinforced by Aksakov's later personal associations, notably with the admiral himself. Particularly in attitudes toward style, traces of Shishkov's principles can be found even in Aksakov's late works. Still, perhaps more important than any specific knowledge Aksakov gained or

7. Aksakov quotes his first published verse in *Reminiscences,* in *Sobranie sochinenii,* 2:146. The notes in the 1955–1966 edition provide another verse 'n a Karamzinian mode by the young Aksakov, 2:480–481.

8. *Reminiscences,* in *Sobranie sochinenii,* 2:86. Subsequent references to Aksakov's works in this edition will appear in the text.

literary orientation he acquired at Kazan was the sense of cultural and social community imparted by his teachers and fellow students there; according to Aksakov's memoirs of his student years, even final public examinations were like family gatherings (2:192). Throughout his life Aksakov tended to seek the company of persons with the same cultural attitudes and interests as his own and to form an intimate circle (kruzhok), typical of the cultural life of the early nineteenth-century gentry.

In 1807 Aksakov withdrew from the university a few months short of finishing in order to seek a post in government service in St. Petersburg. He seems to have acted on the advice of G. I. Kartashevskii, the mathematics teacher at Kazan, with whom Aksakov boarded while at Kazan and who acted as his guardian and tutor. (Kartashevskii married Aksakov's sister Nadezhda some ten years later and eventually became an education official in the government service.) In St. Petersburg, Aksakov held minor posts on several government bodies. Early in 1808 he was appointed as a translator for the Commission for the Codification of the Laws, which was eventually headed by Mikhail Speranskii. The commission was one of the reform-minded projects of the early years of Alexander I's reign, but like most projects of the day, it was ultimately ineffectual. In 1810 Aksakov began to serve on the "Expedition" on Government Revenues, where he seems to have done even less than in his previous post.[9]

Still only in his late teens, he devoted the greater part of his time, as he recounts in his memoirs, to the theater, eventually becoming acquainted with I. E. Shusherin, one of the major actors of the day, and to his literary interests. He gained entrée to the salon of Admiral Shishkov, the redoubtable champion of those espousing a conservative approach in literary style and a rather strident nationalism in politics. Shishkov's salon was attended by some of the leading literary figures, including the major poet of Catherine's day, Gavrila Derzhavin, the fabulist I. I. Dmitriev, and the comedy writer (later director of the Imperial Theater) Prince A. A. Shakhovskoi. Aksakov witnessed the first meetings of Shishkov's circle, the Beseda ("colloquy" or "conversation") of Lovers of the Russian Word, devoted to anti-Sentimentalism and to the defense of nationalistic and archaistic stylistic principles. A very junior and minor observer of this group, which later be-

9. See Mashinskii, S. T. Aksakov, pp. 14–15.

came embroiled in polemics with Arzamas, the group to which Pushkin belonged, thus figuring significantly in the development of the modern literary language, Aksakov would "sit sometimes quietly in a corner of the main drawing room as a silent auditor of what was read and said at these meetings. In conscience I must say that nothing remarkable took place and even my ideas of that time went unsatisfied" (2:302).

In 1811 Aksakov left St. Petersburg for Moscow, spent 1812 in Moscow and then, when Napoleon invaded, returned to Orenburg, for several years thereafter dividing his time among St. Petersburg, Moscow, and Orenburg. He held no post, and literary and theatrical activities of a dilettante nature occupied him during his visits to the capitals. His absorption in such pursuits can be seen in his near total disregard of the events of 1812; indeed, he tarried in Moscow on the eve of Napoleon's invasion in order to participate in productions of plays in which his friend, the actor Iakov Emel'ianovich Shusherin, was appearing. In addition, during these years he worked on translations of Sophocles' *Philoctetes* (from a French version) and Molière's *Ecole des maris*,[10] further indications of his rather conservative literary orientation at the time.

In 1816 at twenty-five, Aksakov embarked on a more settled and responsible existence. In that year he married Olga Semenovna Zaplatina, the daughter of a landowner from the Kursk region. Her father had been an officer under Catherine and had directed mobilization in his district during the Napoleonic wars; her mother had been a Turkish girl captured at the siege of Ochakov in 1788 who had been baptized and raised as a Russian.[11]

Unfortunately, we know little about their courtship and marriage beyond the fact itself; Aksakov does not treat it in his writings, and there are almost no surviving letters from this period of his life. In fact there are few letters from Aksakov to his wife from any period of their forty years of married life because their separations were both infrequent and brief, a fact which may in itself attest to their devotion to one another. Ivan Aksakov, in his sketch of his family, depicts his mother as loving but stricter with the children than the indulgent Sergei Timofeevich and as much more insistently patriotic than her husband, perhaps a reflection of her family's military background. Contrary to the

10. Ibid., pp. 40–41.
11. See I. Aksakov, "Ocherk semeinogo byta Aksakovykh," pp. 14–15.

patterns of the day, they seemed to have shared equally in raising their numerous children. Their marriage and household served as something of a model of traditional Russian hospitality and rectitude for the Slavophiles in the 1840s, but the mistress of the house, who played a much greater role in managing its affairs than her husband did, remains a rather shadowy figure. However, Olga Semenovna seems not to have been absorbed in her large household and the raising of her children to the exclusion of other interests; along with her daughters, she participated in the intellectual discussions taking place in her drawing room on an equal footing with the men. Indeed, the women seem to have displayed more interest in such conversation than the paterfamilias himself, who would often amuse himself with cards.

Following their wedding, Sergei Timofeevich and Olga Semenovna took up residence in Aksakovo and, except for one season in Moscow, remained in the countryside for the next ten years, first at Aksakovo with Sergei Timofeevich's parents and then at Nadezhdino (called Parashino in *Family Chronicle* and *Years of Childhood*). Konstantin was born in 1817, the first of some fourteen children, of whom four died in infancy and one son, Mikhail, in adolescence. Konstantin's birth was precisely recorded by Sergei Timofeevich, much as Stepan Mikhailovich records Sergei Bagrov's birth at the end of *Family Chronicle*: "1817, March 29, on Thursday of Holy Week, at 3:25 in the morning there was born a son, Konstantin, at the village of Aksakovo. Nameday May 27."[12]

Aksakov had seemingly settled down permanently to the uneventful life of a provincial landowner and family man, devoting himself wholeheartedly to his family and to the sports of rod and gun. However, a decade after his marriage, in 1826, he and his family moved from the countryside to Moscow, in or near which Aksakov was to spend the rest of his life. Several factors must have contributed to the decision to move. Sergei Timofeevich would certainly have liked to be closer to the cultural life of Moscow, with which he had renewed contact during a stay in 1821. Olga Semenovna disliked the Orenburg region, which was still a rather raw frontier compared to the Kursk of her own childhood. In addition, Sergei Timofeevich's relations with his parents may have become somewhat strained. More importantly,

12. S. T. Aksakov, "Kniga dlia vsiakoi vsiachiny" (manuscript notebook). LL, *fond* 3 (Aksakovs; GAIS/III), folder 7, item 1, p. 140.

arrangements had to be made for their sons' formal education, and Sergei Timofeevich was reluctant to subject them to life in a distant boarding school of the sort he had endured. This fear was not unfounded. From all accounts, conditions in many schools, both private and state institutions, were grim. Aksakov's youngest son, Mikhail, was the only one to attend school at any distance from home, and he died in St. Petersburg in 1841 at the age of fourteen. However, the decisive factor in the move was probably economic, since Aksakov had not been particularly successful in managing his estate and never would be (3:55). In Moscow he could find a position of some sort in the bureaucracy which would provide a steady cash income.

Aksakov's earlier literary contacts had their potential for practical advantage as well. Admiral Shishkov, Aksakov's mentor during his St. Petersburg years, had become the minister of education in 1826 as part of the conservative wave that followed the Decembrist Revolt and Nicholas I's troubled accession to the throne. Through Shishkov's patronage Aksakov succeeded in securing a position on the Moscow censorship committee, which had been newly reorganized and given considerably enhanced power under the stricter censorship introduced by Nicholas.[13] Aksakov served as a censor from late 1827 to January of 1829, acting as chief censor for part of the time. He was relieved of duties as a consequence of another reorganization of the censorship committee: Shishkov had retired as minister of education in 1828, and K. A. Lieven, the new minister, had no desire to retain his predecessor's protégé on the committee. Aksakov however returned to the censorship committee in June of 1830 and served until February 1832, when he was permanently dismissed for permitting several allegedly scurrilous items to be published. In fact, these ephemeral items were only used as a pretext by Lieven to dismiss Aksakov. The real reason was doubtless his having permitted the publication of a wide-ranging article, "The Nineteenth Century" ("Deviatnadtsatyi vek"), by Ivan Kireevskii. Soon to become a seminal figure in the Slavophile movement, Kireevskii published the article in the first number of his own journal, the European (Evropeets), in late 1831. The journal was closed and Aksakov reprimanded, but his dismissal was to follow shortly.[14]

13. For Aksakov's account of his appointment, see his "Memoir of A. S. Shishkov" (2:308–309) and also his Literary and Theatrical Memoirs (3:68).
14. See Mashinskii, S. T. Aksakov, pp. 168–169.

In 1833 Aksakov managed to gain a post as the inspector of the Konstantin Geodetic School, an institution for training land surveyors. Though hardly a prominent position, it did offer prospects of greater security from political currents than had the censorship position. Instrumental in the restructuring of the school as the Konstantin Geodetic Institute in 1835, Aksakov served quite ably and conscientiously as the first director of the reorganized school until 1838, when he retired from government service at the age of forty-seven, officially for reasons of health, but probably primarily because of the inheritance of sizable proportions from his mother and father, who had died in 1833 and 1837 respectively.

Throughout his years in Moscow, and particularly with the temporarily enhanced resources provided by his inheritances, Aksakov devoted as much time (and certainly a good deal more interest) to his cultural and social activities as he did to his government service. From the 1820s to the 1840s and beyond, his areas of interest were many, including literature, theater, and journalism. His circle of acquaintances, including people both of importance and of insignificance in these various fields, was extremely broad. Such cultural and social pursuits in large part functioned as the urban equivalent of the hunting and fishing which had occupied Sergei Timofeevich while he lived in the country, and both can be viewed as expressions of the rights and privileges of the caste to which Aksakov belonged. Hunting of course had been a right of the nobility since ancient times, but cultural activities as a means of affirming corporate autonomy and personal identity were very much part of the Russian gentry's ethos in the late eighteenth century. Perhaps the most characteristic manifestation of this new attitude toward cultural pursuits were the sometimes lavish private theaters, staffed by serfs, that flourished in the late eighteenth and early nineteenth centuries. By the 1830s conspicuous display was a thing of the past and beyond Aksakov's means in any case, but his attitude toward his cultural pursuits, which might be frivolous in themselves but indicated status, and their range, particularly in theater and literature, provide ample evidence of his roots in the culture of the gentry.

Although the social roots of Aksakov's cultural interests are evident, the intensity of commitment he brought to them often raised them above mere pastimes. Ivan Aksakov draws attention to his father's ability to endow an activity not usually thought of as aesthetic with an artistic dimension and contrasts this with the seriousness of purpose typical of a later day:

> Sergei Timofeevich loved life, he loved pleasure; he was
> an artist in spirit and had the attitude of an artist toward every
> pleasure. A passionate actor, a passionate hunter, a pas-
> sionate cardplayer, he was an artist in all his pursuits—both
> in the field with gun and dog, and at the card table. He
> was subject to all the weaknesses of a passionate person, often
> forgetting the entire world in the fever of his enthusiasm;
> even after he was married he would spend entire days hunting,
> entire nights at cards.[15]

Ivan here touches on a fundamental unifying factor in his father's various interests. Be they fishing or butterfly hunting, acting or declamation of verse, Aksakov was capable of treating them as self-valuable activities that had a serious aesthetic dimension.

Perhaps the most important of these interests was theater, which held a lifelong fascination for Sergei Timofeevich perhaps even greater than that of literature. This interest embraced all aspects of theater, from dramatic text to acting technique to costume and makeup and staging. He began to memorize and declaim verse at an early age; his skill as a reader later provided him with an entrée to Admiral Shishkov's salon in St. Petersburg and led in 1816 to his acquaintance with the aged Derzhavin, who was moved to tears by Aksakov's rendition of his verse. One of Aksakov's greatest regrets in old age was that his poor health and failing eyesight made it difficult for him to read his own works to his family and friends; Konstantin usually read his father's works in public.

Contact with theater proper began for Aksakov during his school days in Kazan, when he first saw the actor Petr Alekseevich Plavil'shchikov perform; as he relates in *Reminiscences*, theater in all its aspects became a passion from that moment. His principal interest, however, was acting, and he confessed in the 1850s that he "had a definite acting talent and even now think that the theater was my true vocation" (2:287). A career on the public stage, as distinct from private theatricals that were sometimes quite elaborate and professional in execution, was precluded for a member of the gentry at a time when most actors

15. I. Aksakov, "Ocherk semeinogo byta Aksakovykh," p. 12.

were the product of serf theaters or still serfs themselves. But Aksakov frequently acted in amateur productions in Kazan, St. Petersburg, and Moscow.

In 1816 he met Mikhail Zagoskin, later the director of the Imperial Theater in Moscow (and author of the historical novel à la Scott, *Iurii Miloslavskii*, 1829). Through this friendship, as well as his own acting skill, Aksakov had entrée backstage in the Moscow theater and was a respected visitor there in the 1820s and 1830s. Aksakov observed the great Russian Romantic tragic actors, Pavel Mochalov and Vasilii Karatygin, and left precise and informed descriptions of their technique in the brief theatrical notices he wrote, usually under pseudonyms, for various journals in the late twenties and early thirties.

He also began a lifelong friendship with the comedian Mikhail Shchepkin, perhaps the greatest Russian actor, whose views on acting technique later influenced Konstantin Stanislavskii. Shchepkin's respect for Aksakov's theatrical expertise is evidenced by his suggestion that Aksakov serve as the nominal director of Gogol's controversial comedy *The Inspector General* (*Revizor*) in its first Moscow production in 1836 (3:185–189). Indeed, he considered Aksakov important to his own development as an actor.[16] Later, with his illness and partial withdrawal from Moscow's cultural life, Aksakov's direct contacts with the theater decreased, although his friendship with Shchepkin endured. He did attend rehearsals of his son Konstantin's play *The Liberation of Moscow in 1612* (*Osvobozhdenie Moskvy v 1612om godu*), which had only a mixed reception and was banned by the censorship after one performance.[17]

In 1854 he attended a performance by the famous French actress Rachel and in letters compared her performance (unfavorably) to that of George, whom he had seen in her St. Petersburg début nearly fifty years before; he found both lacking in the naturalness he considered a hallmark of the Russian school of acting.[18]

Fittingly, Aksakov's formal farewell to the theater took the form of a tribute to one of the chief exponents of that school

16. A. I. Shubert, *Moia zhizn'*, p. 100.
17. S. T. Aksakov to Iu. F. Samarin, 22 December 1850. PD, *fond* 3, inventory 11, fol. 28.
18. S. T. Aksakov to M. G. Kartashevskaia, 3 January 1854. PD, 10 685/xvi s 42, fol. 36–36v.

of acting, his friend Shchepkin. For the fiftieth anniversary of Shchepkin's début, a dinner in his honor was arranged in November of 1855, in large part at Aksakov's insistence, by the literary and theatrical elite of Moscow. To an audience of nearly two hundred, Konstantin Aksakov read Sergei Timofeevich's encomium to Shchepkin, "A Few Words about M. S. Shchepkin" ("Neskol'ko slov o M. S. Shchepkine") (3:610–620). In addition to briefly sketching Shchepkin's career, which began in a serf theater, Aksakov provides a summation of the actor's art which suggests the sources of his lifelong attraction to it. It is an evanescent art,

> producing the strongest and liveliest impression but thereby the least stable as well. There is no greater pleasure, no more gratifying feeling than to move thousands of people with a single word, a single glance. . . . But alas, the effect is fleeting, and if it does not immediately dissipate in the spectators upon their return to the real world, it still weakens and dies along with them. The actor does not leave a testament of his talent. (3:619)

In addition to providing one of the greatest pleasures in his life, Aksakov's familiarity with theater and acting technique surfaces in his works, particularly in *Family Chronicle,* with its characters dominated by a single passion and its occasional theatrical scene.

Another of the traditional activities of the gentry that Aksakov maintained during his Moscow years was that of entertaining. From the time Sergei Timofeevich and Olga Semenovna settled in Moscow to the 1850s, the Aksakov drawing room was the scene of an open house on Saturdays (the day on which Aksakov's literary circle in Kazan had met), functioning as a meeting place for Moscow's cultural luminaries. The gentry, people from the university and the growing profession of journalism such as Pogodin, writers such as Gogol and later Turgenev and Tolstoi, and socially acceptable theater figures such as Shchepkin could gather to enjoy the ample food (some of it brought by cart from the Aksakov estates), genial atmosphere, and stimulating conversation. Activities ranged from cards to authors reading from their new works, to musical performances and, particularly in the later 1830s and 1840s, when Aksakov's sons Konstantin and Ivan and their associates participated more actively, philosophical and political discussion. Aksakov describes such an evening in 1844:

On Saturday there were two groups at our house: Pogodin,
Tomashevskii, Vin, and I played cards in my study, while in
the small drawing room Karolina Karlovna [Pavlova, Russia's first significant woman poet] and her husband, Sverbeev,
Khomiakov, Samarin, Panov, Efremov, and Konstantin
[all important figures in the intellectual or publishing world of
Moscow], of course in the presence of the hostesses (Mother
and Verochka), argued until three in the morning. The
shouting was incredible.[19]

In the 1850s Aksakov spent much of his time in the countryside outside the city, on his estate at Abramtsevo, but even there
guests gathered, often staying several days. Aksakov's eldest
daughter, Vera, who seems to have been as interested as her
more famous brothers in cultural matters, recorded one such occasion in January 1855 in her diary. Aleksei Khomiakov, Shchepkin, and Turgenev were among those present, and as might be expected in such a company, "in the drawing room conversation
took place among Konstantin, Khomiakov, and Turgenev concerning Russia and the Russian common man. Naturally no one
agrees completely with Konstantin's opinion of the Russian, that
is of the peasant."[20] Vera Sergeevna also reports on other activities,
such as outings in carriages and readings of her father's work in
progress, *Family Chronicle*.

For Sergei Timofeevich it was doubtless the literary aspects of
such gatherings (apart from the games of whist) that held the
greatest interest. Throughout his life Aksakov cultivated the
friendship of a strikingly long list of literary figures both great
and small, from Derzhavin, who died in 1816, to the twenty-
eight-year-old Tolstoi, whom Aksakov met in 1856 and who died
in 1910. Thus, in keeping with his idea of literature as a collec-
tive pursuit, in which even minor authors prepare the way for
great ones—a view Aksakov expresses in *Literary and Theatrical
Memoirs* (*Literaturnye i teatral'nye vospominaniia*), 1858—
Aksakov's literary acquaintances spanned virtually the entire
spectrum of what can be termed the literature of the gentry in
Russia. His circle included such diverse figures as the early nineteenth-century dramatist Shakhovskoi, the minor novelist Mi-

19. S. T. Aksakov to I. S. Aksakov, 7 February 1844. LL, *fond* 3 (GAIS/III), folder
3, item 22b.
20. Vera Sergeevna Aksakova, *Dnevnik Very Sergeevny Aksakovoi (1854–5)*, p.
43. The entry is for 25 January 1855.

khail Zagoskin, the poet Karolina Pavlova, and more important authors such as Pushkin and Turgenev, as well as critics such as N. I. Nadezhdin and Vissarion Belinskii.

His association with Gogol, however, was the longest and perhaps most important. Sergei Timofeevich recognized Gogol's talent early and championed the works of the eccentric young author from the Ukraine from their first appearance until Gogol's death in 1852. His support at times took practical form, as his willingness to become involved in the Moscow production of *The Inspector General* and his "loans" to the often financially pressed author indicate. He also urged others to donate money on Gogol's behalf. The Aksakov house was of course open to Gogol whenever he came to Moscow, and he was accorded a place of honor and even reverence in it (an attitude perhaps reflected in Konstantin's enthusiastic 1842 review, hailing *Dead Souls* as a resurrection of the epic). The Aksakov hospitality was extended in the teeth of Gogol's frequent eccentricity, which often amounted to boorishness. Although his whims were catered to and special dishes prepared to his specifications, Gogol is described by one visitor to the Aksakov home as sitting hunched over the dinner table, silent and directing gloomy stares at every one present.[21]

Despite his great respect for Gogol's talent, Aksakov seems to have thought less highly of his personality, finding him erratic, enigmatic, and at times exasperating. Aksakov even broke off relations with him for a while in the mid-forties, when Gogol responded to the news of Sergei Timofeevich's sudden partial blindness with a particularly moralizing letter, advising him to seek consolation in the works of Thomas a Kempis, to be read a chapter (no more) at a time, at a set time every day (after coffee was ideal). Gogol was probably entirely sincere, even if it apparently escaped him that it was Sergei Timofeevich's inability to read that was precisely the problem. Always a foe of religious hypocrisy and doubtless stung by Gogol's lack of ordinary sympathy, Aksakov heatedly replied that he had read Thomas a Kempis before Gogol had ever been born and had no use for mysticism (3:298). Aksakov did not renew his correspondence with Gogol for several years, although the rift was eventually healed. After Gogol's death in 1852, Aksakov recorded this in-

---

21. Avdot'ia Panaeva, *Vospominaniia*, pp. 112–113.

cident and others in *The History of My Acquaintance with Gogol* (*Istoriia moego znakomstva s Gogolem*), based in part on his correspondence with Gogol. Although never completed and unpublished until the 1890s, it contains the first extensive treatment of any aspect of Gogol's rather puzzling personality.[22] Despite the advantage of long personal acquaintance, Askakov, like many later biographers, found himself confused and ultimately baffled by Gogol. In Aksakov's words, "Some friends and associates knew him well, of course; but they knew him only partially" (3:605).

In the 1840s two events altered the pattern of Aksakov's life considerably. In 1843, mainly through the efforts of his practical-minded second son Grigorii (later the governor of Samara Province), Aksakov was able to realize a longstanding desire to acquire a country residence within reach of Moscow by purchasing Abramtsevo, a small estate about thirty-five miles northeast of Moscow and eight miles from the St. Sergius–Trinity Monastery in present-day Zagorsk, one of the centers of the Russian religious tradition. Although originally bought to serve as a summer house, by the later 1840s Abramtsevo became Aksakov's principal residence and at least part of the family often spent the entire year there, despite the old house's unsuitability as a year-round residence. The modest estate, in its charming natural setting, has become doubly noteworthy in Russian cultural life. Visited by such figures as Gogol and Turgenev while the Aksakovs owned it, it was later purchased from the Aksakov family by Savva Mamontov, a wealthy Moscow merchant and patron of the arts. In the 1870s and 1880s the estate became a center for the revival of Russian art (as well as for the preservation of Russian folk art), with such painters as Vasnetsov, Serov, Repin, and Vrubel' associated with it. Today the estate, accessible by train from Moscow, is a museum dedicated to both its sets of illustrious inhabitants, and its lands are part of a nature preserve.[23] Financial considerations and Aksakov's increasing dislike of life in Moscow both contributed to his decision to spend much of his time at Abramtsevo, although after 1849 there were political rea-

22. Aksakov's *History* was first published in 1890. Modern editions usually include the texts of letters between Gogol and Aksakov from the period after Aksakov's narrative breaks off, that is, after 1843.

23. See Tamara Talbot Rice, *A Concise History of Russian Art*, p. 243; in more detail, Camilla Gray, *The Russian Experiment in Art 1863–1922*, pp. 12–29.

sons as well, stemming from his family's brush with Nicholas I's policy of intimidating the open discussion of ideas. Matters of health also played a role, as Aksakov related to an old school-mate in 1854:

> In 1845 I became blind in my left eye; I underwent a great
> deal of treatment in order to save the right one; I caught cold
> in the bad eye (while fishing, of course) and suffered an
> inflammation in it and such rheumatic pains in my head that I
> was on the verge of going mad. In 1847 I was unexpect-
> edly cured by the doctors and since then, although I am often
> ailing, I see, thank God, the light of day with my right
> eye, I can read a bit, write a bit (especially with a pencil), I can
> fish and I can hunt for mushrooms, of which I am a great
> fancier.[24]

Although this gives a fairly accurate picture of his favorite activities at Abramtsevo, Aksakov does not go into detail on one of his principal activities after 1845, namely, his writing—it was his appearance in print that had prompted his old schoolmate to write to him. With the idleness forced on him by life in the country and by the impairment of his eyesight, and partly as distraction from the occasional pain, Aksakov began to devote more time to writing, or rather to dictating, usually to one of his daughters, since he was unable to read or write for long periods himself. Beginning with *Notes on Fishing (Zapiski ob uzhen'e)* and *Notes of a Hunter of Orenburg Province (Zapiski ruzheinogo okhotnika orenburgskoi gubernii)*, 1846 and 1852, he composed and published a series of works, culminating in *Family Chroni-cle* and *Reminiscences (Vospominaniia)*, both published in 1856, and *Years of Childhood*, 1857, that firmly established him as a major figure in the new, realistic Russian fiction that was emerg-ing at the time.

Although he had spent most of his adult life on the fringes of literary life in Moscow and had dabbled in the city's incipient journalism in the late 1820s and early 1830s (usually under pseudonyms, both because of his position on the censorship committee and because of the feeling that a member of the gentry should leave the mundane realities of journalism to parvenus or academics), it was only now, with regular and fairly significant

24. S. T. Aksakov to A. I. Panaev, 3 July 1854. PD, *Razriad* I, inventory 1, item 10, fol. 2v.

production, that Aksakov began to publish frequently and under his own name. Many of his pieces appeared in the *Muscovite (Moskvitianin)*, the principal Moscow-based journal of the 1840s and 1850s. It was a rather stodgy affair, edited by the history professor Mikhail Pogodin, whom Aksakov had known since the 1820s. Pogodin espoused a political position more supportive of the role of the state in Russian history and in current affairs than the Slavophiles or Sergei Timofeevich would have liked, but because of Nicholas I's ban on new journals, the *Muscovite* was the only available journal Aksakov deemed acceptable, and he began his association with it with his biography of Mikhail Zagoskin in 1852. Pogodin's casual editing annoyed Sergei Timofeevich, but he had nowhere else to turn, and continued to publish in it until the emergence of new journals after the death of Nicholas I and the accession of Alexander II in 1856.

There was a practical reason as well for Aksakov's appearance in the *Muscovite*: his family's financial situation had deteriorated steadily, as was the case with many of the gentry. The Orenburg estates and all their 600 "souls" (serfs) were mortgaged to the government, the income from the estates were dropping, and payments were falling due. Receiving payment for pieces too short for publication as books certainly had its attractions for an author saddled with debts in the neighborhood of twenty-two thousand roubles, a substantial sum for the day. In late 1853, after rejecting Pogodin's offer of a loan, Sergei Timofeevich readily accepted his suggestion of payment for articles appearing in the *Muscovite*. Assuming the status of a professional writer so late in life does not seem to have disturbed Aksakov unduly. (Turgenev, whose family background was also impeccable, insisted on, and got, hefty fees from the St. Petersburg journals, whose editors realized that good literature, much more than informative articles or critics' polemics, attracted subscribers.) Aksakov wasted no time in accepting Pogodin's offer: "You thought that I would be insulted by an offer of monetary reward, and perhaps you would have been correct twenty-five years ago; but see what time means: I myself wanted to suggest this to you."[25]

Being paid for his works by no means implied, to Sergei Timofeevich's way of thinking, that he would relinquish any of the privileges accruing to a dilettante of good family. He set Pogodin

25. S. T. Aksakov to M. P. Pogodin, 29 November 1853. LL, Pogodin *fond*, section II, carton 1, storage unit 59, letter 8.

a number of strict conditions, including the right to withhold pieces the censors might mutilate, and insisted on complete autonomy: "In order to receive four thousand roubles, it's necessary to write about forty printer's signatures a year, but in a given year I may not even manage to write ten. So I am not accepting any obligation and I will give you whatever comes, when it comes. Of course, upon your receipt of the articles I will receive my money without delay."[26] The most important piece Aksakov published in the *Muscovite* was the complete first chapter of *Family Chronicle* in 1854; he withheld the second, with its murder of Kurolesov by his serfs, for fear of censorship, and even when that chapter appeared in the first edition of *Family Chronicle* in 1856 the details of the murder were not included.

With the easing of restrictions on new journals in 1856, Aksakov was able to lend his name, by then well known, to several new journals, notably the Slavophile *Russian Conversation (Russkaia beseda)* and Katkov's *Russian Herald (Russkii vestnik)*, a major conservative journal when Dostoevskii appeared in it in the 1860s but closer to the Slavophiles in its early years. In 1856 *Russian Conversation* published the fourth chapter of *Family Chronicle* and *Russian Herald* the fifth, capitalizing on the popularity of the first three chapters, which had appeared in book form earlier in the year. In 1857 Aksakov contributed three chapters of *Years of Childhood* to *Russian Conversation* before the complete work appeared in book form.

This was destined to be Aksakov's last major work. In declining health and often in pain, he became confined to his bed late in 1858 and died in Moscow, apparently of kidney failure, on April 30, 1859. He was buried at the Simonov monastery in Moscow.

Since Aksakov was closely associated with the group of Russian thinkers, among them his own sons Konstantin and Ivan, known to Russian history as the Slavophiles, and since his works are sometimes cited as expressions of Slavophile sentiments, it may be worthwhile to indicate briefly who the Slavophiles were, what their leading ideas were, and how closely we can connect Aksakov's works to them.

Although the term *Slavophile* had existed for some time, it gained currency and became a fixed designation for a specific

26. Ibid.

group of people with a shared complex of ideas in the heat of polemics in the 1840s; the term for their opponents, the so-called Westerners, was established at the same time. Slavophile thought had its roots in Romantic notions concerning the cultural uniqueness and distinct historical mission of each separate people, a doctrine which led Russians conversant with German Romantic philosophy to ponder the question of Russia's specific characteristic and its historical role. Ivan Kireevskii (1806–1856) first articulated in the 1830s the central ideas which would come to be termed Slavophile. These included a rejection of Western European culture as a model for Russia because of the West's spiritually desiccating emphasis on rationalism and individualism, viewed as forces that had fragmented the individual personality and destroyed the social fabric, both political and religious, in the West. By contrast, Russia, by virtue of its ancient political structure and Orthodox religion, was thought to foster the integral wholeness of the personality and provide social bonds of a noncoercive nature based not on the power of ruler over ruled but on the unanimous, free consent of the governed (although this unanimity and freedom by no means implied economic or social equality). Russia had been a community rather than a conglomeration; its ultimate mission was to preserve this community and even eventually to offer it as a model to other nations as an escape from the social chaos and spiritual alienation to which unbridled rationalism would inevitably lead.

If such a historiosophic scheme is applied to Russia's actual history, Peter the Great, the man who did the most to change Russia's established customs and to transform her at least partially into something like a Western, rational state, emerges not as a great reformer but as a problematic, even negative figure, whose rational apparatus for governing the state had stifled and still continued to stifle the traditional (and superior) Russian approach to social organization. The Slavophiles saw the role of the state as that of a guardian, regulator, conservator, and protector of the community, and were vehemently opposed to the "Official Nationalist" school of Pogodin and S. P. Shevyrev, who, like Karamzin, saw the state as the crucial factor in Russian history and political life. They also opposed the bureaucratic, centralized, and all-controlling (in intention, at least) government of Nicholas I, which did in fact view the Slavophiles with some concern, as it did independence of thought from any direction.

The Slavophiles were hardly in total agreement or entirely uniform in their ideas; however, the core of ideas or central paradigm first worked out by Kireevskii was shared by other figures in the movement, with individual modifications or particular emphases. Kireevskii's close contemporary Aleksei Khomiakov (1804–1860), much more than Kireevskii himself, was responsible for the wider propagation of Slavophile views. In addition to being a formidable polemicist and skilled debater, he wrote prolifically on subjects ranging from agriculture to comparative Indo-European philology; in addition, belying the stereotype of the Slavophiles as Moscow-bound eccentrics, he was quite cosmopolitan, with correspondents throughout Europe and with a particular interest in England (a visit to which country he enjoyed in 1847). Khomiakov's major contribution to Slavophile thought per se draws on his interests in theology, specifically ecclesiology (he remains an influential figure in Russian Orthodox theology), and it was he who most fully developed the notion of *sobornost'* (communality or collegiality) as the determining feature of Orthodoxy as opposed to Roman Catholicism or Protestantism, whose faults he saw as excessive authoritarianism and excessive individualism respectively. Khomiakov in large measure transferred this model of the church to the social or political sphere; much more than Kireevskii, who traced the unique features of Russia's social organization to the nation's prehistory and ancient history, Khomiakov emphasized Russia's religious experience, with its integration of the individual into a community characterized by mutual love and freedom.

While Kireevskii and Khomiakov remained on a general theoretical level, the younger Slavophiles, Sergei Timofeevich's sons Konstantin (1817–1860) and Ivan (1823–1886), as well as Iurii Samarin (1819–1876), all sought more direct impact on public attitudes and even on policy, notably through journalism. Kireevskii had edited the *European* in 1832, but it was closed after two issues; he edited, with assistance from other Slavophiles, Pogodin's *Muscovite (Moskvitianin)* in 1845. They were all involved in the various *Moscow Miscellanies (Moskovskie sborniki)* in 1846, 1847, and 1852, engaging in more extensive journalistic activity after the end of Nicholas I's regime. Ivan Aksakov and Iurii Samarin also entered government service. Ivan eventually (in the 1860s and later) became a spokesman of Pan-Slavism, a much more strident and chauvinistic movement that abandoned many of "classical" Slavophilism's reservations about the state and its power and also took great interest in the affairs of other Slavic peoples, notably in the Balkans. (The term *Slavophile* was in part a misnomer, in that the Slavophiles of the 1840s and 1850s had virtually no interest in the other Slavic peoples or their political aspirations.)

Of these three junior figures, Konstantin Aksakov is the most significant, if also the most thoroughly impractical. Like Khomiakov, Konstantin entertained a wide range of interests, including literature and language (his master's essay, defended in 1847, was on Lomonosov as a poet, while some of his linguistic speculations are important to the later development of linguistic theory in Russia). In contradistinction to Khomiakov and Kireevskii, Konstantin Aksakov saw the ideal model of Russian society neither in the remote past nor in the church, but in the village commune (*obshchina* or *mir*), with its insistence on unanimous decisions—a far cry in Slavophile eyes from the factionalism of Western democracy, of which the United States was the extreme example. Despite his extreme idealization of it, Konstantin's emphasis on the commune and its role as a model for Russian political life as a whole was not without its pragmatic dimension; the village assembly was an actually functioning political institution in the Russian village, even if it operated under a host of restrictions. It had only to be granted wider scope to become viable, a point Konstantin argued on the eve of the Emancipation. This focus on an actual political form, rather than on the forms derived from a lost past or the ecclesiastic sphere, as championed by Kireevskii and Khomiakov respectively, thrust Konstantin much closer to the brink of action, even if it was only symbolic. For example, in the 1840s he dressed himself in the Old Russian fashion, for he was stridently anti-Petrine, in large part because of the modern Russian state's attempts to limit the commune. Potentially more important was his 1855 memorandum to the new tsar, Alexander II, "On the Internal State of Russia," in which Konstantin urged reform based on the recognition that the Russian people were nonrevolutionary and nonpolitical, their support for past revolts having been grounded in personal allegiance to rulers whose claims were felt to be legitimate. He called particularly for greater freedom of speech and a recognition of the state's need to consult the people, whom the state serves as an executive instrument rather than ruling as an

absolute, unquestioned master. Konstantin concluded his memorandum with an appeal for the reestablishment of ancient harmony:

> Let there be reserved for the government unlimited freedom
> *to rule*, which is its prerogative, and for the people full
> freedom of social and spiritual *life* under the government's
> protection. Let *the government have the right to action*
> and consequently the power of law; let *the people have the*
> *right of opinion* and consequently the freedom of speech.
>   That is the Russian civil order! That is the only true civil
> order![27]

As is apparent even from this brief summary, the Slavophiles
first formulated a configuration of notions about Russia, its nature, and mission that has had enormous importance for Russian
thought and literature throughout the rest of the nineteenth century and even down to the present. Perhaps equally as important
as the content of their theories is the fact that they and their
ideological opponents, the Westerners, were the first groups in
Russia to take a principled and public stand—as public as censorship allowed—and to urge that the right to do so be respected
by the government. Aware of the absence of any real possibility
of effective political action, they were among the first to stress
the crucial role of public opinion, a concept to which they often
appealed.

In part, their sense of identity and worth stemmed from the
social cohesion of the Slavophiles. Unlike their opponents, the
Westerners, whose ranks included such social newcomers as Belinskii, the Slavophiles were very much of a similar background,
that of the comfortably landed gentry. Kireevskii, whose mother
was a relative of the poet Zhukovskii, tutor to Alexander II, and
who had ties with the Elagin family through his mother's second
marriage, was probably the wealthiest and best connected of the
group. Khomiakov's mother was a Kireevskaia, the Sverbeevs
and Elagins (and hence the Kireevskiis) were related by marriage,
and there were other, more indirect links as well, some involving
the Aksakovs. This is hardly surprising, for in addition to being
an intellectual and cultural center for the gentry, Moscow was
also its principal marriage market and long the gentry's social
center.[28]

27. Konstantin Aksakov, "On the Internal State of Russia," p. 251.
28. See V. I. Kuleshov, *Slavianofily i russkaia literatura*, p. 25n.

The Aksakovs were the most beset by money problems, but even their poverty was relative. Living principally in Moscow, their families concerned themselves with cultural and intellectual matters (Petr Kireevskii, Ivan's brother, was an early collector of Russian folk songs) and entertained one another, if not lavishly, then amply and regularly. Traditional hospitality and intellectual curiosity converged in a round of salons and open houses, providing an almost endless series of opportunities for stimulating conversation and semipublic debate. In the 1840s Ivan Kireevskii entertained on Wednesdays, his mother Avdot'ia Petrovna Elagina on Sundays, the beautiful Ekaterina Aleksandrovna Sverbeeva on Fridays, the Aksakovs on Saturdays, and Khomiakov, Petr Chaadaev, and others at less regular intervals. In addition, some of the younger figures in the movement, such as Konstantin Aksakov and Iurii Samarin, had studied together at Moscow University, a common meeting ground in the 1830s for both future Slavophiles and future Westerners such as Aleksandr Herzen.

Given such close interconnections, Sergei Timofeevich's general sympathy for the Slavophiles is hardly surprising; they were, after all, the younger generation of his own set and included his own sons. On a practical level too their doctrines were congenial, tending to approve the status quo as far as the gentry's economic position was concerned and to enhance the gentry's significance in the political sphere. Sergei Timofeevich's joining Konstantin in affecting Old Russian attire is understandable, especially given the emotional closeness between him and his eldest son. On the other hand, solidarity to the point of occasional action on social and familial grounds partially masks Sergei Timofeevich's indifference to specific Slavophile issues and tenets, and indeed to public affairs and philosophical issues generally. As his son Ivan states, he was "aloof from any civic interests, and his attitude toward them was indifferent; nature and literature were his primary interests. Even the year 1812, when Sergei Timofeevich Aksakov was already twenty-two years old, left him with no special recollections."[29] He could view with practical skepticism even his eldest son's most cherished notions; certainly he found Konstantin's idealization of the Russian village and its mir completely naïve and unrealistic, ill grounded in

29. I. Aksakov, "Ocherk semeinogo byta Aksakovykh," p. 13.

the often harsh facts of village life. Memoirs often depict Sergei Timofeevich playing cards with his cronies in another room at social gatherings while fierce debates raged in the drawing room, and only purely literary discussions or readings seem to have been able to claim his interest. The whole set of his personality, formed in an earlier, less theoretical day, would seem to have been against the abstract philosophizing of the sort so much in vogue in the Moscow of the 1840s.

We may briefly consider Aksakov's works in the light of Slavophilism, although such evidence, of course, remains circumstantial. In his works there are only broad coincidences between his theories and those of the Slavophiles, not well-articulated demonstrations of Slavophilism. Given their memoiristic base, Aksakov's works are perforce set in the post-Petrine Russia of the eighteenth century, a period dominated by a Westernized state generally distasteful to the Slavophiles. While the Bagrov/Aksakov estate under Stepan Mikhailovich may be a model of an organic society, it occupies only a small part of Aksakov's total work, and its less attractive sides (as well as its equally possible opposite, in the Kurolesov chapter) are apparent. More important, despite the fact that Konstantin Aksakov was the main propagandist of the peasant commune, Sergei Timofeevich devotes little space to peasants and almost none to their social organization. In addition, in his works, organic integration seems possible only on the personal, psychological level, when the individual confronts nature without the mediation of any society whatever, whereas the Slavophiles focused on social integration above all.

While the degree of affinity between Aksakov's texts and Slavophilism is a matter of the interpretation of those texts and thus endlessly and perhaps fruitlessly debatable, a clear gap also appears if we consider the Slavophiles' own literary norms and practices.[30] They were considerably more conservative than Sergei Timofeevich, even though he was older than any of them. Their own literary efforts, taken as a whole, evince a hierarchy of forms that seems almost to have stepped intact out of the eighteenth

30. See K. N. Lomunov, S. S. Dmitriev, A. S. Kurilov, eds., *Literaturnye vzgliady i tvorchestvo slavianofilov: 1830–1850–ye gody*, section 3. For the most thorough discussion of Slavophilism as an ideology, see Andrzej Walicki, *The Slavophile Controversy: History of a Conservative Utopia in Nineteenth-Century Russian Thought.*

century. It was characterized by some drama (most of it historical and some of it in verse), an overwhelming proportion of verse, and a nearly total disregard of prose fiction, at a time when such figures as Gogol, Lermontov, Turgenev, Goncharov, the young Dostoevskii, Tolstoi, and others—Sergei Timofeevich among them —were beginning to create an enormous body of prose literature, in some cases deliberately abandoning verse to do so. Even the verse of the Slavophiles suggests conventions that were in eclipse —odic and civic verse, Zhukovskian epistles and elegies— while the intimate lyric was perhaps the most significant poetic form of the day. Of the major poets only Fedor Tiutchev, who had affiliations with the Slavophiles, noticeably echoes such earlier forms.

Although the Slavophiles themselves neglected prose fiction, they were well aware of the literary scene and were anxious to attract leading talents to their cause. Konstantin Aksakov's enthusiasm over Gogol, as well as his and others' attempts in the 1850s to court first the liberal Turgenev and then Tolstoi (whose position at the time wavered from association with St. Petersburg's radical journalists to conservatism, to moralistic rejection of the literary trade altogether) were part of this effort. The Aksakov hospitality was extended and Turgenev, like Gogol earlier, was a guest at Abramtsevo. Friendship with Sergei Timofeevich, himself now an esteemed writer as well as a respected member of the older generation, to some extent served as bait in these efforts. At least with Turgenev, the association with Sergei Timofeevich was based more on shared interests as writers and hunters (and as writers about hunting) than on political views. The fact that their friendship survived the campaign of the early 1850s to enlist Turgenev in the Slavophile cause suggests that philosophical or political acceptability was hardly uppermost in Sergei Timofeevich's selection of friends.

When the Slavophiles discussed current literature, they necessarily had to discuss prose, since fiction, much of it stemming from the Westerner-oriented, socially critical Natural School, was dominant in the journals and among the reading public. Here again, Slavophile tastes are revealing. Their highest praise, despite the authors' disregard of the peasant, was accorded works like Gogol's *Dead Souls* or Sergei Timofeevich's work, which they praised for their impartial epic contemplation. In both cases, the appeal to epic suggests the underlying nostalgia of form and the implicit dislike of prose dealing with contemporary issues.

The Slavophiles did not deny that the fiction of the 1840s and 1850s was useful in bringing adverse social conditions to general attention, but found much of current literature flawed by its rationalism. In a sense, it was itself a symptom of the social fragmentation caused by Westernization. It could describe the illness accurately but could neither explain the causes nor offer any cure other than more Westernization, an approach the Slavophiles felt was doomed to inevitable failure. Thus they called for works that provided values consistent with their interpretation of Russian life, works on which a new community could be built. The only works other than the epic in which the Slavophiles found such values reflected were those in which peasants were presented in a manner deemed sympathetic and positive, stressing their internal, permanent, spiritual qualities rather than fortuitous external circumstances such as material poverty. Of major authors, only Turgenev received unstinting praise from the Slavophiles, and that for his *Sportsman's Sketches*. In general, however, the Slavophiles found that their call for positive treatment of the Russian people went unheeded by first-rate authors, who often had different priorities. Even the praise for Sergei Timofeevich's works as models of epic contemplation and as masterpieces of the Russian language veils the fact that there was little in his works to bolster Slavophile views directly. In fact, Sergei Timofeevich's most extended and sympathetic treatment of Russian peasants can be found in his first prose work, "The Blizzard," which was written before the elaboration of the Slavophile position and remained virtually unknown until it was republished in 1858.

Thus, on formal grounds, Aksakov's works were much more in keeping with the significant innovations and experiments that characterized Russian fiction in the 1840s and 1850s than were the Slavophiles, who favored older forms and neglected or ignored (insofar as they could) the possibilities presented by a new, realistic prose. In terms of content, Aksakov seldom chose to depict the very subject, the Russian peasant in his age-old commune, deemed most worthy of portrayal by the Slavophiles, particularly by Konstantin Aksakov. Whatever the degree of Sergei Timofeevich's personal sympathy with or adherence to Slavophile ideas (and the evidence strongly suggests a sense of social solidarity rather than intellectual conviction as the basis for his alliance with the Slavophiles), his actual works reveal relatively little that can be termed exclusively a reflection of Slavophile tenets. Indeed, this very avoidance of explicit ideological commitment in favor of a generalized nostalgic or pastoral orientation with which readers of various political positions could (and can) identify helped assure his immediate and lasting success with readers.

Much more important to Aksakov than abstract ideals was his commitment to his caste and above all to his family. Aksakov was far from being a snob, as his cordial relations with individuals of various social backgrounds who shared his passions attest. Shchepkin, born a serf and still technically owned by a master long after he had become a leading actor, was perhaps Aksakov's closest friend in the theatrical world. In the early 1850s Aksakov's plan (scuttled by the censorship) to launch a journal in which hunters of whatever class or region would be both readers and contributors indicates his tendency to value expertise over social station. Still, he certainly found much to agree with in the Slavophiles' view that the gentry (or at least part of it) were a sort of civic conscience which, as the reflective segment of the population, spoke for Russia as a whole vis-à-vis the state. Such a role necessarily implied freedom of speech, more important to the Slavophiles than political action, which they delegated entirely to the state; the gentry was to be an unofficial parliament with powers of debate but not of legislation. Indeed, it was Nicholas I's often gratuitously harsh restrictions on freedom of expression, restrictions extending to Aksakov's own hardly controversial writings, that Sergei Timofeevich found most onerous.

In the main, however, Aksakov's interests remained within the confines of theater, literature, his acquaintances among the Moscow gentry, and above all his own family. Indeed, his family formed the indispensable core of Aksakov's life, in sharp contrast to other Russian authors such as Pushkin, Lermontov, Turgenev, or Goncharov, for whom family life was of little importance. The Aksakov family as a whole exhibited a pronounced sense of the family as a protective circle closed against external threats from whatever quarter. It constituted a refuge, and considerable effort seems to have been expended to keep it intact and unchanged; only two of the younger generation married during Aksakov's lifetime.

The family most clearly served as a defense against the outside world in the case of Konstantin. His one foray abroad in 1838 ended in a sudden return to the safety of Moscow and home, and on several occasions in the late 1830s and early 1840s, Konstantin rather formally and emotionally ended friendships formed in his student days, ostensibly because of ideological differences. His withdrawal into the emotional security of the unchanging family (Konstantin seems to have had no romantic entanglements and never married) permitted increasingly overt and explicit expression of philosophical and political opinion, and this outspokenness eventually brought him into conflict with Nicholas's increasingly repressive regime.

Needless to say, in this conflict between state and family, Sergei Timofeevich upheld the rights of his family, though he perhaps assessed the situation somewhat more realistically than either of his two sons. The incidents in question, which provide Aksakov's biography with its one touch of political drama, occurred in the spring of 1849 and involved, in separate ways, both Ivan and Konstantin Aksakov.

Konstantin, in order to dramatize his call for a return to the virtues of Old Russia, had at various times in the 1840s dressed in his version of Old Russian attire. At first this was accounted mere eccentricity, and Petr Chaadaev's comment that peasants in the streets of Moscow took Konstantin for a Persian rather than an ancient Russian accurately conveys the general amused toleration of such quixotic behavior. In the wake of the events of 1848 in Western Europe, however, the situation had become rather more serious; any deviation from official positions was viewed with great suspicion. In this tenser atmosphere, Sergei Timofeevich explicitly allied himself with his son, like him letting his beard grow and adopting Old Russian clothing, as "a protest and a demonstration," as he called it, although his total adherence to Konstantin's social views is open to some doubt.

Nicholas I's attempts to cow the Slavophiles were rather crude, if temporarily effective. In March of 1849, Iurii Samarin was arrested for comments, in private letters that had been read by the police, critical of official policy toward non-Orthodox believers in the Riga area, where he served in the bureaucracy. Ivan

Aksakov was arrested in St. Petersburg, where he worked in the government service, under similar circumstances. The two young men were soon released, Ivan on March 22, after interrogation. The transcript of his interrogation bears marginal comments by Nicholas himself, indicating at how high a level this operation against the Slavophiles had originated.[31] The arrests shocked the Samarin and Aksakov families and dismayed the Slavophiles generally, who felt their loyalty to Russia was above question. (Nicholas was in fact moving against both right and left at the time; the Petrashevskii circle, one of whose members was the young Dostoevskii, was broken up in April 1849, with much more serious consequences for those arrested, since they lacked the social standing of an Aksakov or Samarin.)

A farcical sequel followed closely on the heels of the near-tragedy of Ivan's arrest. In April 1849 an order from the Ministry of Internal Affairs, aimed in part at Konstantin Aksakov, forbade the wearing of beards by members of the gentry, on the grounds that Peter had banned the beard and also that beards had become "the mark and sign of a certain mode of ideas" in the West,[32] although the Slavophiles could hardly be accused of radicalism of any sort. Despite protestations of loyalty and appeals by Sergei Timofeevich and Konstantin to the chief of police in Moscow, father and son were served with an order to appear at police headquarters and sign a statement that they had shaved their beards. Konstantin complied, and, since he considered Old Russian garb senseless without a beard, never wore it again. On grounds of ill health, Sergei Timofeevich's signature was obtained at home, and he in fact disregarded the order and continued to wear a beard, as well as a *zipun*, a loose-fitting jacket of Old Russian style. Since he was not the real target and seldom appeared in public, his defiance was disregarded. Konstantin, along with his father, withdrew even more from the public arena, spending the next several years primarily at Abramtsevo, determined "to shut ourselves up in the countryside forever," as Sergei Timofeevich put it.[33] During these years Sergei Timofeevich turned more and more to writing, eventually emerging as a professional author.

31. The transcript is published in *I. S. Aksakov v ego pis'makh*, 2:147–163.
32. In the words of A. F. Orlov, head of the Third Section (the secret police). Ibid., p. 142.
33. Ibid., p. 142n.

In his actions in 1849 Sergei Timofeevich was probably motivated as much by his desire to protect his eldest son as by philosophical convictions (although his sense of the rights of the gentry is not to be discounted). While Aksakov was close to all his children, his relationship with his eldest son might well be termed excessive. Sergei Timofeevich had taken care of Konstantin in his infancy, behavior almost unheard of for men among the gentry at the time.[34] In later years, the two were virtually never apart, even sharing the same room. Sergei Timofeevich's overprotectiveness with Konstantin rendered his son relatively helpless in practical matters, a situation he regretted but from which both father and son presumably benefited emotionally. Sergei Timofeevich laid bare the contradictions of his relationship with his eldest son in a rather frank epistolary confession to Ivan, but his letter offers no real solution, only a perpetuation of the withdrawal into the family characteristic of the Aksakovs generally. At the time of the letter, 1844, Konstantin was wearing Old Russian dress, and Sergei Timofeevich's attitude toward his son's behavior differs markedly from his public solidarity five years later, when the issue is no longer confined to the circle of family or close acquaintances:

> Konstantin is acting the holy fool again [iurodstvuet, a word
> with echoes of Old Russian eccentric saints] but never-
> theless his sickly condition is the heaviest stone upon my
> heart . . . the more so in that I am convinced in my conscience
> that the reason for it is we ourselves or even . . . I. . . .
> That is something very hard to bear. How many superlative
> qualities and how much talent will perish or is perishing
> in this unfortunate man without bearing fruit! But this would
> not distress me so much. The main thing is he can never be
> happy in life. Only within his family, surrounded by tender
> familial concern, can he exist and find some comfort.
> The world outside, to which he is not indifferent, will crush
> him. His successes, the highest public esteem for him,
> even that feeling of affability with which he is greeted—mean
> nothing. . . . Society will have its revenge on him for all
> that. This forms the dark side of my inner state.[35]

This self-perpetuating cycle of interdependence persisted until Sergei Timofeevich's death and constituted the hidden, negative

34. I. Aksakov, "Ocherk semeinogo byta Aksakovykh," pp. 11–12.
35. S. T. Aksakov to Ivan Aksakov, 26 June 1844 LL, fond 3 (GAIS/III), carton 22b.

side of the quasi-patriarchal Aksakov home life. Ivan Aksakov attributed his brother's death, little more than a year after that of their father, to tuberculosis aggravated by the shock of his father's death.[36]

If the relationship with Konstantin reveals consequences of an inner-directed style of family life that Sergei Timofeevich preferred to repress, they were offset by the general and genuine warmth of the Aksakov household, with frequent celebration of name-days, holidays, and other family rituals reinforcing family cohesion. The marriage in 1848 of Aksakov's second son, Grigorii (who seems to have been the most independent of the Aksakov children and later became governor of Samara province) to Sofia Aleksandrovna Shishkova (no relation to the admiral) seems to have evoked a certain sense of familial pride in Sergei Timofeevich, who eagerly incorporated Sofia into the charmed circle of the Aksakov family. After first meeting her, he wrote to his son and new daughter-in-law: "And thus my ardent desire has been realized; I have seen you, found out a great deal about you, my dear Sonechka, and have come to love you even more, if that is possible. I have learned even more about you, my dear son Grisha!—or rather, I have seen you now entirely matured."[37] In some of his letters to his daughter-in-law, Sergei Timofeevich affects a folksy, old-fashioned style, not unlike that he later would assign to his fictional patriarch, Stepan Mikhailovich, in *Family Chronicle*.

In general, there seem to be some indirect links between Grigorii's marriage and Sergei Timofeevich's works about his family. He uses his daughter-in-law's given name, Sofia, to replace his mother's name, Maria, in *Family Chronicle* and *Years of Childhood*, retaining his mother's patronymic, Nikolaevna. While this may simply be coincidence, Sergei Timofeevich did in fact write what he termed part of the "family chronicle" for his future daughter-in-law in 1847; not published until 1939, this brief sketch deals with Grigorii, and breaks off with an episode during his son's school days (2:412–416). The attempt to link present and past generations through writing foreshadows one of the explicit purposes of *Family Chronicle* (of which only the static opening sections existed in 1847), and more importantly, the

36. I. Aksakov, "Ocherk semeinogo byta Aksakovykh," p. 12.
37. S. T. Aksakov to G. S. Aksakov and S. A. Aksakova, 27 February 1848. PD, *fond* 3, inventory 16, item 28, fol. 7.

characterization of Grigorii is not unlike that of Stepan Mikhailovich (Grigorii's great-grandfather in real life): great physical
strength, piercing blue eyes, fits of towering but transitory rage.
The characterization of Stepan Mikhailovich may have been
worked out in part in this fragment Sergei Timofeevich intended
for his daughter-in-law, for Stepan Mikhailovich's first fit of rage
in *Family Chronicle* occurs in the third section of the first chapter and was written only after the fragment describing Grigorii.
Finally, *Years of Childhood* was dedicated to his granddaughter
Olga, Grigorii and Sofia's daughter. Thus it would seem that
events in the life of his son—Grigorii was the only child married
at this time and thus the only one continuing the family line—
in part prompted Aksakov's imagination to turn to the generations
of the family prior to his own and to some extent to transpose
present experience into the past. In this case, Stepan Mikhailovich becomes in part a self-projection, perhaps Aksakov's notion
of what a patriarch should be but which he himself in many
ways was not.

   Although Aksakov's relations with his second son and his family may have found some indirect reflection in his work, the
question remains why Aksakov, so late in life, devoted so much
time and effort to his writing. He dictated his last work, the brief
"Sketch of a Winter's Day," during his final illness, when he was
confined to bed and in considerable pain, suggesting that the
need to write had become much more than a pastime. The increasing power and artistry of his works suggest their increasing
importance for their author. Beyond the common human desire
to record for posterity the events of one's youth, currents beneath
the calm surface of Aksakov's life and works suggest deeper,
though infrequently expressed, apprehensions and even fears
that may lie close to the inner sources of his art. Sergei Timofeevich's complex and somewhat guilt-ridden relationship with
his oldest son certainly indicates tensions absent from his work,
but other shapes and shadows emerge if we consider Aksakov's
personal attitude, at the time of his writing, toward some of the
places and people who figure prominently in his works.
   Though one would be hard-pressed to deduce it from *Family
Chronicle* or *Years of Childhood*, Aksakov's own attitude toward
his ancestral estates as they were in the 1850s was extremely
negative. The estates had declined economically by then, but

from the time he left the Orenburg region with his family in 1826 until his death, Aksakov returned to his estates only four or five times over the course of some thirty years. Russian landowners living in the city often left them in the hands of managers, and Aksakov's brothers lived on other family estates in the vicinity of his own. Furthermore, travel was difficult and unpleasant (Aksakov himself particularly disliked having to ferry across the Volga),[38] and his health was not always up to such a journey. Nevertheless, so few trips in over thirty years to such sizable holdings suggest a strong disaffection.[39] This is in part borne out by a comment in a letter Sergei Timofeevich wrote to Grigorii after what would prove to be his final trip to Nadezhdino and another estate in 1851: "God in his wrath created two repulsive places—Vishen'ki and Nadezhdino—I never will go to live in them and will die at Abramtsevo, where we will all reside without leaving until our affairs are straightened out."[40] Why does Aksakov's private opinion differ so greatly from the often idealized picture of the family estates presented in *Family Chronicle* and other works?

Part of the reason may lie in Aksakov's relations as an adult with his parents; this subject is neither mentioned nor alluded to anywhere in Aksakov's writings. In them, any reference to his parents or to other relatives, even in a fictionalized guise, more or less ends with Sergei's departure to St. Petersburg at the end of *Reminiscences*, that is from early 1808. From this point on, only the "public" Aksakov, active in theatrical and literary circles, appears in his works. The only works which are set in the countryside as it was in the period 1810–1830 are the works on hunting, which are basically static with regard to time and in which the only human is the schematic figure of the hunter. As far as we know, Aksakov never entertained any plans for treating this period in any other way. He was generally reticent on the subject of his immediate family (his wife and children appear

38. The episodes involving crossing the Volga in *Years of Childhood* (1:541, 555) are tense and dramatic. In an 1835 letter to his wife, Aksakov describes his fear while crossing the Volga and adds, "I hate big rivers. They are graves." Letter of 24 July 1835. PD, *fond* 3, inventory 15, item 26, fol. 5.

39. To judge by surviving letters, Aksakov made trips to his estates in Orenburg in 1832, 1835, 1839, 1840, and 1852; the evidence is fragmentary and it is possible that other trips were made. None of the known trips seems to have lasted longer than a month or so.

40. S. T. Aksakov to G. S. Aksakov and S. A. Aksakova, July 1851. TsGALI, *fond* 19, inventory 3, storage unit 29, fol. 59.

only in *History of My Acquaintance with Gogol*), but this total silence with regard to the later lives of the two persons who figure most prominently in his works may involve more than decorum.

Ivan Aksakov, in his "Brief Sketch of the Aksakovs' Family Life" (originally intended as the opening of a projected biography of his brother Konstantin), provides some hints of a conflict between Sergei Timofeevich and his parents. According to Ivan, Sergei Timofeevich's mother, Maria Nikolaevna Aksakova, whose portrait in his works seems accurate in its emphasis on the intensity of her emotional relationships, "ceased to love her intensely beloved Serezha as soon as he married."[41] Since Ivan was writing after the deaths of his father and brother, he probably relied on family tradition, as shaped by Sergei Timofeevich himself or by Olga Semenovna. A few surviving letters from Maria Nikolaevna to her son and daughter-in-law to some extent corroborate Ivan's assertion. In them, Maria Nikolaevna expresses interest almost exclusively in her young grandchildren, especially Konstantin, and addresses Sergei Timofeevich only to criticize his overindulgence of his eldest son;[42] one can perhaps trace Aksakov's emotional domination of Konstantin to patterns set by his mother. Maria Nikolaevna's affections seem to have gravitated toward Arkadii, her youngest son, after Sergei Timofeevich's marriage.[43] The preference for perpetual or "frozen" childhood and unchanging family roles seems to have been part of the Aksakov family tradition.

Ivan Aksakov also states rather plainly that the potential for discord between his grandparents, hinted at in *Family Chronicle* and *Years of Childhood*, had in fact been realized in their later lives:

> The once brilliant, passionate Maria Nikolaevna turned into an old, sickly, suspicious, and jealous woman, tormented til the end of her days by the awareness of her husband's insignificance and at the same time by jealousy concerning

41. I. Aksakov, "Ocherk semeinogo byta Aksakovykh," p. 17.

42. N. M. Pavlov, ed., "Iz semeinoi perepiski starikov Aksakovykh," pp. 120–121.

43. Maria Nikolaevna laments, "I have parted with my Arkadii, whom I of course will see no more in this life." Arkadii was leaving home to study in St. Petersburg, but would in fact return to live most of his life on the family estates. The date is August 1818, and Maria Nikolaevna was to live until 1833. Ibid., p. 114.

> him, for she felt that he merely feared her, but that she had lost
> his heart. . . . Both the old people felt that Serezhen'ka
> had left their way of life behind. Everyone in the household
> feared only Maria Nikolaevna. She was the head of the house.[44]

The rift between the older Aksakovs, apparent in the years just
after Aksakov's marriage, may have contributed to Sergei Timofeevich and Olga Semenovna's decision to move to Moscow and
seems to have eventually led to serious conflict in the years
immediately preceding his parents' deaths. Unfortunately, information on this point is very scanty and circumstantial, consisting mainly of a few letters by Sergei Timofeevich from various
dates before and following his mother's death in 1833. To judge
from Sergei Timofeevich's letters to his father from this period,
Timofei Stepanovich had entered into a liaison of some sort with
a serf named Avdot'ia. She herself was married and probably
acted with her husband's knowledge and collusion in exploiting
Timofei Stepanovich's perhaps senile affections. The exact nature of the relationship and the aims of Avdot'ia and her husband
Iakov remain unclear from Aksakov's letters, but Maria Nikolaevna, who had gone blind in the late 1820s, had strong apprehensions about the situation and sought to have the woman removed from Aksakovo. As Sergei Timofeevich wrote his father,
on his last visit to Aksakovo before her unexpected death he had
proposed to his mother that

> she sign over these people to me so that their removal could
> return tranquility to her for the present and even for the
> future. Mother did not agree, fearing your anger towards me
> and your annoyance with herself; she even added the
> following words with dissatisfaction: "That's fine for you!
> You'll leave, but I will remain in your father's hands. I'm blind
> and I depend on him for everything." All my attempts
> to convince her that you would have no reason to get angry,
> that you yourself would be satisfied with this arrangement,
> were unsuccessful. Still, there is no doubt that if Mother's
> death had been from some other disease, if she had seen that
> death was at hand and had made proper dispositions,
> then Iakov and his wife would have been turned over to me or
> to my sister Nadezhda. I can not in conscience decide
> whether Mother's suspicions were justified, but in any case
> this woman's closeness to you, so soon after the death of our

---

44. I. Aksakov, "Ocherk semeinogo byta Aksakovykh," p. 17.

long-suffering mother, lends these suspicions credibility,
offends the memory of the deceased, and offends your
children. You yourself were always a dutiful and respectful
son; put yourself in our place and tell us: Can we not take
offense, can we not wish the removal of Avdot'ia, who
is hateful to us, and can we willingly agree to and cooperate
in her coming close to you ? . . .
. . . .

Nadezhda Timofeevna has two letters from Mother with a
description of all her torments and fears (one of the letters,
despite her blindness, is written in her own hand), and
with requests to take these people, which was put off until
Nadezhda's arrival; finally, two weeks before her death, at
Mother's order, a letter was written by Annushka to brother
Nikolai, requesting that he agree to take Iakov and his wife—
and so the removal of Avdot'ia was our mother's constant,
unchanging wish and desire up until her very death.

There is no doubt about this and no explanations are
necessary. Can our mother's righteous wish be sacred only
while she is alive?[45]

Whatever the precise situation may have been, Timofei Stepanovich was sufficiently angered by his son's rebuke to threaten
Sergei Timofeevich with a paternal curse, to which the latter
replied,

Could I have ever imagined that I, a loving and respectful son,
I even make bold to say, an exemplary one (I pray God
that my own children may be the same toward myself), would
receive such a letter from you, my respected sir and father,
after which I am not to dare to address you as "dear Father"! I
have committed no offense before you, but you, only out
of mercy, do not subject me to a curse. . . . That is really too
hard to bear![46]

In addition, Timofei Stepanovich apparently was upset over
various arrangements that his children were making with their
mother's property. Although Sergei Timofeevich's surviving letters from this period do not indicate the final resolution of l'af-
faire Avdot'ia, within a year his father's anger seems to have
subsided somewhat. Still, with his mother dead and his father
embittered toward him, the whole rather unpleasant episode

45. S. T. Aksakov to T. S. Aksakov, 6 March 1834. PD, *fond* 3, inventory 3,
item 11, fols. 1v–2v.
46. S. T. Aksakov to T. S. Aksakov, 2 May 1834. Ibid., fols. 4–4v.

could not have failed to affect Sergei Timofeevich's emotional attitude toward the countryside and the changes, much for the worse, that had occurred in and among its inhabitants.

On a visit in 1835, accompanied by Konstantin, Sergei Timofeevich visited his mother's grave at Aksakovo. Other experiences on this trip reinforced his sense of loss and of mortality. He wrote his wife,

> On Saturday, at ten in the evening, we arrived at Arkadii's; we
> went directly to Mother's grave. . . . It is not necessary,
> and I am unable, to describe to you, my dear, all the various
> emotions I underwent. . . . That night and even the fol-
> lowing one I could not close my eyes. . . . We inspected her
> room, which remained in that same disorder in which
> it was at the moment of Mother's last departure for Sernye Vody
> [a mineral spa]. A washbasin stands on the floor, which
> she had placed there herself; in general everything was in that
> living disorder which disturbs the soul by presenting the
> past to it as actual and bringing memories back to life.[47]

On this same trip, Aksakov not only had to confront vivid reminders of the irretrievable loss of his mother, but also had to deal with his father. After an initially cool reception, a reconciliation of sorts was reached, although the meeting could hardly have been pleasant.[48]

Even given the tensions of this particular journey, one might assume that Aksakovo would at least retain pleasant associations, since of all the family properties, it was the one on which Sergei Timofeevich had spent the most time as a child. On the contrary, as a letter to his wife suggests, the very familiarity of the place vitiated any positive memories: "I can not live here; everything produces a strong impression on me; I grieve during the days, and nights I literally do not sleep; fishing doesn't distract me."[49] In a marginal comment in the same letter he offers, perhaps as an afterthought, a generalization about his sentiments on the current state of Aksakovo, one with considerable pertinence to his later years and to his works: "A thought which has become a conviction has occurred to my heart: One must live out

---

47. S. T. Aksakov to O. S. Aksakova, 24 July 1835. Ibid., inventory 15, item 26, fols. 5v–6.

48. S. T. Aksakov to O. S. Aksakova, 26 July and 7 August 1835. Ibid., fols. 7 and 9.

49. S. T. Aksakov to O. S. Aksakova, 26 July 1835. Ibid., fol. 7.

one's *old age* in some new place, and not where one had spent his childhood and youth, for there everything constantly reminds you of what you were and what you are."[50] Thus years before Sergei Timofeevich presented the Orenburg region and Bagrovo/ Aksakovo in the highly nostalgic and idealized tones of the first two sections of chapter 1 of *Family Chronicle*, the region and the estate had already become places to be avoided, constantly bringing to mind both the erosion of family concord and the oppressive passage of time.

Moreover, this sense of loss and disillusionment brought about by revisiting the scenes of his earlier life seems not to have been a momentary or transitory one: on a trip to Aksakovo four years later, he found that hunting failed to bring release from the depression occasioned by the sight of the old familiar places, even though his father's death in 1837 had ended all possibility of overt conflict.[51] Aksakov once again, at nearly fifty years of age, expresses in his letters the same sorrowful disillusionment with Aksakovo: "Places here, that is Znamenskoe [Aksakovo], constantly produce one emotion in me—sorrow. I can only sleep while in a tarantas [a kind of carriage]. The places are all just the same, there are the same water, woods, and meadows, but none of the former people. . . . I meet hardly a single familiar face, except for a few old people who can not cease marveling at the fact that I too have gotten old."[52]

Thus not only the remnants of the society of Aksakov's youth, but even the very landscape in its unchangeability have become for him a reminder that *et in Arcadia ego* and an indication of his own changed appearance and dwindling years. In this context, his comments of 1851 on the desolation at Nadezhdino, quoted previously, seem to be not so much a condemnation of that particular estate at that moment (although Aksakov never seems to have particularly liked it) as a late expression of an abiding antipathy toward the present state of the remembered Eden in which he had spent his early years. For all their apparent candor, Aksakov's works pursue a deliberate strategy of avoiding the present and the recent past, with their sorry record of parental rejection, discord, decay, and death, in favor of a bright distant past, one that perhaps never existed and cannot be regained, but one in

50. S. T. Aksakov to O. S. Aksakova, 26 July 1835. Ibid., fols. 7v–8.
51. S. T. Aksakov to O. S. Aksakova, 15 August 1839. Ibid., fol. 39v.
52. S. T. Aksakov to O. S. Aksakova, 5 August 1840. Ibid., fol. 43.

which the secure emotional circle of the family seemed a sure bulwark.

If Aksakov's remembrance and reshaping of the past reflects a psychological need to suppress a harsher present reality, he has differed from his readers only in the degree of intensity of that longing and in his ability to satisfy it through art. On the biographical level, the emotional interdependence of Aksakov and his children may have been for him a form of compensation for the loss of a secure past. Similarly, the purchase of the estate at Abramtsevo, which became the place where Aksakov first turned to serious writing and where he composed many of his works, may have provided him with a pastoral retreat which solved the dilemma of continued life in the city or return to the now detested Orenburg estates. Within the safety of this emotionally neutral space, Aksakov could begin, in his writing, to approach more and more closely his own inner life. In broad outline, the prose works beginning with *Notes on Fishing* move from a rather impersonal and unemotional, generalized pastoral to the observations and historical accounts of the literary memoirs and *Family Chronicle*, to the subjective world of *Reminiscences* and *Years of Childhood*. In the latter works particularly, where Aksakov deals in detail with the relationship between himself and his mother, he abolishes the effects of the intervening years. His final works fix the golden age in artistic form.

Aksakov's life was ostensibly one of family happiness and of cultural dilettantism, but there are undercurrents of disillusionment and embitterment, stemming from conflict with and between his parents, from the submerged emotional tragedy in his own family, and from the passage of time itself. Only through an art that captured the bright world of nature and regained the bliss of the past could Aksakov at least partially ease his carefully veiled anguish at the destruction wrought by time.

2

Early Verse and First Prose

Had Aksakov died in 1840, his place in Russian literature would be minor to the point of insignificance. His theater criticism of the late 1820s and early 30s would attract the attention of historians of the Russian theater, but little else would attract even the most indefatigable collectors of literary minutiae. Aside from these theater articles and a few translations,[1] the corpus of Aksakov's works would have consisted only of a rather small number of verses, generally of indifferent quality and not all published in Aksakov's lifetime, and one short piece in prose, "The Blizzard" ("Buran"), 1833. In short, Aksakov would have merited at most a footnote in a scrupulously inclusive history of Russian literature.

Although at the age of fifty Aksakov still had before him the literary career on which his reputation would rest, his early verse and his one original prose piece prior to 1840 deserve some brief attention in the light of their author's subsequent development as a major author of the mid-nineteenth century. While these early works do not of course go far to explain the larger-scale and more successful late works, they do reveal themes and modes of expressing those themes that acquire considerable importance in Aksakov's last two decades. In addition, they provide a certain amount of evidence suggesting that even in his late works Aksakov's style owes a debt to the theories of his early mentor, Admiral A. S. Shishkov.

1. Aksakov, in the years from 1812 to 1830, translated a number of works, most attesting to his theatrical interests and conservative literary bent. His translations include Sophocles' *Philoctetes* (from a French version by La Harpe), Molière's *L'Ecole des maris* and *L'Avare*, Boileau's eighth and tenth *Satires*, and Sir Walter Scott's *Peverel of the Peaks*. Aksakov undertook the latter only to complete a translation (from a French version) undertaken by his friend Aleksandr Ivanovich Pisarev, who died in 1828. For details, see Mashinskii, *S. T. Aksakov*, pp. 40–42, 139, 146–149.

The young Aksakov first became acquainted with Shishkov's *Discussion of the Old and New Style of the Russian Language* (*Rassuzhdenie o starom i novom sloge rossiiskogo iazyka*) in 1806, when he was co-editor of a student journal. His enthusiasm for Shishkov's theories was so great that he was moved to exclude from *Journal of Our Activities* (*Zhurnal nashikh zaniatii*), "so far as I could, the idyllic direction of my friend [Aleksandr Panaev] and blind imitation of Karamzin."[2] In his "Memoir of Aleksandr Semenovich Shishkov" ("Vospominanie ob A. S. Shishkove"), Aksakov maintains with some humorous irony that his discovery of Shishkov's book confirmed his own nationalist sentiments and his literary attitudes: "Of course, I acknowledged him as an incontrovertible authority, the wisest and most intelligent of men! I believed in every word of his book as in a sacred thing! My Russian leanings and my hostility to everything foreign were perceptibly strengthened, and my vague sense of nationalism developed to the point of exclusiveness" (2:268). While Aksakov may exaggerate his adolescent nationalism for humorous effect, his sympathy for Shishkov's ideas, political and literary, continued during his years in St. Petersburg, where he was an almost daily guest of Shishkov's and an observer of the first meetings of the Beseda ("conversation"), Shishkov's conservative literary salon, at which the main activities were readings, literary discussions, and amateur theatricals. Despite the great difference in their ages, Aksakov became a literary confidant of Shishkov's and found his discussions with the admiral reflected in the latter's *Dialogues on Literature* (*Razgovory o slovesnosti*), 1811 (2:282).

Aksakov certainly shared Shishkov's nationalism, and late in his own life considered the admiral a forerunner of mid-nineteenth-century Slavophilism (a view the Slavophiles themselves probably did not share), pointing out that the term *Slavophile* had been applied to Shishkov derisively in the early nineteenth century (2:270). For Shishkov, as Aksakov states, "the judgment and censure of social morality was inseparably linked with the task of literature" (2:312–313). Discussion of literature was merely the battlefield on which combat for higher stakes was conducted; though Shiskov directed much of his own effort toward literary polemic, the real premises of his position were

---

2. Reminiscences (*Vospominaniia*) in *Sobranie sochinenii*, 2:148.

political and ethical. Thus his literary doctrine is hardly a coherent theory, but is confined almost entirely to matters of style,
where pernicious foreign influences were most immediately
apparent. Aksakov, at least in later life, was never as vehement a
moralist or nationalist as Shishkov, and one may entertain doubts
as to the seriousness of his interest in his mentor's political doctrines even in his early years. However, he does seem to have
shared, in practice if not in explicit theory, Shishkov's basic
premise of the autonomy of every language, based on national
uniqueness. The main corollary to this was the necessity for
maintaining semantic exactitude in style, and Shishkov, an amateur lexicographer, considered lexical precision the surest means
to this end. Here of course Shishkov directly challenged Karamzin's advocacy of a vague, rather neutral style suitable to
the elevated norms of the salon; for Karamzin, the imitation of
French vocabulary, syntax, and word order was predicated on
the universality of human feelings, even in individuals of different nations, and the need to express those similar feelings in
similar ways.

The defense of the autonomy of Russian constitutes the major
goal of Shishkov's *Discussion of the Old and New Style of
the Russian Language*. In this work, Shishkov attacks the use
of French, particularly in education, and protests even more
strongly against the imitation of French in Russian, but he also
advances a positive argument for the independence of Russian
from foreign influence, namely, the organic nature of any language and the historical, intrinsic development of its semantic
system: "In every language there is a multitude of words or terms,
which in the course of long usage by various writers have acquired varied senses, or depict various concepts, and thus signi-
fication may be likened to a circle formed by a rock thrown into
the water and constantly expanding its limits" (pp. 29–30).

The insistence on the historically determined specificity of the
lexicon of each language implies the avoidance of direct borrow-
ing of foreign words. Shishkov also rejected the artificial restriction of vocabulary typical of Karamzinian style, and on the
stylistic and syntactic levels he opposed the excessive use of
metaphor and the delicate phrasing favored by the Russian Sen-
timentalists in imitation of their French models. Shishkov argues
that such practices not only ape French usage unnecessarily but
also lead to patent illogicality: "Rapture . . . over foreign, often

absurd, writings engenders . . . the desire to imitate and love for these and similar odd expressions: 'a tender heart which sleeps delicately beneath a transparent haze . . .'" (p. 65).

Thus the style of Sentimentalism as a whole, not merely its borrowings or calques, constitutes a degradation of true Russian style, which, according to Shishkov, possesses the virtues of simplicity, power, and exactitude. It should be noted that in his late works, and in a few of his verses of the 1820s, addressed to his brother, Aksakov at least in part retains a basic Sentimentalist goal, the communication of universal feelings. In order to effect this communication, however, he employs a style much closer to the norms of the Shishkov school, with which his association was much longer and considerably more intimate.

The roots of certain aspects of Aksakov's later style can be seen in Shishkov's development of the positive side of his theories in his *Dialogues on Literature*. Having rejected the mellifluous vagueness of the Karamzin school, Shishkov instead advances lexical precision as the primary determinant of style. If concrete and definite terminology seems at first prosaic, it nevertheless has the advantage of realizing more fully the potentialities of the word, which, thus isolated, acquires increased semantic import. Even the components of the word, its roots and affixes, are exploited as important sources of meaning, nuance, and aesthetic potential. All this directly opposes the Karamzinian approach, in which the phrase serves as the basic unit and determines use and order of words: "Words, not only by their own particular meaning, but even by the significance of prefixes or particles connected with them, give a phrase much force and beauty" (p. 144).

Since every element of a word possesses a specific significance, an author's use of it must be based on conscious decision, drawing on a thorough comprehension of the choices available and the total meaning of the word actually chosen. The choice of a word depends for Shishkov on the historical use of a given word, and thus requires etymological and philological knowledge and understanding of the organic growth of a root and its derivatives. (Such philological preoccupation was common later among the Slavophiles as well, including Konstantin Aksakov.) In the search for the proper, historically given meaning of a word, Shishkov considers the earliest texts normative, insofar as they permit access directly "into the repository of versification and of eloquence. There are three such sources: first, the sacred or religious books; second, chronicles and all accounts similar to them; third, the language of the folk" (p. 50). Of these sources, the third represents an innovation on Shishkov's part and is probably a point of the greatest eventual significance for Aksakov. Shishkov goes beyond his predecessors on the subject (principally Lomonosov), not only tolerating the use of the common language (that is, the language of non-Westernized classes) for elevated subjects or genres, but indeed finding in it "beautiful thoughts and expressions. It is evident that the Muses, occasionally fleeing from the learned, love to visit simple cottages" (p. 102). Although Shishkov does not advocate total acceptance of the common language, he considers its use a surer means of attaining authenticity than the imitation of foreign models: "The common language, somewhat purified of its rudeness, renewed and adapted to our present literature, would draw us closer to that pleasant innocence, those natural feelings, by distancing ourselves from which we are becoming *mincing prattlers* rather than truly eloquent writers" (pp. 155–156).

Shishkov's views are relevant both to Aksakov's early verse and to his later prose in the following points: the insistence on lexical precision, the avoidance of excessive metaphor, and the positive assessment of the use of the common language on any level, valued as a means of renewing the literary language by a return to simplicity. In his verse of the 1820s ("The Angler's Lament") and his later prose, Aksakov frequently has recourse to popular, even peasant language, although the reasons for this are not entirely the same as Shishkov's. Shishkov viewed popular language as a repository of vital archaisms; this, rather than any populist bias, is probably the reason why he accords it equal value with Slavonic religious writings or Old Russian secular works.

If Aksakov ever fully shared this archaistic attitude, he certainly lost it in subsequent decades; his late prose often employs regionalisms, technical terms and other items from the popular language, but they are used because they are the precise terms, not because of their popular or archaic features per se. He uses technical theatrical terms in much the same way, even though many of these terms are of foreign origin, because they are professionally correct. However, when Aksakov is not dealing with a specific occupation, location, or group, and there is no need to establish the narrator's expert knowledge of the subject, he employs a rather neutral prose (in memoirs of literary figures, for example, or in analyses of inner states and feelings) and usually avoids deliberate archaisms, regionalisms, popular or professional terms, or other stylistically marked terms. Foreign terms are accepted if they have become a part of cultivated Russian, and in general there are no a priori principles of inclusion or exclusion. Of course, to do otherwise in the post-Pushkin period would be impossible; even in his day Shishkov was fighting a rear-guard battle.

Aksakov's continued interest in matters of style, particularly vocabulary, can be seen even late in his career. He reproaches Turgenev for neglecting matters of "language and style" ("iazyk i slog")[3] in Turgenev's review of *Notes of a Hunter of Orenburg Province*, and in a letter discussing Turgenev's "The Way Station" ("Postoialyi dvor"), he criticizes the author for using regionalisms solely for local color:

> With regard to the language of the story, I came across words that were imprecise and improperly used. In addition, I consider it a mistake to use words and expressions which are local, provincial, and for the comprehension of which one must have a dictionary of regional dialects. Language must be generally comprehensible, Russian. Instead of imparting a seeming local coloration, such words mar the general impression, at least at first reading.[4]

One might note that modern editions of Aksakov's own works are often provided with brief glossaries of regional terms, but in his comment to Turgenev Aksakov is objecting to regionalisms that are either totally unmotivated, or motivated solely by a desire for local color. Thus even late in his career, Aksakov retains allegiance to the Shishkovite principles of rational clarity and lexical exactitude, which permits the use of necessary popular or local terms but does not encourage overindulgence in them.

Aksakov's original verse, more than his early prose or translations, provides some (admittedly slight) indication of the evolution of his style beyond the rather lofty norms of Shishkov. In addition, his verse, especially that of the 1820s, a potentially more intimate form than the prose of the time, gives some hint of the themes that will become central in his prose of the 1840s and

3. S. T. Aksakov to I. S. Turgenev, January 1853, in Maikov, ed., "Pis'ma Aksakovykh," no. 9, p. 11.
4. S. T. Aksakov to I. S. Turgenev, 9 March 1853, in ibid., p. 26.

1850s, when prose had become acceptable as a vehicle for the expression of the personal.

Aksakov's earliest known verse appeared in the February 1807 volume of *Journal of Our Activities*, the handwritten journal of the students of the University of Kazan, when the poet was all of sixteen. These two poems, entitled "To a Nightingale" and "To One Who is Unfaithful" ("K solov'iu" and "K nevernoi"),[5] "are melancholy love lyrics written before Aksakov's acquaintance with Shishkov's *Discussion* and his conversion to its author's views. They are, as Aksakov points out in his *Reminiscences*, Karamzinian in diction and theme, the clearest indication we have of Aksakov's brief flirtation with Karamzinism. Inept concatenations of Sentimental clichés, they display the derivative quality that characterizes Aksakov's verse for the next several decades, whether the model is Sentimental or more traditional. At times, Aksakov's adherence to his models takes the form of direct imitation of a specific poem, for example, "A Cossack of the Urals" ("Ural'skii kazak"), 1821, modeled on Pushkin's "The Black Shawl" ("Chernaia shal'"); other poems are exercises in a specific genre, such as the fable (3:647, 633, 650).

However, it should be borne in mind that the basically conservative Shishkovite tendency to which Aksakov soon shifted his allegiance put relatively little value on originality. Imitation is not without its uses, after all, particularly polemical ones. In "An Elegy in the New Taste" ("Elegiia v novom vkuse"), 1821, Aksakov directly and effectively expressed his continued hostility to the stylistic excesses of Sentimentalism and its successors, notably Zhukovskian Romanticism, and his attachment to Shishkov's principles. Aksakov later termed his mock-elegy "a protest against the misty-meditative poems engendered by imitation of Zhukovskii" (3:51). The poem's epigraph, from Horace's *Ars poetica*—*nugae canorae* ("tinkling trifles")—ironically calls attention to the role of sound in verse, and the pseudonymous signature Podrazhaev ("Imitator") completes the polemical framing of the poem. In the text itself, through a rapid and unrelenting catalogue of the standard epithets, stereotyped metaphors, and needless (and untranslatable) diminutives of the mellifluous elegies of the Zhukovskii school (the last two features in partic-

5. The first poem is quoted by Aksakov himself in *Reminiscences* (2:146); the second is published in the commentary to it in the 1955 edition of his works (2:480–481).

ular violate Shishkovite norms of exactitude), Aksakov points out and ridicules the frequent vacuity of such verse:

> Molchit ugriumyi bor . . . luch' solntsa dogoraet . . .
> Brodiashchii veterok v listochkakh umiraet . . .
>   S bezbrezhnoi vysoty
> Prokhlada snizoshla na lone temnoty. (3:645)

> The gloomy pine forest is silent . . . the sun's ray flickers . . .
> The errant breeze expires in the leaves . . .
>   From the limitless heights
> Coolness has descended upon the bosom of darkness.

Two other early poems of Aksakov's, the verse epistles to A. I. Kaznacheev and P. A. Viazemskii (1814 and 1821 respectively; 3:636, 643) are also of a polemical nature. Composed in the wake of the Napoleonic invasion, the first, with true Shiskhovite blending of language and civic morality, excoriates Russian Francophilism as the source of moral decay. The ladies of Russian high society, instead of foregoing all things French at a time of war, rush to embrace (both literally and figuratively) captured French officers, thereby dashing conservative hopes that

> we would be ashamed of blind imitation,
> return to our customs, to our native tongue. (3:636)

As a true disciple of Shishkov, Aksakov sees the only salvation for Russian society specifically in the abandonment of the French language:

> We should drive out their language,
>   forget it forever. Now
> whoever doesn't speak it—is not a person,
> In polite society he is not received,
> Be he intelligent and learned—he is called
>   an ignoramus. (3:637–638)

Kaznacheev, to whom the poem is addressed, was Shishkov's nephew, which reinforces the link between the poem and the admiral. In many respects, this epistle, composed after Aksakov's longest period of direct contact with Shishkov, is his most thoroughly Shishkovian effort, not only in its rather archaic diction but also in its ascription of the lapses in public morality to thoughtless imitation of French customs and uncritical use of the French language. However, the implicit attitude of disdain for society in general and the advocacy of stoic patience in the face of its ephemeral frivolities point as well to Aksakov's later, frequently expressed dislike of Moscow's social whirl.

Aksakov's other "public" epistle, to Prince P. A. Viazemskii, is a polemical reply to Viazemskii's epistle to M. T. Kachenovskii, editor of the journal *Herald of Europe* (*Vestnik Evropy*), and seeks to defend the editor from Viazemskii's charge that he is a petty critic. In it, Aksakov rejects Viazemskii's Romantic premise of the superiority of the artist and asserts that rational, critical analysis of a poem is the surest way of ascertaining genius (3:643). The stance is reminiscent of Shishkov's rationalistic attacks on Karamzin, and is still discernible thirty years later, in Aksakov's comments on Turgenev's style and in his references to his own works as constructions.

These two "public" epistles contrast with a group of intimate epistles written in the 1820s that seem to mark the inception of themes that were to persist throughout Aksakov's creative career. The beginning of this line of poetry can be seen in a fragment "Behold My Homeland" ("Vot rodina moia"), 1816, which describes Aksakov's native Orenburg region:

> Vot rodina moia . . . Vot dikie pustyni!
> Vot blagodarnaia orataiu zemlia!
> Dubovye lesa, i zlachnye doliny
> I tuchnoi zhatvoiu pokrytye polia!
>
> Vot gory, do nebes chelo svoe vsnosiashchi,
> Mladye otrasli Rifeiskikh drevnikh gor,
> I reki, s penoiu mezh propastei letiashchi,
> Razlivom po lugam pleniaiushchie vzor! (3:642)
>
> Behold my homeland . . . Behold the wild wastes!
> Behold the land grateful to the plowman!
> Oak forests and valleys of grain
> And fields covered with rich harvest!
>
> Behold the mountains, raising their brow to the heavens,
> The young spurs of the Ripaian mountains,
> And rivers, flying with foam 'midst chasms,
> Enchanting the sight with their flooded meadows.

The hyperbole and elevated vocabulary (*orataiu, chelo, zlachnye*) suggest such eighteenth-century models as Lomonosov and Derzhavin, favorites of Shishkovite archaists, and the impersonality echoes Aksakov's public epistles, but there is no longer any concern with matters of literary style or questions of the conduct

of Russia's elite. Instead, the basic geography of Aksakov's world
is established: forest, steppe, mountains, lakes, and rivers, specifically, those of Orenburg. In three epistles to his brother Arkadii
(dated 1823, 1824, and 1830), the subjective significance of this
world, the aspect which becomes most important in his prose,
first emerges.

The intimate and minor character of these three epistles should
be noted (only one was published in Aksakov's lifetime). Perhaps because they are addressed to a younger brother, they are in
iambic tetrameter rather than the more elevated hexameter of the
epistles to Kaznacheev and Viazemskii, and strive to strike a tone
of intimate conversation that is absent in the earlier works.

The first, subtitled "About Hunting" ("Ob okhote"), consists of
a brief evocation of the unexpected lure for Aksakov and his
brother of a season traditionally associated with ending and loss
—autumn:

> It . . . does not delight as joy does,
> Does not force us to grieve
> It . . . is a secret of the heart . . . Enough
> Of explaining the inexplicable. (3:661)

A catalog of migratory game birds, with brief but precise indications of their habitats and habits, follows. This short epistle may
be considered a germ of the encyclopedic *Notes of a Hunter of
Orenburg Province* (*Zapiski ruzheinogo okhotnika orenburgskoi
gubernii*), 1852, not only in its precise description of various
game, but also because it implies that hunting is an authentic
passion, unintelligible to those who do not share it.

The second epistle, "Autumn" ("Osen'"), subtitled "To My
Brother Arkadii Timofeevich in Petersburg" ("Bratu Arkadiiu
Timofeevichu v Peterburg"), and dated a year after the first epistle, touches even more basic themes bound up for Aksakov with
the family estates in Orenburg: themes of the past and familial
ties. Although the poem concludes in rather trite formulae, the
major portion of it consists of an evocation of the past, specifically Aksakov's close friendship with his brother and the rustic
joys of the family estate, Aksakovo. A return to Aksakovo serves
as the occasion for the poem:

> I have been to Aksakovo and—sadness
> did not leave me anywhere.
> Everything reminded me of you,
> The house seemed to me dull, empty. (3:664)

Aksakov's letters of the 1830s suggest that, because of the current unpleasantness of his relations with his parents, this nostalgic attitude toward Aksakovo had become not merely a poetic stance but a permanent conviction. In a manner that adumbrates Aksakov's prose, his nostalgia is immediately given a locus, in which every detail metonymically objectifies and reinforces the basic emotion. The millpond (prud) of the estate, its gloomy autumnal appearance pathetically matching the poet's, serves as the focal point of this objectification:

> Everywhere I see the same thing;
> Everywhere the traces of your sport
> And of your kind concern for me:
> Wavering in the wind and waves
> There stand abandoned stakes
> Which you, with a firm hand,
> Had plunged deep
> into the muddy bottom of the shallows . . .
> They speak to me in eloquent words
> of the past. (3:665)

In later works, as well as in letters such as the one describing his mother's room, Aksakov frequently employs such "traces" (sledy), here mentioned explicitly, as signs of an absent person and of the emotional bond with that person. Such objects evoke for Aksakov not only the individual, but also the complex of actions associated with the object. Only this dynamic memory linking the observer, the absent person, and the objects associated with the actions of that person can withstand time's inexorable alteration and destruction.

Time is yet another element in Aksakov's work that first appears in this epistle:

> We shall find alteration in each other;
> The traces of the Almighty's fatal hand,
> Of Saturn's awesome flow,
> We shall see even upon ourselves.
> The past is forever hidden,
> Nothing will bring this back,
> And be it however painful, but indeed,
> Everything will be the same—yet not the same. (3:666)

Although the cosmic imagery in the second and third lines suggests Derzhavin, the great eighteenth-century poet of time, the last two lines, in emphasizing a personal perception of and reac-

tion to the changes wrought by time, point more to the later
Aksakov.

"Autumn" is postscripted with a declaration of Aksakov's
abandonment of poetry, but he composed a third epistle to his
brother in 1830, when their positions had been reversed, with
Sergei Timofeevich in the city (Moscow) and Arkadii Timofeevich in the country. More elevated in tone than the first two epistles, the third incorporates the last two stanzas of "Behold My
Homeland" of 1816, except that the lofty optimism for the future
expressed in that fragment has been abandoned. The destructive
element of time has been introduced, and Aksakov foresees the
intrusion of new settlers and new exploitation in Orenburg:

> And you will not recognize yourself
> Under their unclean hands!
> They will trample your meadows, fell the forest,
> Even sully the waters—the image of heaven! (3:674)

For the present, however, the still-virginal beauty of Orenburg is
opposed to the pollution rampant in Moscow even in spring, the
season of rebirth. Askakov employs the motif of flight from the
corruption of the city to the pastoral world of Orenburg, to his
brother,

> For whom, as for me, are repellent
> The capitals with their glitter and noise.
> To you I fly in imagination;
> With you I sit, with you I walk,
> I hunt, fish on the millpond,
> But I share my excitement with no one . . .
>   and I argue about verses
> And headaches. (3:675)

The opposition of urban and rural, not stated in the two previous
epistles, is clearly sketched here; although such sentiments can
be found even earlier in Aksakov's letters, it is only with this
epistle that a basic theme of his late works finds direct literary
expression.

Of Aksakov's original verse up to 1830, one remaining effort
should be mentioned: "The Angler's Lament" ("Rybach'e gore"),
1824, subtitled "A Russian Idyll" ("Russkaia idilliia") (3:668). A
rather ambitious poem for Aksakov, it is a dramatic dialogue
between two fishermen on the inevitable subject of the one that
got away. Of all of Aksakov's works written before 1830, "The

Angler's Lament" most clearly recalls Shishkov's advocacy of the use of common language; indeed it often shades into the specialized language of fishermen. However, its rather unusual metrical scheme (basically amphibrachic pentameter) suggests affinities with nineteenth-century verse, in which amphibrachs became more common, especially in forms reflecting the purported inner life of the simple folk, notably the ballad, popularized by Zhukovskii. The use of a dialogue form, for the personages of which the otherwise insignificant event is important, permits not only the unelevated, conversational tone, but also a technical precision of description to the point that footnotes are provided by the author (he often does the same in his books on hunting and fishing).

Perhaps the most important aspect of the poem is its elevation and poeticizing of the trivial, or at least of the minor, a tendency Aksakov would pursue throughout his later literary career. One method of investing the ordinary with significance is to fragment actions into a series of specific acts:

> I pulled out all the lines, one after another,
> And set the bait right, threw them back,—
>   and again smoke my forgotten pipe
> And await again a lucky moment. (3:669)

The focus, for purposes of emphasis, on process rather than result (or on stressing result by depicting processes leading to it) can be seen as a prosaicized form of the retardation typical of both epic and pastoral. In addition to this pastoral device, "The Angler's Lament" also echoes the tradition of pastoral poetry in its humorous and anecdotal quality, its dialogue form, and its concluding affirmation of gentle friendship. Thus the poem is Aksakov's most "literary" pastoral of the period, far exceeding his epistles to his brother in this respect. Although it will drop the apparatus of verse pastoral, Aksakov's late prose will retain and intensify certain pastoral features, notably catalogue and retardation.

After 1830 Aksakov's few further efforts in verse consist of occasional pieces celebrating family anniversaries or events of importance to the family (such as the purchase of Abramtsevo in 1843); there are however a few poems on themes pertaining to nature, one of which will be discussed in connection with the hunting books. Even before 1830 Aksakov's verse is obviously

minor and certainly reveals no great poetic talent; still, given the
dominance of verse in Russia in the early nineteenth century, it
would perhaps be more surprising if someone with Aksakov's
literary interests and tendency to imitation had not tried his
hand at verse. Despite its weakness, some of Aksakov's verse
hesitantly touches both the themes and the devices characteristic
of his later prose, suggesting that Aksakov's sensibility and style
are the fruit of a long internal and organic development, most of
it hidden from our view, rather than merely a reflection of contemporary trends.

In his early period, Aksakov, like most of his contemporaries
and particularly the Shishkovites, felt verse to be the preferred,
indeed the only, artistic literary medium, with prose limited to
pragmatic functions such as criticism. (It was not a Shishkovite
but the Sentimentalist Karamzin who wrote some of the first
serious modern literary prose in Russian.) In this respect, Aksakov's first prose work, "The Blizzard" ("Buran"), 1833, a brief
sketch which appeared in the almanac *Day Star* (*Dennitsa*),
edited by Aksakov's friend M. A. Maksimovich, is of considerable
interest. It is apparent from the date of the sketch that Aksakov
began to consider the possibilities of artistic prose considerably
before the rash of realist prose appeared at the time of his later
works in the 1840s and 1850s. In fact, the date makes it clear that
he first tried prose in the period of poetic prose concomitant
with the protracted breakdown of Romanticism. Although "The
Blizzard" is much more definitely a work of poetic prose than
his later works, its existence suggests that one should not attrib-
ute Aksakov's later interest in prose solely to the flowering of
realist prose in the forties and fifties. "The Blizzard," like some
of Aksakov's verse of the late 1820s, indicates that Aksakov was
attuned and responsive to contemporary trends, but his Shishkovite antecedents and dilettante stance also instilled a certain
aloofness toward new literary movements, even when Aksakov
was willing to experiment with their techniques.

"The Blizzard" originally appeared anonymously for fear that
Aksakov's name on the piece would evoke hostile criticism of
the whole almanac from Ksenofont Polevoi, with whom Aksakov
had had unfriendly relations during his service as a censor. Aksakov republished the work in 1858, with an introduction in
which he stresses two points: the authenticity of the incident

related, which he maintains was a "real event, which occurred not far from my village," and the role of memory, which serves as the source of the descriptions of nature ("pictures of its [Orenburg's] nature were fresh in my memory") (2:404–405). The stress on memory as a primary source may well reflect Aksakov's attitudes or those he ascribes to his readers in 1858 more than it does the creative process in 1833; the subject and even some of the phrasing of "The Blizzard" are based on a verse fragment preserved in Aksakov's notebook, entitled *Book for All and Sundry* (*Kniga dlia vsiakoi vsiachiny*),[6] which he used from 1815 to sometime in the late 1820s, and which is at present in the Aksakov material in the Lenin Library. Thus Aksakov's earliest prose work draws directly on his previous poetic output and indicates a deliberate shift of literary values in favor of prose. It is, of course, a prose derived from poetry, as one might well expect in the age of Gogol. Aksakov is in his way in step with the developments within Russian literature at the time, for prose with all the ornaments of verse was characteristic of the 1830s. Aksakov's later prose is much less overtly "poetic," but its background in verse and poetic prose is at times discernible.

"The Blizzard" consists of a brief description (five pages in the 1955 edition of Aksakov's works) of a group of peasant drovers caught in the open steppe of the Orenburg region by a sudden blizzard. The text divides into two clearly differentiated stylistic levels, each associated with one of the two thematic elements in the sketch: nature and man.

Nature, as befits a lofty subject, is presented in a style that incorporates some of the distinctly poetic features of the underlying verse fragment, such as syntactic parallelisms, repetitions, simile, and personification, with an emphasis on visual effects:

> Solntse sklonialos' k zapadu i kosymi luchami skol'zia
> po neobozrimym gromadam snegov, odevalo ikh brilliantovoi
> koroiu, a izurodovannaia nalipnuvshim ineem roshcha, v
> snegovom i ledianom svoem ubore, predstavliala izdali chudnye
> i raznovidnye obeliski osypannye takzhe almaznym bles-
> kom. Vse bylo velikolepno. (2:408)

> The sun was inclining toward the west and, slipping with its
> slanted rays over the immense mountains of the snows,
> it clothed them with a diamond crust, and the grove, distorted

---

6. Published in the notes to "The Blizzard" in ibid., 2:499–500.

by clinging frost, presented from afar wondrous and variously
shaped obelisks also bestrewn with a diamond glitter. All
was magnificent.

The verse fragment in Aksakov's *Book for All and Sundry* is
clearly the inspiration for such prose:

> Siiaet solntse, vozdukh tikh,
> Nedvizhny derev vershiny,
> Spokoiny snezhnye puchiny.
> Almaznyi blesk gorit na nikh
> I oslepliaet vzor prel'shchennyi. (2:499)

> The sun shines, the air is still,
> The treetops are motionless,
> The snowy abysses are calm.
> A diamond glitter burns on them
> And dazzles the enticed gaze.

The peasants, in contrast to the landscape, are described in a
style that tends to avoid poetic effects and stresses the specific
and practical elements of action in the peasant's behavior:

> With great effort they dragged the old man's sled forward, and
> they first drove past Petrovich's horse, which had been
> pushed off the road to one side, and then pulled it out of the
> snowdrift and Petrovich became the last. (2:409)

The peasants are further characterized by their language, which
is even more directed to action, and consists of brief semantic
clusters related by parallel grammatical structures lacking conjunction of any sort. In the following example, there are two
units, one describing conditions and one prescribing actions;
each of these two units consists of three grammatically similar
subunits. Aksakov also employs some regionalisms and popular
vocabulary (as he also does in "The Angler's Lament"), such as
kaliakat', *negozhe*, and *umet*:

> "Polno kaliakat', rebiata. Do umeta daleko, noch' blizka, delo
> negozhe. Beri vozzhi, sadis', pogoniai loshadei." (2:407)

> "Enough prattling, fellows. It is far to the way station, night
> is near, things look bad. Take the reins, sit down, get the
> horses moving."

These colloquialisms and regionalisms are used more insistently and emphatically here than in later works, which do not

usually deal directly with peasants, and in any case avoid the strong stylistic polarity of "The Blizzard." Particularly noticeable in the first stylistic level and absent from the second are the mannered similes and metaphors reminiscent of Bestuzhev-Marlinskii, the most violent imagist of Russian Romantic prose:

> . . . belovatoe oblako, kak golova ogromnogo zveria. (2:408)

> . . . slyshalsia kak budto otdalennyi plach mladentsa, a inogda voi golodnogo volka . . . (2:409)

> . . . a whitish cloud, like the head of an enormous beast.

> . . . there was heard something like the crying of an infant, and sometimes like the wail of a hungry wolf . . .

The theme of "The Blizzard" rests on the interaction of these two stylistically defined levels, and it is in theme, rather than in style, that "The Blizzard" most directly foreshadows the later Aksakov. The basic pattern of the story is the journey, but the determinant of action is nature rather than man. The text can be divided into sections consisting of a change in the state of nature, an interpretation of this change by the peasants (or by the eldest among them), and their adaptive reaction based on this interpretation. Nature proceeds from relatively benign frozen beauty, in which the peasants feel at ease, joke, and play, through incipient storm, to full blizzard (metaphors of snakes and animals appear in this section), culminating in total chaos:

> A white gloom enveloped all, impenetrable, like the murk of the darkest autumn night! Everything merged, everything became mixed: earth, air, sky turned into an abyss of boiling snowy dust, which blinded the eyes, took away the breath, roared, whistled, moaned, groaned, beat, tossed, twisted from all sides, from above and below, twined like a snake and smothered all. (2:409)

Compare the verse fragment from *Book for All and Sundry*:

> A white gloom enveloped all with its wings,
> Night fell, the blizzard came on! It
> Whistles, hisses, roars, whines,
> Now upwards, now down twists in a column,
> The boiling snowy dust on all sides
> Blinds the eyes and suffocates. (2:499–500)

Finally, the storm subsides, and the reemerging steppe is compared to a frozen sea (2:410).

Faced with this potential for titanic force in nature, humanity's only adequate response consists in developing to the full the ability to interpret nature through its signs and to set a course of action in harmony with it. Thus wisdom, of a practical but vital sort, depends on interpreting, and acting in accordance with, nature's ceaseless messages, which are apparent to the trained and receptive observer. The peasants in "The Blizzard" are divided ethically by this criterion into the wise and the foolish. *Neopytnye* ("inexperienced, untested") (2: 408, 410) is a key term for the distinction; the inexperienced are also young, implying that full understanding of nature requires long study. The old peasant demonstrates his ability to decode nature's language by interpreting ice on trees as a sign of a good harvest in the coming year, while the young peasant resorts to superstition, calling the phenomenon, which means nothing to him, the work of a forest spirit (*leshii*) (2:407). He has not lived long enough, or, more importantly, has not observed carefully enough, to apprehend the seemingly remote and arbitrary connection between sign and signified.

The old peasant has developed an exceptional ability to interpret visual signs; his first perception of the coming storm comes when he "looks attentively in all directions" (2:407). Safety for the others depends on obedience to

> the stern voice of the old man, made wise by years of experience, whose penetrating gaze had foreseen a tempest in the light darkness, in the stillness. (2:408)

At each stage of the storm the old man advises the correct course of action, first haste, then a slow pace, and finally, with the horses exhausted and no refuge in sight, the construction of an emergency shelter of upturned sleds, beneath which to wait out the blizzard. Some young and inexperienced (*neopytnye*) peasants rebel at this seemingly certain death and decide to continue their journey, and of course perish. Those who understand nature, or obey those who do, experience only a surrogate death, consisting of burial in the snow, and are reborn, dug out on the third day by a passing group of drovers and revived from a semiconscious state by being rubbed with snow. (2:411).

Although somewhat melodramatically expressed in "The Blizzard," the theme of awareness of the environment and adjustment to it remains one of Aksakov's crucial concerns throughout his subsequent career. This theme constitutes the core of his works on hunting, but it plays an important role as well in *Family Chronicle* and particularly in *Years of Childhood*, concerned as it is with the child's developing perception of the world around him, both physical and social.

The action of "The Blizzard" can be viewed more dynamically as a plot or fable, one which involves a test culminating in a final ordeal that only those who have learned the lessons of experience can survive. Although presented literally in "The Blizzard," such initiatory experiences run through many of Aksakov's prose works, providing the central or most dramatic moments in them (the hunting books also initiate, in a sense, but here it is the reader who vicariously becomes a hunter). Thus Aksakov begins his career in prose with an isolated version of one of his central patterns of action. An exercise in a given literary mode, "The Blizzard" adumbrates the works of its author's final decades.

3

The Strategy of the Hunter

Aksakov's works during his real literary career, from the 1840s until his death in 1859, can be seen, from one point of view, as a series of attempts to enter literature, specifically, prose literature, through genres that were either nonliterary or on the edge of literature ("The Blizzard" was Aksakov's only earlier original prose work and derives in part from a fragment of poetry). The later 1840s and 1850s were of course a period of great ferment in Russian literature, of debuts and literary experimentation, primarily in realistic prose and often in forms that had previously been deemed peripheral or subliterary: sketches, notes, memoirs, in a certain sense even the novel itself. Aksakov was by far the oldest of these debutants, but as though to compensate for this fact, many of his works can be considered successive debuts, presenting themselves as new forms or as novel recombinations of existing forms.

Aksakov's first two lengthy prose works, *Notes on Fishing* (*Zapiski ob uzhen'e*), 1846, and *Notes of a Hunter of Orenburg Province* (*Zapiski ruzheinogo okhotnika orenburgskoi gubernii*), 1852, represent the initial stage, both chronologically and conceptually, in Aksakov's campaign for literary stature. They are the furthest of all of Aksakov's works from the standard literary forms, for they are ostensibly handbooks for the angler or hunter, texts which seem to have a purely practical orientation and to lack obvious aesthetic value. However, they also aspire to interest the nonhunting audience and employ a stylistic and structural complexity beyond the requirements of the practical manual.

As a serious hunter and angler, Aksakov was familiar with earlier works on the subject, such as V. A. Levshin's *Book for Hunters of Beasts and Birds* (*Kniga dlia okhotnikov do zverinoi i ptichei lovli*), 1810–1812, which he mentions ironically in the second edition of *Notes on Fishing*.[1] Aksakov intended both his books to meet standards of accuracy and literacy lacking in previous books on the subject: "In Russian, insofar as I know, until the present there has not been printed even a single line about fishing in general or angling in particular that is written by a literate sportsman, intimately knowledgeable in his subject" (4:13). If Aksakov considered his books on fishing and hunting to be improvements on the practical level, their predecessors must have had even less value as literary models.[2] However, the literary potential of a work concerned primarily with nature may have been suggested to Aksakov not by hunting manuals, Russian or foreign, but by writings of naturalists, such as an article entitled "Scenes from the Life of a Naturalist" ("Stseny iz zhizni naturalista") that appeared in N. I. Nadezhdin's *Telescope* (*Teleskop*) in 1832. As Nadezhdin's unofficial associate in *Telescope* and *Rumor* (*Molva*), its supplement, Aksakov was presumably aware of the article; in addition, in his capacity as censor he passed the particular issue of *Telescope* in which the article appeared. "Scenes" consists of a translation of excerpts from J. J. Audubon's *Ornithological Biography* which were quoted at length in a review of the book in *Blackwood's Magazine* for July and August 1831. Although Audubon's brief appearance in *Telescope* can hardly be considered a major influence on Aksakov's hunting books, the precedent of an engaging, yet generally accurate and informative account of natural history in a remote area is worth noting. In particular, Audubon's sometimes excessive willingness to enter his narrative in the first person and generally to employ his narrating self to validate the entire text is pertinent to the narrative strategy of Aksakov's own hunting books.

From the start, Aksakov intended his works on hunting and fishing to be simultaneously pragmatic and aesthetic and to be the reflection of a definite, if not overly specific, observing personality. The orientation of this personality toward nature was of crucial significance, as he indicated in a letter to Gogol: "I have undertaken to write a book about angling, not only in its technical aspect, but in relation to nature in general; my passionate

1. Mashinskii, S. T. *Aksakov*, pp. 320–321 and p. 320n2. Aksakov refers to Levshin's book in *Sobranie sochinenii*, vol. 4, p. 118n2.
2. A. V. Chicherin, "Russkoe slovo Sergeia Aksakova," pp. 120–121, draws attention to earlier works on hunting, but the 1793 article he cites is exclusively practical.

angler likewise passionately loves the beauties of nature as well; in a word, I have fallen in love with my work and I hope that this book will be pleasant not only for the lover of fishing, but also for everyone whose heart is open to the impressions of early morning, late evening, luxuriant midday, etc."[3] Aksakov's mastery of the technical aspect of fishing can be judged by the frequent mention of fishing, alone or with Konstantin, in his letters. According to a record book dating from the early forties, some 1,500 fish were landed at Abramtsevo from June to October 1846, and like numbers in the summers of 1845 and 1847; fish caught are often tabulated by date and species. Despite this considerable experience, Aksakov distrusted his unaided memory in the description of each species, and strove, like a painter, for complete accuracy of depiction: "I am continuing the dictation of my little book on fishing nearly every morning; at present I'm writing about the fish, but I have forgotten some, and in general it is necessary to describe their appearance from nature; and so all this will be corrected later on."[4]

Having established technical exactness and reliability as the foundation on which the book rests and the source from which its deeper theme draws its validity, Aksakov remained apprehensive about the value of his *Notes* for the nonfisherman. Praise from Mikhail Pogodin after the book's appearance reassured him that a larger audience would accept his book and that critical opinion, which keenly interested Aksakov throughout his late-blooming career as a writer, would be favorable: "Particularly important for me is the fact that you are not a sportsman and even dislike this form of sport. Therefore, independent of fishing, my little book must have some interest. Reality, truth, sincerity can be sensed in it. I admit that I found all this in it, but I see little reason that others should find it."[5] The qualities of reality, truth, and sincerity that Aksakov considers his book's primary values for the nonfisherman depend on the establishment of the authenticity (as distinct from the accuracy) of the *Notes*.

3. S. T. Aksakov to N. V. Gogol, 22 November 1845, included in *Istoriia moego znakomstva s Gogolem*, in *Sobranie sochinenii*, 3:326. Of the times Aksakov mentions, midday is particularly common in traditional pastoral.

4. S. T. Aksakov to family, 25 November 1845. TsGALI, *fond* 10, inventory 3, storage unit 15, fol. 13.

5. S. T. Aksakov to M. P. Pogodin, 16 May 1847. LL, Pogodin, *fond* II, carton I, item 57, letter 5.

Aksakov sought to achieve this authenticity by emphasizing his identity with the narrator-observer, whose devotion to and experience in angling is such that he has become an expert. Thus the work is not merely an impersonal, informative book; it is "not a treatise on angling, not a natural history of fish. My little book is no more and no less than the simple notes of a passionate sportsman" (4:13).

The entire text, in both its technical and artistic aspects, becomes an expression of this unifying personality, which reveals itself primarily through its memories. Although restricted to one area of activity, *Notes on Fishing* represents an attempt to record a specific individual's experience, as Aksakov indicates in a letter to his son Ivan from the autumn of 1845: "My book is developing in an unexpected manner. With each day this labor becomes more pleasant for me. I have raised from the bottom much that was forgotten, decayed in the dim repository of my memories. A good deal of myself, of my youthful impressions, will be in this book if I succeed in writing it the way I sometimes imagine it. For people close to me, and for all those who love me, it will have a double worth."[6] Thus Aksakov's first book, in addition to its characteristic blending of genres, also established another recurrent feature of Aksakov's prose: its intensely personal quality of memory. The process of composing each work becomes for Aksakov a means of revivifying the past; the completed work is a form of ordering and preserving a particular aspect of his past, endowing it with value perhaps not apparent in the evanescent moment of experience.

Following the successful appearance of *Notes on Fishing* in 1847, Aksakov undertook a more ambitious project employing the same basic form: a book on hunting. Once again he could draw on a lifetime of observation and expertise, as attested by records he maintained of migration dates in Orenburg province from 1811 to 1826,[7] daily entries of birds bagged, and yearly totals in the hundreds (898 birds in 1813). Aksakov was indeed the passionate hunter he claims to have been in his youth. Brief

6. S. T. Aksakov to Ivan Aksakov. PD, *fond* 3, inventory 3, item 13, fol. 103. The date of this letter is missing, but it was probably written in the autumn of 1845.

7. "Prilet dichi i nekotorykh drugikh ptits v orenburgskoi gubernii," *Sobranie sochinenii,* 4:504–514.

descriptions in Aksakov's hand of hare, snipe, ducks, and other game have been preserved;[8] Aksakov later employed these early notes in writing his serious work on the subject.

Notes of a Hunter required greater effort than *Notes on Fishing*, not only because of its greater length but also because of the greater significance Aksakov attached to it, both as a personal document and as a literary effort. In its initial concept, however, it was intended as a companion to *Notes on Fishing*: "If God fulfills my wish and I spend this winter in the country, then I will start to write another little book 'on hunting with a gun'; from the age of twelve to thirty-six [i.e., when Aksakov left for Moscow in 1826], I was absolutely madly devoted to this form of hunting. I have already written 'Arrival of Birds in the Spring'; I think that even a nonhunter can read this fragment with pleasure."[9]

Like *Notes on Fishing*, which Aksakov also referred to as a little, minor book (*knizhka*), this book was to draw on his own past and was addressed to two audiences, the primary one consisting of hunters and the secondary and larger one composed of readers who were only tangentially concerned with the facts of hunting, if at all. Aksakov realized that the second audience must be captured by his style and rhetoric, and he displays considerable concern for the organization and tone: "I've written an enormous article of eight and a half printer's sheets on the grouse. . . . Konsta and Vera praise it highly; but I, while admitting its worth with regard to liveliness and veracity of the description, still see a multitude of shortcomings. . . . The main shortcoming consists in the fact that much is not in its proper place."[10]

Of even more concern to Aksakov than internal order was the problem of creating and maintaining a tone of narration that was in harmony with the subject. During the winter of 1849–1850, when Aksakov was working regularly on his *Notes of a Hunter*, his letters frequently allude to his efforts to avoid any too-apparent departure from the hunter's sensibility in the direction of a self-conscious perception of nature as intrinsically beautiful. Such direct reaction to nature figures more prominently in *Notes on Fishing*, where it suits the somewhat more meditative activity

8. "Opisanie raznoi dichi v nashikh mestakh" (12 folios), LL, *fond* 3, folder 5, item 2a.

9. S. T. Aksakov to N. V. Gogol, 21 June 1848, in *Sobranie sochinenii*, 3:364.

10. S. T. Aksakov to Ivan Aksakov, 24 November 1849, in A. A. Dunin, "Materialy po istorii russkoi literatury i kul'tury: I. S. Aksakov v Iaroslavle," p. 117.

of angling, but even there it is never excessively indulged: "I constantly hold myself in check, lest I get carried away in describing nature and subjects extraneous to hunting. . . . I fear, like fire, senile prattle."[11] In another letter, Aksakov expresses even more clearly his fear of lapsing too readily into a facilely poetic stance: "I can't find the proper tone, can't establish boundaries for myself with accuracy; everything I've written till now displeases me. It's the account of a simple hunter with an unconscious poetic sensitivity, who in the simplicity of his heart isn't aware that he is describing nature poetically. It's a man of letters pretending to be a simple man."[12] To allow the narrator to turn into a naïve poet, or worse, a hackneyed littérateur, would undermine the claim to authenticity implicit throughout the text and call into question the general reliability of the narrator, whose knowledge and memory support the entire text.

Maintaining "a unified depiction, written in the same spirit"[13] was perhaps more difficult in Notes of a Hunter than in Notes on Fishing, if only because of the differences in stereotype between the somewhat reflective and even garrulous angler and the more taciturn and active hunter. That Aksakov was well aware of the narrator he was creating is further attested by his comments on Turgenev's sympathetic review of the book. While thanking Turgenev for the praise, doubly valuable because Turgenev himself was a serious hunter, and so a member both of the primary and secondary audiences Aksakov was addressing, he takes exception to Turgenev's mention of Shakespeare and Pushkin, for fear that they might "crush my insignificant persona with their enormous personalities".[14] Aksakov is of course hardly using persona in its modern sense, but he seems to be contrasting Shakespeare and Pushkin as creative individuals not so much with himself as with the hunter-narrator he has created for his work.

Following the completion of Notes of a Hunter and its publication in 1852, Aksakov turned to other subjects, primarily literary memoirs, but he did not completely abandon his interest in the subject of hunting. The second edition of Notes on Fishing (Zapiski ob uzhen'e ryby) appeared in 1853, with some addi-

11. S. T. Aksakov to Ivan Aksakov, 1 December 1849, ibid., p. 123.
12. S. T. Aksakov to Ivan Aksakov, 17 February 1850. LL, fond 3, folder 3, item 22g.
13. S. T. Aksakov to Ivan Aksakov, 3 February 1850. Ibid.
14. S. T. Aksakov to I. S. Turgenev, January 1853, in Maikov, ed., "Pis'ma Aksakovykh," no. 9, p. 11.

tions, the most important being a section "On Fish in General" ("O rybakh voobshche"). Aksakov also planned to start an annual journal for hunters, but permission to begin a periodical was denied, and the articles he had intended for it eventually appeared in the *Muscovite* and in a separate volume entitled *Tales and Reminiscences of a Hunter on Various Types of Hunting* (*Rasskazy i vospominaniia okhotnika o raznykh okhotakh*), 1855. Limited to a discussion of various specialized types of hunting such as falconry and snaring with which Aksakov was familiar in his youth, the articles in *Tales and Reminiscences* tend to assume the form of a memoir more consistently than either of its two predecessors. The final interpenetration of memoir and hunt can be seen in the late "Butterfly Collecting" ("Sobiranie babochek"), 1858, which serves both as the conclusion of Aksakov's memoirs of the University of Kazan and as a discussion of butterfly collecting. While minor, these later texts are helpful in defining Aksakov's notion of the hunt and in elucidating the significance of hunting as a human activity, the major theme of *Notes on Fishing* and *Notes of a Hunter*.

Hunting (*okhota*) of one sort or another constitutes the sole human activity depicted in Aksakov's first three books. The narrator is a hunter, his memories are restricted to that one activity, and his style is partly determined by his being a hunter; his audience, at least the primary (if largely fictive) one, is composed of hunters. The Russian word *okhota* can signify not only the pursuit and capture of wild animals but also any partiality or desire, even a hobby.[15] Aksakov includes both of these meanings in his notion of *okhota*, as can be seen by considering the various activities he chooses to discuss as forms of *okhota*: angling, hunting of game proper, whether with gun, falcon, trap, or snare, collecting butterflies, and even gathering mushrooms. Keeping songbirds, pigeons, and small animals are also included as "hunts that are, so to speak, profitless, which are rewarded only by pleasure" (4:469), but such hobbies clearly skirt the edges of what Aksakov includes in the idea of *okhota*.

The hunt is not fully defined by object, but neither is it adequately determined by the instruments; rod and gun are merely

---

15. Etymologically the word *okhota* is related to the verb *khotet'*, to want, and may have acquired the meaning "hunt" in East Slavic languages from use as a replacement for tabooed words dealing with hunting. Cf. M. Vasmer, *Russisches etymologisches Wörterbuch*.

the most generalized means, as is clear from his discussion of special techniques in *Tales and Reminiscences*. What, then, characterizes a valid object of hunting and what constitutes a valid method? In "Comments and Observations of a Lover of Mushroom Gathering," written in 1856, Aksakov discusses the object of the hunt in some detail:

> Among the number of various types of *okhota*, the placid *okhota* of going for mushrooms, or gathering mushrooms, has its place. . . . I am even prepared to prefer gathering mushrooms, because it is necessary to seek them out, consequently it is also possible not to find them; there is here involved a certain skill, knowledge of the habitat of mushrooms, knowledge of the locale, and luck. . . . Here there is uncertainty, unexpectedness, there is success and failure, and all this together arouses desire [*okhota*] in man and forms its particular interest. (4:590)

The gathering of mushrooms shares an essential characteristic with other forms of the hunt and indeed its attraction seems to rest almost entirely in that characteristic: one may find mushrooms, but it is also possible not to find them. The element of risk, of probability but not total predictability, is essential. For a hunt to have value, this factor of uncertainty must be preserved even by conscious effort, and Aksakov dismisses the shooting of grouse, attracted by a decoy, from a comfortable blind, with the telling question: "But where then is the hunt?" (4:410). A relationship must be maintained in which "the superiority of the hunter over the hunted cannot be absolute."[16] Hunting involves the pursuit and attempted capture of an elusive being, by means which do not completely eliminate the prey's ability to escape.

A true hunt may involve a certain self-handicapping, in which the hunter's potential for technological advantage is consciously curbed in order to maintain the equilibrium of action. Thus mushroom gathering is oddly enough a perfect hunt; no instruments of any sort are needed and the outcome depends entirely on the hunter's keenness, knowledge, and skill, which alone provide a marginal advantage over the elusive, if sessile, prey. Hunting thus entails a certain ethical dimension: practice, training, and internal discipline outweigh instruments in the hunt and contribute significantly to the pleasure of the pursuit.

16. Ortega y Gasset's phrase, in *Meditations on Hunting*, p. 57.

Hunting, in the context of the modern world at any rate, demands an acceptance of the terms suggested by nature and thereby a return to it. That the essence of the hunt does not lie in the means of hunting is suggested by a letter from Aksakov to Turgenev, in which he states that he tended to avoid descriptions of equipment in *Notes of a Hunter* because he was rather behind the times in this regard.[17]

In addition to the risk or gamble, hunting also touches another chord in man. As Aksakov says in the opening of *Notes on Fishing*, there is an irrational pull in hunting activities and he directs his text in the first instance to those "fishermen by inclination, *okhotniki* for whom the words 'fishing pole' and 'fishing' are magic words, acting powerfully on the soul. . . . Angling, like other forms of hunting [*okhoty*], can be both a simple inclination and a powerful passion" (4:9).

Part of the power of hunting derives from its effect on the hunter, from the fact that, as a nonrational but not purposeless or unstructured activity, hunting liberates the hunter from his ordinary circumstances. It places him in a situation in which only his own choices and action determine the result and in which his skill alone is capable of countering all attempts by the prey to avoid capture. Thus another disadvantage of technology in hunting may be overdetermination; simpler equipment permits the human being to stand independent in what Ortega y Gasset calls the venatic relationship.

The hunter, having chosen to limit the instruments that reason could provide, becomes an *okhotnik-artist*, a hunter-artist (4:44). The artist for Aksakov is the product not only of passion but also of practice, and he stresses the importance of skill or craft (*umen'e*) in hunting. At times, reversing his stylistic precepts for ironic effect, he resorts to a less technical vocabulary than a true hunter would use in order to point out the degree of competence required: "No, there is nothing simpler, it seems, than to take a fishing pole, put a worm or a bit of bread on the hook, toss it into the water, and when the bobber starts to sink, pull a fish out onto the bank. That's all true, but it's no less true that there exists great skill in fishing. To acquire this skill requires a great deal of experience" (4:44). *Umen'e*, which raises hunting to the level of an art, depends directly on the development of the two key vir-

17. S. T. Aksakov to I. S. Turgenev, January 1853, in Maikov, ed., "Pis'ma Aksakovykh," no. 9, p. 10.

tues of the hunter, *opytnost'* ("experience") and *nabliudatel'nost'*
("power of observation"). The two qualities function reciprocally, with interdependent levels of development, but they are
distinguishable at least in concept. In "The Blizzard" (1834), Aksakov had already established the centrality of experience, the
attainment of or approach to perfection in interaction with the
environment. Although the concept is dealt with more prosa-
ically in the hunting books, it remains crucial to the ethic of the
hunter, whose ability to locate and capture his prey depends on
constantly selecting the one valid course of action.

Experience depends on observation, the second essential quality in the hunter, which transcends passive observation and involves an empathetic identification of the hunter with the quarry.
In *Notes on Fishing* Aksakov declares: "For the real fisherman,
the hunter-artist, study of the habits of fish is necessary, but this
is a most difficult and obscure undertaking, although fish dwell
in transparent chambers. Their habits must be guessed at; there
are very little data and therefore it is essential to possess insight
and imagination, as well as so much effort and worry!" (4:44).
Like the old peasant in "The Blizzard," the observer engages in a
constant interpretation of and adjustment to his environment,
although for the hunter the primary source of information is not
nature as a whole so much as his prey within the context of
nature. Thus the stark opposition and even antagonism of man
and nature that underlies "The Blizzard" is attenuated or even
effaced in the works on hunting, where the hunter elects his
temporary position of integration with nature rather than being
permanently subject to it and seeking only to survive. This miti-
gation of nature as an omnipotent force continues as Aksakov's
works focus more and more on the world of human society, so
that nature is rather peripheral in *Tales and Reminiscences* and
becomes the benign environment of the butterflies in "Butterfly
Collecting," Aksakov's last lengthy work with a hunting theme.

One of the principal merits of Aksakov's works on hunting,
viewed as works of literature, lies in their transposition of the
pattern of the hunt itself into the structure and style of the text.
In this regard *Notes on Fishing* and *Notes of a Hunter* are excellent examples of the fallacy of imitative action, since all the
details and their ordering are relevant to the passion of hunting
and derivative from the narrator's observation or experience.
Furthermore, the manner of presenting these details is intended

to engender in the reader attitudes similar to those of the hunter. That the two virtues of the hunter are central to his hunting books may be seen in the first paragraph of *Notes of a Hunter*: "I will speak as well about that which my long experience, passionate hunting, and powers of observation have noted" (4:147).

The reader is meant to become a hunter, however briefly, by reading a text that requires him to participate in verbally presented patterns of action and, more importantly, in the mode of being and perceiving that is characteristic of the hunter. The step to independent action (i.e., whether the text is to be didactic) is of course the reader's choice, but he is provided with a clear model of both the hunter and the hunt. The discussions of equipment and its use, of methods of stalking or fishing a given species, constitute a demonstration of experience; the descriptions of individual species and their behavior are a summation of the narrator's observation. The discussion of each species within the encyclopedic format of *Notes on Fishing* and *Notes of a Hunter* is organized as a brief hunt for that particular species. The pattern followed actually predates the start of serious work on *Notes on Fishing*; in a notebook entitled "Description of Various Game in Our Parts," dating from Aksakov's period of residence in Orenburg province, the marginal headings indicate the kernels from which each description is generated and the basic sequence of such elements. Thus, for the great snipe:

> Shape and color of their feathers
> habitat
> food
> nests and young
> methods of capture
> shooting great snipe
> how and when to shoot great snipe
> flavor of their meat.[18]

In the early, unformed attempt at describing game, Aksakov often departs from the hunting order, such that other entries in the notebook display striking incongruities: "The flavor of their meat is first-rate and woodcock in general is considered prime game. They arrive early and disappear very late."[19] Aksakov observes the

18. "Opisanie raznoi dichi v nashikh mestakh." LL, *fond* 3, folder 5, item 2a, fols. 4–7.
19. Ibid., fols. 8v–9.

basic order much more consistently in both *Notes on Fishing* and *Notes of a Hunter*, and of course develops each element much more fully. In its later development the formulaic pattern of recording reveals its inner correlation with the pattern of the hunt itself and deepens the significance of each stage of the process.

First, the quarry must be positively identified. Aksakov regularly begins the discussion of a species with consideration of the names by which it is known, particularly their etymology:

> The folk don't know at all the word *forel'*; they call this handsome fish *pestriak*,[20] or in the collective, *pestrushka*—a most fitting name, for the entire fish is spotted with black, red, and white dots. (*Notes on Fishing*; 4:128)

> [The mallard] is also called *kriakva* and *kriakusha*. Obviously, all three names derive from the word *kriakat'* [to quack], fully expressing the voice, or cry, of the duck. (*Notes of a Hunter*; 4:266)

The name of the prey, however important, is preliminary to the physical description. The fullness of this description, that is, the degree of observation displayed by the narrator-hunter, derives directly from the hunt, and is roughly proportional to the desirability of the given species as a quarry. Species such as frogs, songbirds, or birds of prey are outside the hunter's goal-defined field of vision and are excluded from consideration. Other species may have only a temporary value; the diving ducks, who arrive before other birds, evoked in Aksakov a certain respect, which he expressed in true hunterly fashion by seeking to shoot them. "Fine gratitude and respect, nonhunters will say, but we have our own logic: the more a bird is respected, the more one tries to bag it" (4:292).

This hierarchy of respect and empathy is reflected in the etiquette of description observed by Aksakov. In *Notes on Fishing*, a small fish, the *golets* ("loach"), fairly insignificant as game, is described in one sentence that is really a nondescription, being organized in negative terms: "Its name, from *golyi* [naked, bare], derives from the character of the skin: it is bare, there are no scales at all on it; the fish is very slim and slippery, of some indefinite color, grayish-yellowish or whitish, with irregular, un-

---

20. *Forel'*, "trout," from German *Forelle*. *Pestryi*, "variegated, motley." Such etymologizing might also be taken as an echo of Shishkovite interest in word origins.

clear spots, more or less dark" (4:76). In contrast, a larger species, the *okun'* ("perch"), whose game value is generally accepted— "almost all anglers like to fish for perch very much, and many prefer it to all other types of fishing" (4:112)—is anatomized into constituent parts, each of which is carefully described:[21]

> The perch is rather broad in figure, somewhat humpbacked, covered with scales of a greenish, somewhat golden color; on its back it has a crest with sharp spines and between it and the tail, a swim fin; the tail and particularly the ventral fins are red, the stomach whitish, the eyes yellowish with black pupils; across the whole body lie five bands, which make the perch variegated and in general very handsome. (4:112)

Although identification remains the organizing principle, the amount of information exceeds the level necessary, particularly for a common species like the perch. A certain aesthetic emerges, based on observation of and empathy for a valued species, recording features for their own sake (such as the perch's eyes). The relationship of value to detail appears with especial clarity in the description of the woodcock in *Notes of a Hunter*. The woodcock is easily defined as the only forest-dwelling bird of a snipelike appearance, but its exceptional desirability as game, determined in part by its comparative rarity and elusiveness, prompts a detailed and appreciative description:

> The woodcock, incontrovertibly, is most excellent, prime game in all respects; it even takes pride of place in the noble snipe family, to which it belongs, by the excellent flavor of its meat, by its similarity to them in its mottled plumage, by the beauty of its large black eyes, by its speed and twisting in flight, by its manner of procuring food, and even by the difficulty in shooting it. . . . The woodcock is very handsome. All the spots, or mottlings, of its feathers consist of dark, reddish, gray-ashen shades, too subtle to describe, as with other snipe species. On the upper part of the woodcock's head lie four transverse stripes, or elongated spots, of a dark color; there is more reddish color on the back and upper side of the wings, while the lower side, crop, and stomach are lighter and covered with regular transverse ash-gray bands; the tail is rather short, its underfeathers are somewhat longer than

---

21. Chicherin, "Russkoe slovo Sergeia Aksakova," p. 120, draws attention to the coloristic aspects of Aksakov's descriptions.

the uppers, very dark, even black, and each one ends with
a small white spot on the underside, red-gray on the upper
side. (4:436)

The description of the woodcock illustrates well the relation between the fullness, even excess, of description and the hunter's
positive attitude toward his prey; not only is the bird compared
to its near relatives and defined in terms of its similarity to them,
but the direct description depends on approximations and comparisons of parts one with the other.

Following the identification of the prey (including its name)
and the preliminary assessment of its value, the focus shifts to
the next phase of the hunt, or rather, to the beginning of the
hunt proper, in which the observation and experience of the
hunter operate synergetically to force the prey to appear and
then to effect its capture. Space and time of course function as
the primary coordinates of any search, and both *Notes on Fishing*
and *Notes of a Hunter* reflect the importance of these factors in
their organization. A special section in each book deals with
selecting a place ("O vybore mesta"); in *Notes on Fishing* mill-
ponds are especially recommended, and four types of habitat
(marsh, water, steppe, and forest) are discussed in *Notes of a
Hunter*, all game being classified according to one of these four
habitats. For each species of fish or game, there is of course a
specific niche within this larger framework; the hunter must
know the place where a given quarry is most likely to appear. In
Notes on Fishing, the key term, introducing the discussion of
niche, is the verb *vodit'sia*, implying not only presence, but also
permanence, including breeding: "Ruffs inhabit [vodiatsia] only
pure waters and, in great numbers, rivers with sandy or clay
bottoms, as well as lakes flooded by high water in spring" (4:88).
In *Notes of a Hunter* such regularity is not observed, partly because general descriptions of habitat open each major section of
the text and partly because habitat for birds is often also a function of season.

The factor of time is even more crucial than that of place in
gaining the appearance of the prey, and is usually specified to a
greater degree in the discussion of each species. The hunter must
consider and allow for such variables as time of day, time of
year, and weather. The presence, movements, habits, and location of his quarry, as well as its value (a fish's or bird's flavor or
weight) may be affected by these variables. For example, the

tench (*lin'*) in early spring will bite in most locations, in the summer only in the weedy margins and upper reaches of mill-ponds, never in an undammed river (4:105). With birds, some of which are present in a given region only during migration or are most abundant or easily found at this time, the migratory habits of most species constitute the primary temporal restrictions on hunting. A special discussion of spring migration, "Passage and Arrival of Game" ("Prolet i prilet dichi") (4:168ff.), in *Notes of a Hunter* complements the information on the arrival of each species in the article devoted to it. "The first isolated appearance of woodcock in the spring sometimes occurs very early, so that there are no thawed areas anywhere. . . . Then, with the onset of warm weather and mild spring (almost always about April 12 in Orenburg province), there begins the mass passage of woodcock" (4:437). Departure is also noted: "By and large, woodcock disappear around the middle of October" (4:440).

Within these limits, movements and activities such as courtship, nesting, and the raising of young are recorded; again the degree of inclusiveness is usually a function of desirability. The descriptions of the daily and annual patterns of behavior of each species of fish and bird marks the fullest development of observation; behavior is presented as a constantly self-modifying system in continuous dynamic interaction with all aspects of the environment. At this point the hunter, having exerted all his effort to understand the quarry and make it appear, now demonstrates his own power of interpreting the environment by turning to the active employment of experience in order to effect a capture, to intervene in the environment and its processes in a manner that does not essentially violate the operation of the system and thereby affirms the human being's rightful place in it.

After thus exhaustively fixing the identity of the prey, the hunter's attention shifts to the means by which it is captured, the bait, hook, shot, and so on. This is frequently followed by the direct appearance of the hunter himself, the narrator in the role of reminiscer, recalling specific incidents from his past experience in hunting the particular species. By shifting from the general to the particular at this point, Aksakov established his narrator as the emblematic hunter, who demonstrates concretely the successful conclusion of the exercise of the hunter's observation and experience:

> Eighteen twenty-two is a particularly memorable year for
> me . . . all the woodcock, without exception, flocked to the
> low brush growing in damp and clammy places, stayed
> there until November 8 and grew incredibly plump! Abandon-
> ing all other forms of hunt, I tirelessly, daily went out after
> woodcock: November 6 I killed eight, on the seventh,
> twelve. . . . In the roots of unpassable brush around a small
> spring-fed marsh, my tireless dog flushed a woodcock, which
> I at once killed. (4:339–340)

After the climax of the hunt there frequently follows, in both *Notes on Fishing* and *Notes of a Hunter*, a comment on the flavor of the particular fish or game bird and the recommended method of preparation. The highly respected snipe, along with the wood-cock, are even accorded the honor of a page and a half in "On the Flavor of the Meat and the Preparation of Snipe Species" ("O vkuse miasa i prigotovlenii bekasinykh porod") (4:201–203). Al-though this feature at first glance may seem to serve only as practical advice, its persistent repetition suggests that the refer-ence to eating also functions in the dynamic pattern of the seg-ments of both volumes of Aksakov's *Notes*. Eating serves as a coda to the capture and celebrates the successful conclusion of the hunt by formalizing the hunter's mastery over the prey by the ritual of consumption. The correct decoding of the prey's mes-sage culminates in the total identification of hunter and prey; the communication of the hunt ends in a form of communion.

Aksakov's hunting works are of course to be distinguished from traditional literary or poetic pastoral (although that in itself is a rather amorphous and commodious category), first of all by their narrative authenticity and secondly by their emphasis on the hunt, the occasional brutality of which contrasts with the usual pastoral emphasis on ease and accommodation among all denizens of the pastoral region. It may be worth noting, however, that Aksakov begins with the most indolent and "harmless" form of the hunt, angling, and devotes little or no attention in the en-tirety of his hunting works to the pursuit of very large game such as wolves or bear; of the traditionally aristocratic forms of hunt-ing, only falconry seems to have attracted Aksakov's attention to any degree.[22] Still, broad areas of affinity with the themes and

22. Only one brief article, "Okhota s iastrebom za perepelkami" [Hunting Quail with a Hawk], included in *Tales and Reminiscences of a Hunter*, and a prefatory

some of the devices of literary pastoral can be discerned, particularly if we consider the origins of pastoral in Theocritus and disregard later accretions and embellishments.[23]

Of all widely accepted forms or modes, pastoral is perhaps the most diffuse, emphasizing "separation and dispersal, not unity" and presenting "a loose combination of independent elements."[24] Aksakov's two books of *Notes*, although hardly formless, consist of discrete, rather rigidly constructed units devoted to individual species. This paratactic, bead-like combination of units (also reflected in the disjunct elements in the first chapter of *Family Chronicle*) is predicated on the intrinsic worth of each species, which merits full and individual attention by the hunter and thus by the reader. The pastoral, like the epic, "refuses to prescribe an absolute hierarchy of values; each element or inhabitant of the pastoral world is savored as independently important."[25]

One of the most common devices of Theocritan pastoral is the catalogue, which also presents objects sequentially yet independently. Although Aksakov does not make extensive use of simple catalogues per se, his detailed inventories of equipment for hunting or fishing, as well as his elaborate descriptions of prized game, are in part motivated by a similar sense of fondness for things in themselves. More importantly, the detailed lists in later works (the menu at the wedding banquet in *Family Chronicle*, chapter 4, for example) can be compared to such pastoral catalogues. In addition, such enumeration of things could be described as the "nominal" form of the epic retardation of action which Aksakov so often employs in describing significant acts, in works ranging from his epistles to his brother, through his hunting works, to the major works of his last years.

Pastoral of course rests on the assumption of man's being part of nature, one element equal to others in a harmonious whole, and thus often involves a flight from the city and its concerns, at least on the part of the reader. The opposition of city and nature

---

note to an 1856 edition of Tsar Aleksei Mikhailovich's *Rules of Falconry*, a seventeenth century handbook, deal with this form of hunting. *Sobranie sochinenii*, 4: 480–503, 584–589.

23. Aksakov's hunting works could be strictly labeled as prose georgic because of their didactic element. However, the broader category seems more useful in light of Aksakov's other works.

24. Thomas G. Rosenmeyer, *The Green Cabinet: Theocritus and the European Pastoral Lyric*, p. 47.

25. Ibid., pp. 104, 53.

(or of the urban and the rustic) is an essential one for Aksakov. This can be noted in his verse epistles to Arkadii Timofeevich, but even earlier, in his St. Petersburg days, Aksakov develops the contrast at length in a letter to his sister Nadezhda Timofeevna:

> You, my dear friend, write that strolling in the country is dull. I am amazed at this; is it possible to prefer our stone and brick walks to the soft earth, clad with grass and mottled with flowers; our dismal gardens, in which every little leaf is weighted down with dust and every tree, like a slave, is forcibly positioned in order, to your happy varied groves, in which freedom and joy reign and which beneficent nature and not art, our gardens' cold attendant, planted like a loving mother. . . . Wherever I direct my glances, everywhere there is bondage— there is no spot where cursed people have not distorted nature.[26]

Although the emotional depth of this letter, which, like many of Aksakov's early efforts in literature, suggests a rhetorical exercise, may be open to doubt, the attributes it assigns to city and country do remain constant for Aksakov and the preference for the country becomes an internalized and strongly held conviction, even as its expression becomes less and less strident. The city is frequently characterized by excessive rationality, force, imposed order, monotony, and illness, while the country is associated with freedom, variety, health, and natural order arising from the absence of boundaries. The world of urban society also provides its own characteristic form of release, namely theater, which is really a transcendence of convention rather than an escape from it. Thus the angler and the actor are paradoxically complementary, one free through the rejection of social artificiality, the other by total mastery of artifice; both are of course artists in the Aksakovian sense by virtue of their immersion in their chosen avocation.

In his later years, including the period during which he wrote his hunting books, Aksakov often expresses dissatisfaction in his letters with the vacuous vulgarity (*poshlost'*) of Moscow life, with its "banal round of daily conversation with guests and daily playing of whist-solitaire with Zagoskin."[27] The country remains the primary source of vital energy, its power if anything intensified from Aksakov's younger days:

26. S. T. Aksakov to N. T. Aksakova, undated. PD, 1068/xvi, item 42, fol. 1–1v.
27. S. T. Aksakov to Ivan Aksakov, in Dunin, "Materialy," p. 123.

> The country beneficently embraced me with its fresh scent of
> young leaves and flowering shrubs, with its space, its quiet
> and peace. I don't know how to explain it to you, such peace
> has flowed into my soul. Toward the end of my stay in
> Moscow I was on edge from morning till night.[28]

Nature's primary qualities are in fact negative ones, the absence
of features typical of the city and its social relations; the country
lacks boundaries, noise, and motion. "What a marvelous effect
Bogorodskoe is having on me! It is infusing some sort of stillness,
peace, calm (*tishinu, mir, spokoistvie*) into my embittered heart!"[29]
The terms *tishina, mir,* and *spokoistvie,* as well as *chudo* ("marvel," "miracle"), form a constellation in Aksakov's letters and in
his writings whenever he feels moved to express the effect of
nature on himself or others.

The hunt provides the most reliable means of perceiving and
truly assimilating these qualities of nature. In the introduction to
Notes on Fishing, Aksakov, arguing that *okhota* draws hunters
closer to nature (4:10), explicitly states that fishing (and by implication all hunting) affords modern man an excellent means of
overcoming the effects of urban, social existence and of regaining
his primeval relationship with nature: "The sense of nature is
born in us, from the rude savage to the most educated person.
Unnatural upbringing, a forced, false direction, a false life—all
this together tends to stifle the powerful voice of nature and
often stifles or gives a distorted development to this sense" (4:10).
The corrupted or distorted sense of nature perceives its environment only globally, maintaining its distance and relying on
already canonized notions of the beautiful. In other words, it
prevents true involvement in nature. Such is the city-dweller's
reaction "to a beautiful locale, a picturesque distant view, a magnificent sunrise, to a bright moonlit night; but this is still not
love of nature; this is love of landscape, scenery, of the prismatic
refractions of light" (4:10). Nature cannot be adequately approached through the fallacious categories appropriate to such
conventional areas of human activity as painting, theater, or science, none of which can ever surpass the limits of human rationality and society. People capable only of such perceptions are in
essence dead; after a superficial glance at nature, they "are al-

28. S. T. Aksakov to Ivan Aksakov, 26 May 1849. PD, *fond* 3, inventory 3, item
13, fol. 3.
29. To O. S. Aksakova, 15 June 1836. Ibid., inventory 15, item 26, fol. 30.

ready thinking about their banal petty affairs and hurry home,
into their filthy whirlpool, into the dusty, choking atmosphere of
the city" (4:10–11).

Opposed to this dead world of the city and its sterile inhabitants is the true world of nature: country, peace, stillness,
quiet (derevnia, mir, tishina, spokoistvie) (4:11). It is accessible
through observation, the hunter's manner of looking at the world:

> Flee there from idleness, emptiness and lack of interests; flee
> there as well from restless, external activity. . . . On a
> green, flowering bank, above the dark depths of a river or lake,
> in the shade of bushes, under the canopy of a giant black
> poplar or leafy alder, silently shaking its leaves in the bright
> mirror of the water, on which your floats bob or lie motion-
> lessly—seeming passions grow still, supposed tempests fall
> quiet, egotistic dreams dissolve, unrealizable hopes fly
> away! Nature enters into its eternal rights, you hear her voice,
> muffled temporarily by the vanity, bustle, laughter, shouts
> and all the banality of human speech. (4:11)

Aksakov's hunting works seek to impart a particular way of
seeing the natural world, or rather to cleanse the reader's vision
of the categories and accretions of "refined" or "civilized" modes
of perception. Of course the underlying purpose of the pastoral
mode as such is to bring the reader to see the things of nature
whole and unique. Aksakov's fisherman or hunter, like Robert
Frost, sees "both the subject of vision and its perspective; the
mode of perception is embodied in the images themselves," so
that "the unity between the thing observed and the way of seeing,
between object and thought, between man's work . . . and his
esthetic experience," reemerges with all its pristine force.[30] Pastoral vision is cleansed vision.

The fisherman or hunter, and by implication Aksakov's reader,
escapes the constraints and restrictions of society and enters
nature, perceiving it from within, himself a part of it; he conducts a constant dialogue with it as a free and equal denizen of
the primeval world. The basic constituents of this newly perceived cosmos are earth, water, and vegetation, especially trees,
all of them archaic loci of being and life, of the sacred; in combination they are the major features of traditional models of the
world.[31] For Aksakov, "water is alive; it moves and imparts life,"

30. John F. Lynen, The Pastoral Art of Robert Frost, p. 22.
31. Mircea Eliade, Patterns in Comparative Religion, p. 269.

"forests are the conservers of water," and a tree "presents . . . the visible phenomena of organic life" (4:245, 377, 386). The world of stillness and freshness is not only beneficial to man and his psyche, but is in fact the source and wellspring of life. Aksakov pays appropriate and stylistically characteristic tribute to this in one of his most striking catalogues, unusual both for its length and for its extreme particularization of description, action, and sound:

> On the branches of trees, in thickets of green leaves and generally in the forest there live the motley, beautiful, various-voiced, infinitely varied species of birds: wood and black grouse boom their mating-call, hazel-hens shriek, woodcock whistle on their mating flights, each species of wild dove coos in its own manner, thrushes cheep and clack, sadly, melodi-ously, orioles chirp back and forth, variegated cuckoos moan, piebald woodpeckers trumpet, jays rattle; waxwings, wood larks, hawfinches and all the numerous tribe of tiny, winged singers fill the air with various voices and vivify the still-ness of the forests; on the branches and in the hollows of trees birds build their nests, lay their eggs and raise their young. (4:381)

This catalogue of species and calls, its lexical diversity and pre-cision pointing to Aksakov's Shishkovite antecedents, presents a stylistic analogue of the fullness of life, which the tree and its attendant species, arranged in a more or less ascending order from the ground to the treetops, represents.

Although Aksakov indirectly indicates his awareness of the symbolic power of water and trees, as well as of man's need to escape the city and time and reestablish his relations with the primitive realities that persist in the natural environment, direct statement of this theme in the hunting books is rare. Rather, as befits the persona of the simple hunter or fisherman uncon-cerned with the world of urban society or literary artifice, it is achieved through the oblique means of inclusion and repetition. The pastoral and even mythic perception of nature, central to Aksakov's general view of nature and to his hunting books, ap-pears explicitly in his "Epistle to M. A. Dmitriev" ("Poslanie k M. A. Dmitrievu"), a poem employing a verse form that is consid-erably less innovative than his prose. Aksakov intended to use the concluding lines of this poem, one of the few from his later years that are not concerned with family matters, as an epigraph for the second edition of *Notes of a Hunter* (1853), but because of objections by the censor to the word *freedom* (*svoboda*), the plan was dropped; the lines did appear, however inconsistently from the point of view of the censor, in the second edition of *Notes on Fishing.* In the "Epistle," Aksakov opposes to the world of nature his unquiet old age.

> Net serdechnoi tishiny,
> Mir dushevnyi nevozmozhen
> Posredi mirskoi volny! (3:686)

> There is no quiet in the heart,
> Peace of spirit is impossible
> Midst the mundane wave.

Beset by the chaos of life in society and by the physical inroads of age, Aksakov finds in nature peace and renewal:

> Est' odnako primiritel',
> Vechno iunyi i zhivoi,
> Chudotvorets i tselitel',—
> Ukhozhu k nemu poroi.
> Ukhozhu ia v mir prirody,
> Mir spokoistviia, svobody,
> V tsarstvo ryb i kulikov,
> Na svoi rodnye vody,
> Na prostor stepnykh lugov,
> V ten' prokhladnuiu lesov,
> I— v svoi mladye gody! (3:686)

> There is however a reconciler,
> Eternally young and vital,
> A wonder-worker and healer—
> I escape to it at times.
> I escape to the world of nature,
> A world of peace and freedom,
> To the realm of fish and snipe,
> To my own native waters,
> To the expanse of the steppe meadows,
> Into the cool shade of the forests,
> And—into the years of my own youth!

Here in a limited space are all the essential characteristics of nature that pervade Aksakov's hunting books (and function in his other works as well); the microcosm of space, water, and trees overflows with life and is endowed with the characteristic features of peace, silence, and healing. However, Aksakov's separate realm of peace, freedom, life, and beauty clearly resides not only in nature but also in the representation of nature, the realm of fish and snipe which are the subjects of his first two books. Thus art and nature merge in their psychological significance; both reconcile humanity and its environment by affording people the opportunity of experiencing or re-creating a world in which the apparent contradictions of existence dissolve in a harmonious reintegration. The last line, adumbrating the theme of memory and the past that becomes central in his subsequent works, suggests the equal powers of memory, art, and nature as means of overcoming time. All of Aksakov's works are essentially unified attempts to escape his own condition.

4

Family Chronicle:
The Fiction of History

To study the evolution of *Family Chronicle* (*Semeinaia khronika*) is to trace Aksakov's development as a major figure in Russian fiction, for it is only with the completion of that work in 1856 that he secured an incontestable place in literature. Aksakov began to compose material that would be incorporated into *Family Chronicle* in the 1840s, which suggests that he was already looking beyond his *Notes on Fishing*. A part of the first *otryvok* ("fragment," Aksakov's term for the chapters of his work), comprising the sections "Migration" and "Orenburg Province" ("Pereselenie" and "Orenburgskaia guberniia"), appeared in *Moscow Literary and Scholarly Miscellany* (*Moskovskii literaturnyi i uchenyi sbornik*), the first Slavophile almanac, in 1846. However, after the appearance of *Notes on Fishing* in that same year, Aksakov began its sequel, *Notes of a Hunter*. Except for a brief fragment dealing with his son Grigorii and intended for his daughter-in-law rather than for inclusion in a longer work, Aksakov set aside any work pertaining to family history, partly because of his growing preoccupation with his hunting notes and partly because of dissatisfaction with his attempts to continue the brief passages already written: "*Family Chronicle* is somehow going sluggishly. It seems it's necessary to alter the plan: abbreviate the details and not observe strict sequence."[1]

Having made the basic decision in favor of an episodic narrative rather than a uniform chronology, Aksakov apparently abandoned *Family Chronicle* until after the publication of *Notes of a Hunter* in 1852; in January of that year he informed Turgenev,

1. S. T. Aksakov to N. V. Gogol, 21 June 1848, included in *Istoriia moego znakomstva s Gogolem*, in *Sobranie sochinenii*, 4:365.

"I'll try to continue *Family Chronicle*."[2] However, serious work on it was further delayed for almost two years. In the interim, he devoted his literary attention to the various hunting articles originally intended for the hunters' journal he planned and which were finally published as *Tales and Reminiscences of a Hunter on Various Types of Hunting* in 1855. In a new departure for Aksakov, he also began to write biographical memoirs, recording his encounters and acquaintances with various figures he felt to be of significance for Russian letters and culture. He regarded many of these people as precursors of Slavophilism, which needed to elaborate an indigenous past to validate its claims of being the truly Russian intellectual movement. This group of works includes "Acquaintance with Derzhavin" ("Znakomstvo s Derzhavinym"), 1852; "Memoir of Aleksandr Semenovich Shishkov" ("Vospominanie ob Aleksandre Semenoviche Shishkove"), 1854, published with *Family Chronicle* in 1856; and *History of My Acquaintance with Gogol* (*Istoriia moego znakomstva s Gogolem*), begun in January 1854, but never completed. It is perhaps in these works—with the exception of the memoir of Gogol, which was not intended for publication— that Aksakov most overtly echoes the Slavophile concerns of his sons and associates, for he assumes the role of chronicler and guardian of an indigenous and specifically Russian cultural tradition. Even here, Aksakov seems far from the extreme positions of Slavophiles like Konstantin who were more interested in a political revival than in continuing a literary tradition.

Aksakov intended the pieces on Shishkov and Derzhavin and a theatrical memoir, "Iakov Emel'ianovich Shusherin and Theatrical Celebrities Contemporary with Him" ("Iakov Emel'ianovich Shusherin i sovremennye emu teatral'nye znamenitosti"), 1854, to be the concluding articles in a compendious volume which he outlined to Pogodin in November 1853. The volume was planned in response to Pogodin's offer to pay Aksakov for further contributions to the *Muscovite*.

> The fragments of *Family Chronicle* and fragments of my memoirs, of course (I speak without any ceremony), would be advantageous for the journal; but the censorship will cut them to shreds, and I can't agree to that. I have also hit on the idea of forming an entire volume out of them: the first

2. S. T. Aksakov to I. S. Turgenev, 12 January 1852, in Maikov, ed., "Pis'ma Aksakovykh," no. 8, p. 463.

half—out of the *Chronicle*, and the second—of memoirs. The latter will consist of the following articles: "Life in Ufa," "Moving to the Country," "Grandfather's Death," "Kazan Gymnasium," "Nadezhda Ivanovna Kuroedova," "We're Rich," "Kazan University," "Moving to Petersburg for Service," "Iakov Emel'ianovich Shusherin," "Memoir of A. S. Shishkov," "Acquaintance with Derzhavin."[3]

To judge from this plan, even as late as 1853 Aksakov was not completely clear as to the dimensions and contents of *Family Chronicle*, but the "second half" that it was to balance would be massive, considering the length of the sketches that were completed or in progress at the time of the letter. Of course the division into two halves may also refer less to length than to principle, the first half being essentially a reconstruction of the time before Aksakov's birth and the second consisting of an account of his own childhood and events to which he was an eyewitness. Regardless of the degree of clarity of formulation, by 1853 Aksakov obviously already had envisioned a program in which each of his literary efforts after his hunting works occupied a definite place; this was to be an encyclopedic effort of which his own prehistory, childhood, education, and entrance into the society of the capital were to be the subjects. Of course this plan gives no indication of the considerable differences in theme and technique in the various works that did eventually emerge, and should not be taken as indicating complete uniformity of purpose from work to work. In any case, such a plan was rather far from full realization in 1853; Aksakov may have wanted mainly to whet Pogodin's appetite for more material.

At the time of his letter to Pogodin, only "Derzhavin" had been completed and only "Shishkov" and "Kazan Gymnasium" were definitely in progress. "Shusherin" was begun in December of 1853, completed in March of 1854, and published in the *Muscovite* in May of that year, thus completing the St. Petersburg section of Aksakov's plan. The "first half," *Family Chronicle*, did not attain its final form until the second edition, with five chapters, in 1856; the intermediate sections evolved into *Reminiscences* (*Vospominaniia*), covering Aksakov's school years, which was published with *Family Chronicle* in 1856, and *Years of*

---

3. S. T. Aksakov to M. P. Pogodin, 29 November 1853. LL, Pogodin *fond*, section II, carton 1, storage unit 59, letter 8.

Childhood of Young Bagrov (*Detskie gody Bagrova-vnuka*), which was not completed until 1857.

Though Aksakov said nothing about its contents in his letter to Pogodin, he resumed work on *Family Chronicle* during the productive winter of 1853–1854. Aksakov probably wanted to take up Pogodin's offer of payment for material for the *Muscovite*, and *Family Chronicle* was the only suitable candidate among contemplated works or works in progress. The major undertaking of the winter, *History of My Acquaintance with Gogol*, was not intended for publication in the foreseeable future; in addition, Aksakov feared disastrous censorship of "Memoir of A. S. Shishkov," since he commented in it on the antecedents of Slavophilism. He also preferred not to have "Acquaintance with Derzhavin" published apart from the total sequence of which it was to be the conclusion. By January 1854 Aksakov thus had several projects under way, but still nothing he deemed suitable for the *Muscovite* that was simultaneously capable of surviving the censor. On January 5 he asked Pogodin, "Should I give you the continuation of the *Chronicle* which was published in 1846 in Panov's miscellany? Only it is too bound up with the published fragment and will be unintelligible without it."[4]

The offer was repeated a week later; a month later, on February 5, Aksakov announced that the first fragment was completed, and offered Pogodin some advice on its publication that indicates Aksakov's estimation of his own worth as a literary property:

> I have ready and even copied out "The First Fragment from
> the *Family Chronicle*." I will send it to you in a week,
> only I request that you do not print it in small type and not in
> "Miscellany." For me it's all the same; without any egotism
> I can say that I will be sought out even in "Miscellany;" but I
> know that others will upbraid you for it, find in it a sign
> of disrespect on your part toward me, and the devil knows
> what. Why do them a favor?[5]

Having completed the third and fourth sections of the fragment, whose first two sections had appeared eight years earlier, Aksakov continued working on "Shusherin," which was earmarked for publication, and on *History of My Acquaintance with*

---

4. S. T. Aksakov to M. P. Pogodin, 5 January 1854. Ibid., storage unit 60, letter 1.

5. S. T. Aksakov to M. P. Pogodin, 5 February 1854. Ibid., storage unit 59, letter 4.

Gogol. "Shusherin" was completed in March, at which time Aksakov began work on the second fragment of *Family Chronicle.* "I am already dictating the seventh notebook of the history of our acquaintance with Gogol; and as this work is wearying, I am writing for recreation and diversion an episode from the family chronicle: the marriage and life of Mikhaila Maksimovich Kuroedov."[6] Kuroedov was the real name of the unscrupulous adventurer who married Aksakov's cousin and who is called Mikhaila Maksimovich Kurolesov in the published text.

The timing and motive of the work on this fragment is interesting, for of the five chapters of *Family Chronicle,* the second is the one least connected with Aksakov's own past and is also the one in which literary patterns are most fully and overtly employed. The composition of the chapter clearly served as a counterpoint to the painstaking, factual work on *History of My Acquaintance with Gogol,* for which Aksakov, drawing on letters and his own memory, strove to present as complete and accurate a historical account as possible.

With various interruptions, Aksakov completed the second fragment in the autumn of 1854, informing Pogodin on November 24: "I just yesterday finished the second fragment of *Family Chronicle:* but it is still raw: I have to correct it and give it a final firing. It can be included in the first January issue. I am only afraid of the censorship. The contents—a master-tyrant of the age of Catherine."[7] A month later, Aksakov sent Pogodin a fair copy with the comment: "I would particularly wish that the censor not mutilate it. As it is, I have already excised much of interest and put dots instead. If the censor cuts a great deal—better not to print it."[8]

The most important omission made by Aksakov in anticipation of the censor consists of the account of Kurolesov's death by arsenic poisoning at the hands of two of his house serfs. Two manuscripts of the second fragment survive, both now in the Lenin Library. The first, incomplete, is dated 15 December 1854, and contains the full version of the murder; the second, evi-

6. S. T. Aksakov to Ivan Aksakov, 23 March 1854. PD, *fond* 3, inventory 3, item 14, fol. 27.

7. S. T. Aksakov to M. P. Pogodin, 24 November 1854. LL, Pogodin *fond,* section II, carton 1, storage unit 60, letter 21.

8. S. T. Aksakov to M. P. Pogodin, 19 December 1854. Ibid., storage unit 59, letter 10. (The archivist assigned this letter to the 1853 files. But the letter's mention of the "second fragment" suggests a date in late 1854.)

dently the one intended for publication, since the historical names Aksakov, Kuroedov, Nadezhda and so on are changed to the fictional Bagrov, Kurolesov, Praskov'ia, etc., omits the account in favor of implications of Kurolesov's murder, with no mention of the exact method.[9] (The original version was restored in later editions, beginning with the fourth in 1870). Even with the omission of the most offensive point, the censorship forbade publication in January 1855. Aksakov found the action absurd and became fearful for the projected publication of the entire *Family Chronicle* and *Memoirs*, as he confided to his friend A. I. Panaev:

> I don't expect anything good. Judging by the way things have
> begun, it must be assumed that instead of a large volume
> a small one will appear, and the articles will be mutilated.
> See, my dear friend, how every intellectual activity of people
> who are the most well-intentioned is persecuted, and all
> this thanks to stupid executors of the censorship code who are
> zealous to the point of baseness, although the code was
> written in a spirit of legal freedom.[10]

In the light of the various difficulties that Aksakov and his sons had suffered at the hands of the censorship, his latest difficulty was hardly unexpected, but it did prove to be his final brush with the bureaucracy of Nicholas I. The change in the publishing world after Nicholas's death was doubtless a factor not only in encouraging Aksakov to publish many items already written, but also in stimulating him to new writing.

Aksakov began the third fragment in May of 1854, two months after he had begun the still-unfinished second fragment. It apparently owes its inception to a sudden creative urge following a brief illness:

> Recuperation from serious illness is in itself an unusually
> pleasant sensation. I have experienced it several times in my
> life and have experienced it to some extent in the past
> several days; but since my illness was short lived, this sensa-
> tion lasted only one morning. That very morning I managed
> to feel such freshness of imagination and such a desire
> to express it that I started to write a fragment of *Family*

9. LL, *fond* 3, folder I, items 2a and 2b. 2a is dated 1854 December 15 (fol. 13v).

10. S. T. Aksakov to A. I. Panaev, 29 January 1855. PD, *Razriad* I, inventory 1, item 10, fol. 18v.

> Chronicle, one of the most heartfelt, based on the memory of
> the person dearest of all to me from bygone life, that is,
> my mother.[11]

In a letter to Turgenev on 11 June, Aksakov repeats the statement
that this fragment is one of the most "heartfelt," adding, "I am so
far quite satisfied, but I am unable to continue."[12] Whether the
inability to continue stemmed from a lapse of the initial post-
illness inspiration or from external factors—his sister, Nadezhda
Timofeevna Kartashevskaia, did not relish the possibility of char-
acterizations of their parents appearing in print—it was of short
duration. Aksakov resumed work on the third fragment shortly
after his letter to Turgenev in order to relieve the pain of an acute
toothache. On this occasion, inspiration gave way to a contrasting attitude also typical of Aksakov's relation to his art, one that
stresses the rhetorical and mechanistic aspects of his literary
activity:

> Sitting in a shut-up room, of necessity I have to occupy myself
> with something and therefore I have already nearly completed
> a fragment of Family Chronicle; but I'm afraid that it will
> taste of leeches, poultices, gargles, and drops for the nerves.
> The order of construction turned out to be unworkable
> and I had constantly to cut it up and then sew up the seams,
> which will doubtless be noticeable to the reader. However,
> this article will hardly do for publication.[13]

Despite the sharp difference in Aksakov's approach to his
work between April and June, it is the same fragment which is
under discussion, a good indication of Aksakov's stereoscopic
attitude toward literature: poetic expression of emotion coupled
with a deliberately constructed artifact. By autumn the third
fragment was in sufficiently final form to be read to Iu. F. Samarin, who reacted favorably. "His elation aroused in me the desire to write another fragment of the same type—see how weak a
thing man is!"[14] However, this desire was not immediately realized. By January of 1855 the first three fragments of Family
Chronicle were completed; the second and third were read aloud

11. S. T. Aksakov to K. A. Trutovskii, 27 May 1854, in K. A. Trutovskii,
"Vospominaniia o S. T. Aksakove," no. 3, p. 130.
12. S. T. Aksakov to I. S. Turgenev, 11 June 1854, in Maikov, ed., "Pis'ma
Aksakovykh," no. 11, p. 17.
13. S. T. Aksakov to Ivan Aksakov, 27 June 1854. PD, fond 3, inventory 3, item
14, fol. 52.
14. S. T. Aksakov to Ivan Aksakov, 7 October 1854. Ibid., fol. 77v.

to Turgenev, Khomiakov, and other houseguests at Abramtsevo and met with general enthusiastic approval. According to Aksakov's daughter, Vera, the second fragment occasioned considerable discussion on the subject of criminal acts and unwarranted cruelty on the part of landowners.[15]

At this time, Aksakov also completed *Reminiscences*, concerning his school days at the gymnasium and university of Kazan. Despite his assertion to Pogodin two years earlier that both personal considerations and the probable attitude of the censor precluded publication during his lifetime, Aksakov decided to attempt to bring out a volume that would include most of the material he had originally outlined to Pogodin. The obstacle of family opposition was met head on; the firmness of Aksakov's decision to publish was communicated to his beloved sister Nadezhda in St. Petersburg in a letter to her daughter, Maria Grigor'evna:

> In a year, if I'm still alive, there should appear an enormous volume of my *Chronicles* and *Memoirs*. This year is dedicated to corrections, to excluding things from the printed version, and to reworkings for the censorship. All this I must read to you in advance and I am very much afraid that I will encounter strong opposition from your mama. The [part of] the *Chronicle* about Grandfather and Grandmother she tolerated, but when matters came to Father and Mother, to her husband G. I. Kartashevskii [Aksakov's mathematics teacher at Kazan], and to herself, then I don't know, what will brother Serezhen'ka do with his little sister Nadezhen'ka? Will he succeed in calming the alarmed minds of his brothers and sisters by the difference in names and surnames between *Chronicle* and *Reminiscences*, by the concealment of proper names by initials or invented names?—I don't know, but the book will be published. I wish to humor my own vanity—and that is all.[16]

The last sentence is in Aksakov's own hand, indicating a particular emphasis, for his letters were usually dictated to his scribe during the last fifteen years of his life because of his poor eyesight.

15. V. S. Aksakova, *Dnevnik Very Sergeevny Aksakovoi*, p. 44. (The entry is for 26 January 1855.)
16. S. T. Aksakov to M. G. Kartashevskaia, 26 January 1855. PD, 10 685/XVI s. 42, storage unit 59, fols. 43–43v.

Having discounted the opposition of his relatives, Aksakov devoted the greater part of 1855 to preparing his manuscript for publication and to dealing with the censor. Fortunately, the thaw that followed the death of Nicholas I in February 1855 mitigated the severity and capriciousness that had characterized the censorship during the last years of Nicholas's reign. *Family Chronicle and Reminiscences* was approved for publication in October of 1855 and appeared in early January 1856, meeting with great popular and critical success. Aksakov followed the critical notices closely, and took their favorable nature as a sign that he had arrived as a writer, though belatedly, and as a confirmation of his intention to continue *Family Chronicle*.

Referring in particular to Pavel Annenkov's review in the *Contemporary* (*Sovremennik*), Aksakov requested Turgenev, who was in St. Petersburg at the time, to offer Annenkov "my sincere gratitude and add for yourself (as a secret) that he has confirmed me in the intention to write a fourth fragment of *Family Chronicle*, in which the life of the young Bagrovs will show its future development and which it has been so far impossible for me to touch."[17] The planned continuation in fact became two fragments, both completed within a comparatively short period of time. On April 12, Aksakov informed his niece, Maria Kartashevskaia, that "all this time I have been writing the stay of the young couple in Aksakovo. There was a reading; they said that it was better than the preceding."[18]

On May 15 a reading of the fifth and final fragment was held for a select group, "on whose judgment and impressions I can rely."[19] The two fragments appeared respectively in the June 1856 issue of *Russian Conversation* (*Russkaia beseda*), the newly launched journal of the Moscow Slavophiles, and in the August issue of Mikhail Katkov's *Russian Herald* (*Russkii vestnik*), which the Slavophiles had brief hopes of dominating; they were then included in the second edition of *Family Chronicle*, which appeared in late 1856.

Aksakov began his major literary career with his books on hunting, which functioned both as mundane manuals and as

17. S. T. Aksakov to I. S. Turgenev, 12 March 1856, in Maikov, ed., "Pis'ma Aksakovykh," no. 12, pp. 582–583.
18. S. T. Aksakov to M. G. Kartashevskaia, 12 April 1856. PD, 10 685/xvi s. 42, storage unit 59, fol. 52v.
19. S. T. Aksakov to A. I. Panaev, 15 May 1856. PD, *Razriad* I, inventory 1, item 10, fol. 8.

literature, at least in some sense. The memoirs written during the period 1852–1855, by discussing figures with whom Aksakov associated because of shared interests such as literature and theater, also function as autobiography. As Aksakov commented to Pogodin concerning "Derzhavin," "In this article I say a great deal about myself."[20] *Family Chronicle* may likewise be called a dual text, employing a form usually considered to be on the fringes of literature as a foundation on which to erect a text with a clear literary structure. As Aksakov's outline to Pogodin suggests, *Family Chronicle* in its final version forms an integral part of a sequence dealing with Aksakov's antecedents, his own birth (with which *Family Chronicle* concludes), education, and entrance into society. In this sequence, of which only the period of earliest childhood remained entirely untreated at the time of the completion of *Family Chronicle*, the *Chronicle* serves as a prehistory, an inquiry into the causes that shaped Aksakov's own existence.

Defining oneself by tracing one's ancestry is typical of the initial stages of an autobiography. Criticism of the time tended to treat Aksakov's works as such, not least because of the appearance of other autobiographical works in the journals of the 1850s that reflected interest in the historical and "real" rather than the artifice of fiction.[21] Aksakov shared with such works the aim of preserving the past from oblivion, and, like them, *Family Chronicle* (as well as its sequels) aspires to minor history, dealing with lives and incidents which are totally peripheral to the realm of major events (for instance, the Pugachev rebellion is only mentioned in passing in *Family Chronicle*). Events and characters acquire significance only through their pertinence to the subject of the autobiography. On the pretext of conforming to the conventions of the personal or microcosmic history, Aksakov provides himself with a blank canvas on which to create an imaginative reconstruction of the past, which owes as much to traditional fiction as it does to history or autobiography, but which relies on the reader's acceptance of the historical or

20. S. T. Aksakov to M. P. Pogodin, 1 September 1854. LL, Pogodin *fond*, section II, carton 1, storage unit 60, letter 16.

21. For instance, excerpts of Andrei Bolotov's *Life and Adventures (Zhizn' i prikliucheniia Andreia Bolotova, opisannye im samim dlia svoikh potomkov)*, written in the 1790s, appeared in *Notes of the Fatherland (Otechestvennye zapiski)* in 1850 and 1851; S. P. Zhikharev's *A Student's Diary (Dnevnik studenta)* appeared in the *Muscovite*, in which Aksakov himself published, in 1853.

autobiographical premise of the text in order to endow the fiction with apparent authenticity. The strategy is, of course, similar to that employed in the practical pastoral of the hunting books. The general pattern of events in *Family Chronicle* (Stepan Mikhailovich's settling of the new land, the Kurolesov incident, the courtship, marriage, and early married life of the younger Bagrovs) does apparently conform to the sequence of events in Aksakov's own family in the later eighteenth century, as is suggested by his sister's reluctance to see the book published. However, *Family Chronicle* resists identification as autobiography or history pure and simple, as indeed it defies complete categorization as fiction. Since these two forms differ radically in their existential import, the perceptive reader is forced to accept ambiguity and to recognize the unique status of the text in question.

If we consider briefly the means by which this unique quality of *Family Chronicle* is achieved, we might first examine an element, the narrator, that was crucial in the organization of the hunting books as well. Here the narrator serves as the primary focus not only of the autobiographical aspect of the text, but also of its historical veracity. From the first sentence: "It became confining for my grandfather to live in Simbirsk province" (1:73), the narrator defines the characters in terms of their family relationship to himself, thereby involving them in the actuality of the narrative act and in his own presumably real existence. In addition, as a further reinforcement of the immediacy of discourse, the narrator overtly assumes the role of historian, conspicuously marshaling and at times displaying his sources; descriptions of events often draw on oral sources (preferably eyewitnesses themselves), or on documentary evidence. For instance, the narrator himself recalls one of Stepan Mikhailovich's fits of rage: "I saw him in such a state in my childhood, which occurred many years after the time which I am relating—and the impression remains alive to this day" (1:90).

Similarly, the narrator refers in footnotes to objects or places mentioned in the text that he himself saw at some later date, such as Kurolesov's cat-of-nine-tails (1:118n.) or the swarms of rats that infested the house at Karataevka (1:216n.). He even gives biographical footnotes that extend beyond the time boundaries of the narrative and nearly coincide with the present, such as the one on Evseich, Aksakov's *diad'ka*, or male nurse, whose death in 1841 is reported (1:253n.). Second-hand evidence is labeled as such and the reliability of the witness assessed: "This I remember clearly; the rest was often recounted to me" (1:90). "Reliable witnesses assured me that the lives of those punished [by Kurolesov] were saved only by wrapping their tortured bodies in the warm, just-removed skins of sheep that had been slaughtered on the spot" (1:124).

Letters are presented as actual documents which the narrator claims to have seen, and which, as a historian, he favors over oral accounts; at the same time, he avoids actual quotation from them: "I judge his joy not so much from reports as from his letter to Sofia Nikolavna, which I myself have read; . . . unfortunately, I recall only a few words from this letter" (1:244–245).

As a historian, the narrator asserts his emotional distance from the events he impartially records "as an impartial transmitter of oral traditions" (1:247). He allows himself an occasional historian's irony: "They called him [a stylishly free-thinking landowner] a Voltairean, those, it goes without saying, who had heard of Voltaire" (1:227), and at times disagrees with the opinions of his subjects, ascribing to them an equality of judgment with himself: "Aleksei Stepanovich so loved this spot that he even preferred it to Bagrovo. I do not agree with him, but I also came to love the quiet little house on the bank of the Kinel'" (1:211).

However, the narrator does not appear as historian uniformly throughout the text, and the use of the historian's mask depends on the effect Aksakov wants to make on his reader. The historian-narrator makes his appearance most insistently at certain crucial points in order to confirm the reality of the events being recounted, thereby ostentatiously disrupting and denying the literary pattern that the action might otherwise seem to approach. For instance, Stepan Mikhailovich's fit of rage, one of the high points of the rather plotless first chapter, is described as something witnessed by the narrator himself; in the third chapter, the narrator offers comments on the style of Aleksei Stepanovich's letter to his parents, which provides the turning point of the chapter.

The most extended example of this use of history to break up an incipiently over-literary pattern occurs at the dénouement of the second chapter ("Mikhaila Maksimovich Kurolesov"), in which a sustained narrative of rather shocking discoveries and events (owing, as we shall see, a debt to Gothic fiction) is disrupted by a series of authorial comments relating to the causes of such events. Aksakov uses the term *sobytie* (event), by which he usually implies an actual occurrence: "How did all this occur, I am asked. . . . The event was accomplished quite simply" (1:132). "It is not difficult to guess how Kurolesov's untimely death came about" (1:135). The precise details of Kurolesov's murder become known only through the deathbed confession of one of his poisoners (1:136). The narrator is dependent on this single source for his account, that is, he is not omniscient on this occasion, but deliberately flaunts his restriction to what he can learn through historical methods.

At the same time, this exposition of sources also disrupts the time sequence of the narrative; the narrator chooses to interrupt the flow of his narrative by introducing pertinent information originating at a much later date. "Several decades after this event, my mother, whom Praskov'ia Ivanovna loved very much, asked her, in a moment of heartfelt outpouring and most sincere conversation, about what had happened" (1:135). Similarly, the narrator provides the details of the further career of the clerk Mikhailushka, who prevented, implicitly by bribery, an official investigation of the circumstances of Kurolesov's death. Devoid of any further connection with the plot and indeed holding little intrinsic interest, Mikhailushka's biography serves primarily to display the narrator's commitment to historical completeness (intermittent though that commitment may in fact be), even at moments of literary climax.

The narrator as historian,[22] depending on sources and striving to give a full and dispassionate account, shades imperceptibly into a more literary narrator, one echoing the omnipotent narrator of the eighteenth-century novel. Time in *Family Chronicle* is treated episodically, which neither the true historian nor the true first-person narrator, like that in *Years of Childhood*, permits himself. Such a narrator is singularly appropriate for *Family Chronicle*, set as it is in the eighteenth century; the historian and the more literary narrator do in fact complement one another while sustaining an ambiguity concerning the nature of the text as a whole.

22. This relationship between narrator and narration in the novel characterizes the "authorial novel" in terminology proposed by Franz Stanzel, *Narrative Situations in the Novel*, pp. 38–39. *Family Chronicle* brings the narrator and his fictional world much closer than is typical, according to Stanzel, for the authorial novel.

Aksakov underlined the unresolved quality of his text in the envoi,[23] where the crosscurrents of history and fiction running throughout the work are insistently juxtaposed in a few lines, as if to underline Aksakov's method throughout. He apostrophizes his characters as "my light and dark images, my good and bad people, or rather, images in which there are both light and dark sides, people in whom there is both good and evil" (1:279). The grammatical parallelism deliberately tends to obscure the fact that two logically incompatible notions are being equated. The individuals of *Family Chronicle* are paradoxically both literary figures (*obrazy*, "images," in Aksakov's terms) and actual people, their characteristics either a matter of deliberate shading, of art created by a conscious artist, or the manifestation of innate moral features which are merely recorded by the aloof chronicler. Aksakov preserves and reinforces this ambiguity throughout the envoi; his characters are "not great heroes, not celebrated persons" (1:279). "Heroes" implies literary status, but "celebrated persons" suggests real existence, although one important feature, insignificance, accrues to both modes of being, thus underlining the minor, picturesque nature of the entire work.

This uncertainty is compounded by two parallel yet paradoxical statements, the first of which asserts, "You were people, and your outer and inner life is just as filled with poetry, just as curious and instructive for us, as we and our life will be in our turn curious and instructive for our descendants" (1:279–280). The interesting and instructive life of one's ancestors is poetic,

23. Not all English translations of *Family Chronicle* include the envoi. I offer a complete translation here, somewhat freer than the passages discussed in the text:

> Farewell my images, bright or dark, my people, good or bad—
> or should I rather say, images that have their bright and dark sides,
> people who have both virtues and vices. You are not great heroes, not
> imposing personalities; you trod your path on earth in silence
> and obscurity, and it is a long, a very long time since you left it. But
> you were people, and your inward and outward life was as full
> of poetry, as interesting and instructive to us as we and our life will
> be in turn interesting and instructive to our descendants. You
> were characters in that mighty spectacle which mankind has presented
> on this earth since time immemorial; you played your parts as
> conscientiously as others did, and you deserve as well to be remem-
> bered. By the mighty power of the pen and of print, your descen-
> dants have now become acquainted with you. They have greeted you
> with sympathy and recognized you as brothers, no matter how
> and when you lived, no matter what clothes you wore. May no harsh
> judgment and no heedless word offend your memory. (1:279–280)

hence aesthetic and literary, and is referred to before Aksakov speaks of the intellectual and moral values inherent in the past. In the second statement, he employs the traditional metaphor of human society as a theater, suggesting his artifice in constructing his characters (and thus their lack of any value but aesthetic) and their conformity with ahistorical roles which repeat themselves endlessly, depriving individuals of intrinsic personal value. "You were the same sort of characters in the cast of the great universal spectacle enacted by mankind from time immemorial; just as conscientiously did you play out your roles, as do all people, and likewise deserve to be remembered" (1:280).

The allusion to theater is not without its precedent in the text of *Family Chronicle*; at various points in the course of the work, Aksakov's thorough familiarity with the mechanics of the stage, the principles of drama, and the actor's craft is evident. Stepan Mikhailovich's fits of rage in chapters 1 and 4, as well as Praskov'ia Ivanovna's discovery of Kurolesov's true character in chapter 2, are strongly reminiscent of theatrical tirades and peripeties. The final scene of the novel, in which Stepan Mikhailovich inscribes his grandson's name in the family tree, begins as a dramatic scene—the servant entering his master's bedroom, Stepan Mikhailovich rushing barefoot in his nightclothes to his desk—but ends with a close-up, the writing of the name itself, which would be difficult to show on stage. Thus *Family Chronicle* concludes with a transition to the more intimate perspective of *Years of Childhood*. Aksakov's use of the theater as an implicit metaphor and as a determinant of scale and point of view is not unique. As Richard Freeborn has pointed out, the Russian novel after Gogol often drew on theater.[24]

Despite the strong pull of theater and of ahistorical aesthetic value in Aksakov's characters, the *envoi* still insists that they be "remembered," that is, that they figure as part of history, not as fictions, by virtue of their very faithfulness to the roles assigned them by history. Aksakov thus closes *Family Chronicle* on a note of mystification as to its status and goals, as well as to his own authorial role in it, offering apparent alternatives but simultaneously fusing and confusing them.

That Aksakov deliberately sought to reinforce the ambiguity of this final passage can be concluded from the deletions and

24. Richard Freeborn, *The Rise of the Russian Novel*, p. 119.

emendations contained in the manuscript of the *envoi*.[25] In each instance of a change of phrasing, the net result tends to check too full a development of one or the other line of metaphor suggested by the initial contrast of images and people (*obrazy-liudi*), that is of fact or fiction. Two deleted sentences, one after the first sentence in the final text of the *envoi*, and the second immediately preceding the final sentence, overemphasize the real status of the characters:

1. It is difficult for me to part with you, I have become accustomed to, gotten used to your life! I have become intimate with your faces, characteristics, feelings, and habits!

2. May your dust rest in peace in the comforting earth and may . . .

The first deletion would have established the parity of the characters and the narrator, calling into question his role in the creation of the text and, by implication, the text's status as a structured literary artifact; the second would also accord them real existence.

Changes in another sentence seem to have been made because earlier drafts overemphasized the creative activity of the author. In the final version, no direct mention is made of the author's role: "By the mighty power of writing and print your descendants have now become acquainted with you" (1:280). By presenting writing and printing as impersonal forces, instruments disguised as agents, Aksakov only hints at the author's creative role, which was explicitly stated in the first version of this sentence in the manuscript:

1. I have summoned you forth and by the mighty power of writing and print have acquainted your descendants with you.

In a second version, direct reference to the author's role is reduced, though not eliminated, through a change of voice and suppression of agent:

25. The *envoi* is one of the few passages in the surviving manuscripts of Aksakov's works to contain numerous variants and cancellations, indicating a careful weighing of alternative phrasings. LL, *fond* 3, folder I, item 7, fols. 57–58v. Since Aksakov dictated his works to a scribe because of his partial blindness, he seems usually to have worked out his text in considerable detail in his mind before committing it to paper. Subsequent quotations from the *envoi* are all found in the MS cited above, fols. 58–58v.

2. You have now been summoned forth from the gloom of
   oblivion and by the mighty power of writing and print, your
   descendants have become acquainted with you.

In the final version, the first clause of this variant is dropped
altogether, eliminating both the direct reference to authorial
power and the suggestion that the characters existed in the past.

The metaphorical use of the stage for history and society, with
its implication of the conventional nature of the characters and
the limitation of their significance to the dramatic, to the aesthetic rather than the ethical, was more sharply formulated in its
initial version:

> Vy byli takie zhe iskusnye aktery velikoi vsemirnoi dramy . . .

> You were the same sort of skilled actors in the great universal
> drama . . .

In the final version, *deistvuiushchie litsa* ("characters,"
"dramatis personae") and *zrelishcha* ("spectacle") replace *iskus-
nye aktery* ("skilled actors") and *dramy* ("drama"). The changes
subtly depersonalize the individuals and reduce the precision of
the metaphor, yet at the same time eliminate a too-direct implication that the characters are entirely derived from literary sources
and that history and society can be entirely reduced to or contained by a specific aesthetic form.

The formal distinction between real, historical individuals and
fictional, generalized characters is one that Aksakov seems to
have been conscious of throughout the period of *Family Chronicle*'s composition. In 1853, before he began any concerted effort
to write *Family Chronicle*, he offered Turgenev a critique of the
latter's *Two Generations* (*Dva pokoleniia*; the work is not extant)
in which he comments that "the first part, it seems to me, divides into two halves: into one which is described from reality
having the quality of notes or memoirs, and one which is created
by the fantasy of the author. The first, as fact, has the great
interest of truth, but the second at times does not satisfy my
requirements: somehow the transition from truth to invention is
perceptible."[26] Not only does Aksakov reveal that he was well
aware of two possible modes of shaping and presenting experience, he also takes Turgenev to task for failing to solve the very

26. S. T. Aksakov to I. S. Turgenev, 4 August 1853. In Maikov, ed., "Pis'ma
Aksakovykh," no. 10, p. 482.

problem that Aksakov sets himself in *Family Chronicle*, namely, the complete fusion of the two forms.

In fact, not only in *Family Chronicle*, but in many of his other works, Aksakov comes much closer to the merger of fiction and fact suggested by the *envoi* of *Family Chronicle* than to the clear distinction he indicates in his letter to Turgenev. In *Family Chronicle* the narrator perhaps plays the major role in achieving this effect; however, even in works which are clearly memoiristic and meant to have the "great interest of truth," Aksakov constructs his characters in essentially the same manner that he employs in a partially fictional work such as *Family Chronicle*. Thus "people" and "images" function in similar ways, and the differences between them depend as much on cues provided by other elements of the text as on the characters themselves. That is one reason why the narrator in Aksakov's memoirs is clearly defined, even if he is often only a witness.

Human action is, for Aksakov, in large measure dictated by passions and basically irrational drives. This is hardly surprising in the light of his books on hunting, where the irrational passion of the hunter is matched by the instinctual behavior of his prey.[27] In his memoirs, written for the most part between the completion of *Notes of a Hunter* and the beginning of serious work on *Family Chronicle*, Aksakov defines his subjects—all of them clearly historical individuals and intended to be perceived as such—in terms of one basic desire. Derzhavin, his first full attempt at such a personage ("Acquaintance with Derzhavin" was completed in May of 1852), is totally possessed by his desire to hear his own verse read to him by the much younger Aksakov: "He, in accord with his ardent nature, impatiently desired to listen to me, or, as he himself later expressed it, to hear himself" (2:316). This desire is virtually the only aspect of his personality that is presented, probably because Aksakov's contact with Derzhavin was more or less limited to such readings, and also because Derzhavin was at the time (1815–1816) already an old man, given to the near-senile whims of old age. Still the desire and the reaction to its gratification is strong: "Derzhavin trembled . . . was already embracing me with tears in his eyes" (2:230). However, Aksakov's

---

27. Aksakov resorts to some of his most overt comparisons of the human and the animal in those passages of his hunting books where the animals display strongly instinctual behavior. See, for example, the comparison of the mating ritual of the grouse to a society ball (4:398).

brief biography of Mikhail Nikolaevich Zagoskin, whom Aksakov knew well for more than thirty years, operates on the same principle: Zagoskin is totally consistent, acquiring in childhood a love of reading and "the inclination and ability to *write*."[28] This desire operates as the focus of Zagoskin's life; his family, government career, and theatrical activity (other than the actual composition of plays) are scarcely mentioned; aspects of his personality other than his passion for writing fall outside the range of Aksakov's interest and are treated anecdotally, almost as an epilogue. Shchepkin's career in the theater, discussed in the speech "A Few Words about M. S. Shchepkin" ("Neskol'ko slov o M. S. Shchepkine"), 1855, is also traced from an initial, determining incident, the first appearance on stage of a stage-struck boy.

Aksakov's most ambitious completed biography, "Memoir of A. S. Shishkov," presents Shishkov as an early Slavophile. Again, the absolute consistency and continuity of this one defining trait is stressed. Shishkov, for all his errors, represented "the Russian movement . . . Slavophilism, no matter how oddly Shishkov conceived of it, which he confessed and professed from his early years to the grave, for which he was a martyr . . ."(2:313). This heroic dedication of Shishkov's, in Aksakov's presentation, found its main expression in philology, with its etymological inquiries and stylistic analysis, and in polemics, all directed against the Frenchified innovations of Karamzin and his followers. Aksakov's attention is focused on this passionate squabbling; other aspects of Shishkov's life are neglected, with no explanation of such odd facts, given Shishkov's supposedly all-pervasive Russian sentiment, as his two marriages to non-Orthodox non-Russians. As is the case with Zagoskin, the subject's absent-mindedness is stressed; neglect of areas of life not concerned with the subject's one obsession thus becomes a function of his own personality rather than the result of intentional exclusion on Aksakov's part. With Shishkov, the disjunction between his almost purely intellectual passion and real life becomes comic in its totality:

> That intelligent and learned hero, the defender of the integrity of the language and of Russian distinctiveness, the firm

28. Aksakov, "Biografiia M. N. Zagoskina," in *Sobranie sochinenii* in 5 volumes (Moscow: Pravda, 1966), 4:151.

> and bold accuser of triumphant novelty and the venerator of
> the pious past, this open enemy of blind imitation of the
> foreign—was a complete infant in everyday life; he lived as the
> most undemanding guest in his own home. . . . He knew
> only the scholarly council at the Admiralty and his own study,
> in which he toiled over dictionaries of various Slavic dialects,
> over old manuscripts and church books, studying etymology
> and comparative derivation of words. (2:279)

In both the hunting books and the memoirs, obsession is absolute, shaping the individual throughout life. This quality of
characterization in the memoirs must of course be taken into
account when considering Aksakov's memoirs as historical or
biographical sources; character in them is logically prior to
events and determines them, rather than the reverse, as we might
expect with a modern biography. Only in two cases does Aksakov seem to have granted events superiority over a preestab-
lished character. The first of these is *History of My Acquaintance
with Gogol* (1853–1855), which, as its title indicates, was to be a
full, or nearly full, account of Aksakov's twenty-year association
with Gogol. While factual completeness may not have presented
a major problem, given the letters at Aksakov's disposal in addition to the recollections of his family, the difficulty Aksakov, like
so many after him, encountered in attempting to define Gogol's
enigmatic personality or to reduce it to a single, clear, motivating
factor may have been the reason Aksakov finally abandoned the
project.[29] The other work not dependent on a single guiding passion in a central figure, *Literary and Theatrical Memoirs* (1856–
1858), is a much more diffuse chronicle than any of Aksakov's
other memoiristic works and perhaps his least successful.

Thus in his literary memoirs, which in the main predate *Family Chronicle* and served as a sort of laboratory for working out
methods of characterization, Aksakov's characters are absolute
and integral, the entire range of their emotions determined by
and consistent with the character's obsession, clearly defined at
the outset, often in terms of a childhood "inspiration." Individuals in the memoirs are defined by their passions, but these are

---

29. In both public and private statements on Gogol, Aksakov stresses that few
people knew him well. In a letter to his sons shortly after Gogol's death, he states
that he felt no fear in the presence of Gogol's corpse (despite his usual discomfort
in such a situation) because "for me Gogol was not a person." (S. T. Aksakov to
Ivan and Konstantin Aksakov, 23 February 1852, in *Sobranie sochinenii*, 3:387.)

of a refined and intellectual sort, indeed can be seen as manifestations, at least in Derzhavin and Shishkov, of the eighteenth-century Russian *dvorianin*'s claim to individualizing eccentricity, especially in cultural matters. In *Family Chronicle* even more extreme psychological reductionism obtains, with the characters of *Family Chronicle* approaching more clearly the "types" Aksakov referred to in his letter to Turgenev.

In the memoirs, the passion falls broadly within the area of *okhota* and is tacitly separated from other spheres of life, which are simply not treated. Shishkov, sitting in his study engaged in etymological research, could serve as the emblem of this disjunction. In *Family Chronicle*, this partition of the personality into two parts is absent; more importantly, a character is not defined in terms of *okhoty*—avocations which are basically benign, if somewhat asocial, and apparently eccentric to those who do not share them—but rather in terms of real passion (*strast'*), powerful universals such as rage, love, greed, or sadism, which not only determine a character's entire being but have major social implications as well. If the pursuits of the narrator in the hunting books and of the characters in the literary memoirs are essentially personal and isolated, in *Family Chronicle* the characters' actions are socially involved and other-directed, at times agressively so, with weaker individuals reduced to instruments or victims of the stronger. Aksakov presents a social paradigm in *Family Chronicle* that hardly flatters humankind, though it is rich in potential for dramatic conflict.

Characters in *Family Chronicle* do share one significant trait with the characters of the literary memoirs: inertia. They persist in their given state until (and only if) external factors alter that state, or at least hold it in check. Characters even continue in their passion to their own detriment: the Bagrov women persist in their flagrant dislike of their sister-in-law Sofia Nikolavna to the point of permitting her to be attacked by rats, even though this is sure to, and does, provoke Stepan Mikhailovich's monumental wrath. The most profound and disturbing example of this sort of unilinear, compulsive character is Kurolesov, the outsider whose sadistic drives lead him to self-destruction. Although the social fabric is strong enough to hold other characters in check, Kurolesov is obviously paradigmatic of the potential for absolutism inherent in each character.

Such a method of characterization involves certain problems

when the text involves dramatic action, which the literary memoirs do not. Change in a character may be dramatically necessary, but in a world of absolute passions it can be achieved only
by complete change; only one emotion can be expressed by a
character at a given time, in much the same way that a character
in a hagiography can be only saint or demon, with miracle and
conversion the only possible mechanisms of change. Aksakov's
experience as an actor may be a factor in his approach to change
in a character, since changes in a stage character must be both
rapid and visible. In any case his view of the emotional life
seems not to have been limited to fiction, but to have been an
intrinsic part of his general outlook. In an 1850 letter to his son
Ivan, informing him of the current state of various ailing members of the family, Aksakov clearly states his belief in the mutually exclusive nature of emotions, even those of the same type,
but differing in their object: "Olin'ka [Aksakov's daughter] bore
all this heroically, but I became thoroughly frightened: for I was
already calm on Mother's account. And this shouldn't seem paradoxical to you; in time you will become convinced that one fear
obliterates the force of another."[30]

Alteration in character in *Family Chronicle* reflects this attitude toward the emotions; since changes involve the emergence
of a new and dominant passion, causing a total realignment of
the personality, such changes are invariably major, often climac-
tic events. In some instances they take the form of total personality changes analogous to religious conversions. At the climax of
chapter 2, Praskov'ia Ivanovna's love for Mikhaila Maksimovich
Kurolesov is replaced by righteous wrath (1:127) the morning
after her discovery of his dissolute and sadistic life:

> He glanced around the room: Praskov'ia Ivanovna was
> kneeling and with tears was praying to God, looking at the
> new church cross which was directly in front of the windows
> of the house and which was ablaze from the rising sun;
> there was no icon in the room. . . . Praskov'ia Ivanovna did
> not become confused, stood up, did not permit her husband to
> embrace her and, burning inwardly with righteous wrath,
> coldly and firmly declared to him that she knew everything.
> (1:127–128)

30. S. T. Aksakov to Ivan Aksakov, 22 March 1850. LL, *fond* 3, folder 3,
item 22g.

Similarly, Sofia Nikolavna's state changes from suicidal depression, caused by her stepmother's hostility, to a firm decision to "suffer, bear, and live" after a night of prayer followed by an apparently miraculous lighting of a taper set before her most treasured icon, one of the Virgin given to her by her own dying mother (1:141).

Stepan Mikhailovich, the central figure of the text as a whole, displays emotions that alternate, but the principle of incompatibility of emotional states is perhaps demonstrated even more clearly by the vacillation between the figures of Stepan Mikhailovich the Good and Stepan Mikhailovich the Angry: "That kind, virtuous and even lenient man sometimes darkened with such outbursts of rage that they distorted in him the image of man and rendered him capable at such times of cruel, repulsive acts" (1:90). The two Stepan Mikhailoviches are summed up in the physical detail of his eyes; ordinarily they are "beautiful large dark-blue eyes . . . calm and mild in times of inner quiet" (1:76), but in moments of rage, they alter completely, becoming basilisk-like instruments of aggression rather than transparent means of perception: "He trembled all over, convulsions wrenched his face, savage fire poured from his eyes, which had clouded and darkened from his ferocity" (1:90). Stepan Mikhailovich is capable of existence only in one of these two states at any given time. The possibility of the onset of a fit of rage provides much of the suspense in Stepan Mikhailovich's world, for these states do not alternate randomly. Ordinarily, Stepan Míkhailovich is beneficient, and the transformation to his wrathful counterpart depends on and is caused by inappropriate behavior (again motivated by individual passions) on the part of others. Stepan Mikhailovich's anger serves as the regulator and guarantor of the social order, the mechanism which prevents an anarchy of passions. Other characters weigh their actions by their possible effect on Stepan Mikhailovich's delicately balanced passions, or ignore this balance at their peril.

Since each personality in Aksakov's universe, particularly in the schematic psychological and social world of *Family Chronicle*, is at any particular moment totally homogeneous, change from one state to another necessarily occurs instantaneously and results in the sudden sequential juxtaposition of what are logically two different characters, though they bear the same names. Such discontinuous change obviously cannot originate within the character; external factors become the only available catalysts of alteration. Another legacy of Aksakov's theater experience is perhaps at work. This stimulus is most frequently visual, an object or suddenly perceived scene that reveals a change in the order of the world that the character must respond to. In this respect, the changes in *Family Chronicle*'s characters represent a radical version of the reaction to the visual stimuli of traces (*sledy*) in Aksakov's early epistles and of the system of observation of environment and congruent adjustment of action that structure "The Blizzard" and both *Notes on Fishing* and *Notes of a Hunter.*

Response to such physical, particularly visual, information is typical of Aksakov's own behavior. For instance, the sight of the room recently vacated by his son Grigorii and his bride, following their wedding visit to the Aksakov home, objectifies and intensifies Aksakov's sense of loss at their departure: "I dressed, went through the whole house, passed into your bedroom. . . . Completely empty: the floor covered with scraps of paper, cotton, and all sorts of trash, the disorder of the furniture and other objects—testified that the inhabitants had recently and hurriedly departed. . . . I felt even more depressed."[31]

Visual perception of concrete objects and configurations are likewise crucial to the sudden, even instantaneous, realization by characters in *Family Chronicle* of altered situations with a consequent change in their own personality. Praskov'ia Ivanovna's glimpse of Kurolesov in his revels completely reverses her feeling toward him. Similarily, Sofia Nikolavna's changed position in her father's household vis-à-vis his Kalmyk manservant is brought home to her by her first glimpse of him upon her return from her wedding trip. To heighten the visual impact, the Kalmyk's usurpation of her place is deliberately literalized: "The old man lay in his usual position: by his side, in the very same armchair in which Sofia Nikolavna had always sat, sat the Kalmyk" (1:239). "The first glance at the lackey sitting in the armchair, which had never been the case before, disclosed the true state of affairs to Sofia Nikolavna" (1:241). This concrete perception of the new status of the Kalmyk leads to Sofia Nikolavna's estrangement from her dying father. Even at second hand, it is physical details that elicit response; Stepan Mikhailovich is well

31. S. T. Aksakov to G. S. Aksakov and S. A. Aksakova, 27 February 1848, in Shenrok, "S. T. Aksakov i ego sem'ia," no. 11, p. 49.

aware of his daughters' hostility toward their new sister-in-law, but it is hearing the concrete facts of the rat attack at Karataevka that unleashes his wrath.

Aksakov's characters, from his early writings through *Family Chronicle*, regardless of the ostensible genre in which they appear, conform to a fairly simple and consistent basic structure. In the memoirs, and much of the time in *Family Chronicle*, there is no real action, in the sense of development involving real change in a character; inertial states rather than dynamic processes are the norm. Of course in such a context the changes that do occur in a given character gain dramatic effectiveness against the background of psychological consistency and simplicity.

Yet Aksakov avoids melodrama in *Family Chronicle*. The historical dimension of the work, the insistence by the historian-narrator that he is reporting and not creating, as well as the ambiguity concerning the existential status of the characters and events narrated, preclude easy dismissal of the text as literary artifice, even at moments when that artifice is apparent. Indeed any simplicity of characterization or schematization of events can be perceived as an appropriate and innate feature of the events narrated and of their period, an age of simpler thought and broader gesture than our own.

Thus the past itself becomes the factor which renders legitimate the literary qualities of *Family Chronicle*; the unique and the universal, "people" and "images," interpenetrate in such a way that one can be approached only through the other.

5

Family Chronicle: Structures and Themes

Aksakov's works prior to *Family Chronicle* consisted primarily of self-sufficient, basically atemporal units linked by similarity in structure and theme. In the hunting books, individual notes on various types of game and in the literary memoirs, incidents perhaps rather distant from one another in time, are connected by the persona of the hunter or by the perceiving and recording memoirist. In *Family Chronicle*, the narrator also plays an important role in maintaining the unity of the text. However, as Aksakov's description of each chapter—"a fragment [otryvok] from a family chronicle"—suggests, the discontinuities between parts of *Family Chronicle* are of a distinctly different quality from those in his earlier works; the whole is composed of parts that are not essentially interchangeable, but that differ from one another in kind. Each chapter of *Family Chronicle* exhibits an affinity in its organization and theme with one or more specific literary modes, a fact which makes the overarching presence of the narrator-historian doubly important in maintaining the coherence of the entire text. The sections of earlier works are simply variations on a theme, while in *Years of Childhood*, which is continuous in both chronology and themes, the chapters are continuous. But the more complex interplay between parts in *Family Chronicle* gives the book its rhythm and density, which is not that of a typical novel (since various genres dominate in different parts of *Family Chronicle*), but still suggests a complete and self-contained work, close to the tradition of the cycle of stories in Russian literature from Pushkin's *Tales of Belkin* (*Povesti Belkina*) and Lermontov's *Hero of Our Time* (*Geroi nashego vremeni*), to Babel's *Red Cavalry* (*Konarmiia*). Since each of the chapters of *Family Chronicle* adheres to its own inner norms, separate discussion of each chapter will perhaps best clarify its structure and its position in the work as a whole.

The first chapter of *Family Chronicle* consists of four distinct segments or sub-fragments, composed and published over a fairly lengthy interval of time.[1] The first and third, "Migration" ("Pereselenie") and "New Places" ("Novye mesta"), narrate the foundation and subsequent growth of Novoe Bagrovo, while the second and fourth, "Orenburg Province" ("Orenburgskaia guberniia") and "A Good Day of Stepan Mikhailovich" ("Dobryi den' Stepana Mikhailovicha") are rather sketches cut off from any chronological sequence. Such narrative and temporal inconsistencies are of course appropriate for the beginning of a chronicle, where fragmentation of narrative, interpolations, chronological lacunae, and stylistic variation, all reflecting heterogeneity of sources and varying times of composition, are most frequent. As we move closer to the present, stylistic consistency, fewer gaps, and greater attention to events of lesser significance all become the rule. All four sections of the first chapter, however, despite the variations in kind, are pertinent to a single theme: the human organization of space.

As chronicle openings often do, the first chapter of *Family Chronicle*, also the most remote in time, puts great emphasis on space and the establishment of human order in it. While spatial contrasts and oppositions are important throughout *Family Chronicle*, they are perhaps the primary focus of the first chapter. The opening paragraph of the entire work directly establishes the basic determinants of the world of the first chapter (and less overtly of the work as a whole):

> It became too confining for my grandfather to live in Simbirsk province, on his ancestral holdings, granted to his forefathers by the tsars of Moscow; it became confining not because it was in fact crowded, because there were insufficient forest, pasture, fields, and other necessities—everything was available in abundance—but because the holding, which had belonged unentailed to his great-grandfather, had be-

1. Aksakov, *Semeinaia khronika*, in *Sobranie sochinenii*. The first two sections were published in 1846 in the Slavophile almanac *Moscow Miscellany* (*Moskovskii literaturnyi i uchenyi sbornik*) and reprinted, along with the third and fourth parts of chap. 1, in the *Muscovite* (*Moskvitianin*) in 1854.

> come shared in ownership. . . . For my grandfather, impatient,
> excitable, straightforward and hating domestic squabbles,
> such a life became unbearable. For some time he had been
> hearing about the Ufa district, about its unchartable expanse of
> land. (1:73)

Old Bagrovo, title to which has become entailed because of in-
heritable dowry settlements to female members of the line, is
defined and confined by history and rendered undesirable by the
action of time. Even the style used to describe the situation suggests this entailment: *otchina* ("holding") is archaic in comparison with the standard *votchina*; the phrase *ot tsarei moskovskikh*
("by the tsars of Moscow"), with its legalistic inversion and
archaic use of *ot* for "agent", suggests the style of the very document (*gramota*) by which the original grant was presumably
made. Because it has five owners, Old Bagrovo is imploding,
without clear delineation of its boundaries and of the rights of
the various owners, whose numbers increase as their relationships attenuate over time. In apparent contrast to this confinement is the "boundless expanse" of land in the Ufa district (later
Orenburg Province), the beauties of which are apostrophized in
the second segment as pristine, "fresh, flowering, untrammeled
by heterogenous populations arriving from all directions" (1:83).
By contrast, Old Bagrovo's water supply has been destroyed by
"man, the cursed and triumphant alterer of the face of nature"
(1:87).

The lands of Orenburg are the promised land only in potentia,
however, for they suffer from a complementary defect, their ownership being underdetermined rather than overdetermined. The
aboriginal and semi-nomadic inhabitants, the Bashkirs, dispose
of their land quite gladly in exchange for a feast, but set its
boundaries in the vaguest terms, such as distances from a dead
birch tree to fox pits to a bee tree (1:75), and direct purchase of
Bashkir land invariably entails later dispute.

Old Bagrovo's chaos of confinement and Ufa/Orenburg's chaos
of openness differ in quality but are functionally equivalent.
Stepan Mikhailovich's goal becomes the establishment of a new
space, clearly delineated both internally and externally. His
search takes on aspects of a quest, leading him across the Volga
into areas with various exotic names: Cheremshan, Kandurcha,
the Bugul'minskii, Birskii and Menzelinskii districts (1:78). This
quest can also be viewed as a variant of pastoral retreat to a

purer, simpler society, and of course much of *Family Chronicle* depends on the contrast of city, or at least more developed areas, and the truly rural, which here as in the hunting books is closer to the sources of all being.

Once he has purchased land with a clear title established by the first Russian owner—actually, the title turns out to be more heavily entailed than Stepan Mikhailovich supposed, perhaps suggesting that total pastoral escape is in fact impossible (1:79)—Stepan Mikhailovich begins the process of imposing order. His "promised land," teeming with water and wildlife (1:79–80), is humanized and transformed from totally free nature into a habitable place, a pastoral *locus amoenus.* (In this respect *Family Chronicle* is less uncompromising than the hunting works or *Years of Childhood,* all of which present nature as transcendent). In the process of constructing a new center for a new microcosm, agriculture is initiated, land enclosed,[2] shelter constructed for peasant and master, and at least the promise of the establishment of a new church is made (1:80–81).

The culmination of the construction of this new world (a replica of the old one, but free of the imperfections rendered by time) occurs with the damming of the Buguruslan River and the foundation of the mill. The damming of the river sums up humanity's creative interaction with its environment, the human ability to intervene in the processes of life and time (both suggested by the flowing water) and to create a new order in which human beings may participate. The mill itself, grinding grain into flour, objectifies man's unique ability to convert the things of nature into the things of culture, to humanize his world. The actual construction of the dam and the placement of the mill take on the character of a ritual; every step in the process is minutely described, in order to stress by retardation the importance of the event (a typically Aksakovian emphatic device). The site is carefully selected and the equipment for the mill prepared; the participants are aware that their undertaking signifies the final and most crucial moment in their transformation of the wilderness into habitable space. "The next day at sunrise about a hundred people assembled to *zanimat' zaimku,* that is, to dam the river. There was a sort of concern and triumph on every face; everyone

2. The establishment of boundaries is an ancient means of indicating the organized and even sacred nature of the space within. See Eliade, *Patterns in Comparative Religion,* pp. 370–371.

was ready to do something; the whole village had hardly slept that night" (1:82). The struggle between man and the Buguruslan, "heretofore free, inviolate, its waters surging" (1:82), ends with the synthesis of the two opponents and the imposition of human purpose upon the wilderness. This moment marks the true inception of the life of the new settlement as an organized world, for the mill is the guarantee of an isolated village's self-sufficiency. It is the start of a new history that persists to the present: "Finally, men conquered, the water could no longer force its way through, it stopped, as if collecting its thoughts, turned upon itself, started to run upstream. . . . By evening a millpond had formed. . . . The next day the press began to stamp and the mill to grind—and grinds and stamps to this day" (1:83).

In this new world the central position is occupied by its creator, Stepan Mikhailovich, who not only constructs the physical order but also controls the social organization of New Bagrovo. The initial description of Stepan Mikhailovich establishes his qualifications for this semi-royal or divine role, a role that persists in later fragments of *Family Chronicle*. The first simile used to describe his physical strength indicates his *bogatyr'*-like nature, in particular by comparing the objects' actions rather than their attributes: "In his carefree youth, in feats of strength, he would shake off a heap of his army fellows who had piled on him as a massive oak shakes drops of water from itself after a rain when the wind stirs it" (1:76). The physical power is linked with moral power; during his military service, Stepan Mikhailovich rounded up Volga robbers, who knew him by sight and feared him like fire (1:77). These details are not without purpose, for Aksakov invariably conceived of the events and actions of childhood and youth as directly determinative or emblematic of later life. This is true both of his memoirs (note Zagoskin's early penchant for writing, for example) and of *Family Chronicle* and later works. In the second chapter of *Family Chronicle* the villain Kurolesov significantly has no youth, but first appears as an adult and outsider, and his sinister qualities remain ultimately unexplained.

The section "New Places" in particular emphasizes Stepan Mikhailovich's role in New Bagrovo. Under his guidance, livestock increases to the point of wealth (1:87), and Stepan Mikhailovich concerns himself in particular with the breeding of horses, the preeminent animal of nobility (1:93). He not only rules his own estate, but becomes a magnet for other settlements, both Russian and non-Russian, helping new settlers assimilate into the area of which he is the guardian. He provides material support in the form of seed, supplies, and advice to the arriving Russians, Mordvinians, and others, but he functions also as an establisher of social order, as an oracle and legislator, dispensing justice: "Whoever lied to him once, once deceived him, let that man not approach him. . . . He settled many a family quarrel, ended many a lawsuit at the very start. People came to him from all directions, both by foot and conveyance, for advice, counsel, and judgment—and his words were obeyed as though sacred" (1:89). As a source of justice, Stepan Mikhailovich also displays the fullness of his power negatively, in his rages, which are invariably (and carefully) connected with punishment for wrongdoing; he may be faulted for excess, but he is a just man. He functions as a chthonic deity, both beneficent and punitive, absolute within a firmly delineated area.

In the concluding section of the first fragment, "A Good Day of Stepan Mikhailovich," a single day serves as the framework within which Stepan Mikhailovich's power and his centrality to the entire operation of his universe are displayed. On the economic level, his power expresses itself as mastery over all aspects of the material existence of his estate, beginning with his early morning observation of the livestock, particularly his stallions, proceeding to an inspection of the crops, both his own and his peasants', and concluding (after a substantial midday meal and obligatory nap) with a visit to the mill, where his superior knowledge of the workings of the very heart of his estate averts a breakdown which the miller himself is unable to foresee (1:100). On the social level, Stepan Mikhailovich's elevated status as patriarch and lord of his family, servants, and peasants is stressed from his morning greeting to his wife, whom he graciously allows to kiss his hand, to his evening conference with his *starosta* (elder of the peasants), at which he dispenses justice to the serfs (1:101).

However, throughout the description of Stepan Mikhailovich's "good day" there runs the counter-scenario, constantly alluded to, of his "bad day." This alternative paradigm of Stepan Mikhailovich's actions threatens to become dominant at various points, but the mere thought of inciting his wrath is sufficient to keep social order. The description of his "good day" is really an attempt to encompass in all its phases the realm of which he is the center.

In addition to its spatial and social coherence, the world that Stepan Mikhailovich establishes in the course of the first chapter can be characterized by its special type of time, which is also in a sense coherent. As we have seen, most of the first chapter functions essentially as a foundation myth, explaining how the present order of the world (or at least of this microcosm) was established, a process that culminates in the inauguration of time for Novoe Bagrovo through the construction of the mill. The last sound in "A Good Day" is that of the ceaseless pulse of the mill: "The mill grumbled and the press stamped more closely in the damp nocturnal fog" (1:102). However, the relationship between the last segment of chapter 1 and its predecessors is not simply or primarily chronological. Significant or effective action, which changes states, is limited in the first chapter to the first and third segments; the foundation of the mill completes one process and begins another. Aksakov frequently presents endings that are simultaneously beginnings. "A Good Day," however, rather atypically for Aksakov, presents the static world created by the act of foundation, a world whose myths are secure and in which every act can and need only once more repeat a permanently established and even archetypal action. Thus every action in "A Good Day" takes on the suggestion of a ritual in an endlessly repeating sequence of actions. The form of "A Good Day" suggests this circularity, its action ending at the point in the daily cycle just prior to the moment at which narration began twenty-four hours earlier. The narrative ends with ritualized gestures that affirm the unchanging equilibrium of man and environment: "My grandfather arose from his porch, crossed himself once or twice before the starry sky and lay down to sleep, despite the closeness in the room, on a hot down quilt and ordered the bed-curtains lowered around him" (1:102).

This closed and stable world with which the first chapter ends clearly serves as an emblem, an ideal of a certain sort of existence and relationship with the world. Insofar as *Family Chronicle* can be said to offer an ideal of traditional life, it is in this section that that image is most clearly presented; but its very static quality in the general historical flow of *Family Chronicle* (and of Aksakov's major works as a whole) suggests that Aksakov is deliberately evoking something unattainable, an atemporal vision of harmony, not a real day. In such a situation, all actions become valuable and significant within the system, but no change can occur without the introduction of characters who seek either to be integrated into this system or to diverge from it.[3]

If the first chapter of *Family Chronicle* reveals, through its primitive narrative structure, its affinities with the opening sections of historical chronicles, the second chapter, entitled "Mikhaila Maksimovich Kurolesov," employs a structurally coherent but psychologically primitive form, namely, the Gothic novel. In *Years of Childhood* Aksakov in fact alludes to the literary nature of the events in the life of the chapter's heroine, Praskov'ia Ivanovna, who reappears in the later work: "Praskov'ia Ivanovna, married off by her mother's relatives to a dreadful villain when she was still a child, having suffered in fact all the horrors which we know from old novels and French melodramas, had already been living as a widow for twenty years" (1:478). The intertwining of experience and literature that Aksakov implies in the *envoi* to *Family Chronicle* is here directly stated; the old novels that Aksakov refers to are those of the Gothic school, particularly those of Ann Radcliffe, whose works, according to M. A. Dmitriev, a memoirist and friend of Aksakov's, were as popular in the early nineteenth century in Russia as they were elsewhere in Europe: "But no one enjoyed such fame as Mrs. Radcliffe! The *terrible* and *sensitive*—here were finally two types of reading more to the taste of the public. Reading of this type at last replaced earlier books."[4] Dmitriev adds that the epithet "famous" (*slavnaia*) sometimes preceded the English novelist's name on the title page of translations of her works. Her *Mysteries of Udolpho* (1792), published in a Russian translation in 1802, offers several points of affinity with the second chapter of *Family Chronicle*, especially in the figure of the villain.

---

3. Aksakov's treatment of a single day in Stepan Mikhailovich's life, with its tendency to make that day typical, as well as to treat it atemporally, echoes some of the procedures of the sketch (*ocherk*) popular in Russia in the 1840s. D. S. Likhachev, *Poetika drevnerusskoi literatury*, pp. 312–313. Although Aksakov is treating the past rather than the present, as was characteristic of the sketch, the sketch did evince some interest in remote areas and, more importantly, avoided intrigue. As he often does, Aksakov is combining forms for his own purpose, here mixing sketch, poetry, epic, and history. On the *ocherk*, see A. S. Tseitlin, *Stanovlenie realizma v russkoi literatury: Russkii fiziologicheskii ocherk*.

4. M. A. Dmitriev, *Melochi iz zapasa moei pamiati*, pp. 47–48.

Aksakov's contact with the Gothic novel was not limited to his youth, and two novels that utilize Gothic elements may have suggested to Aksakov the possibilities inherent in employing Gothic motifs without giving full rein to Gothic sensibilities. Elizabeth Inchbald's *A Simple Story* (1791)[5] employs a Gothic motif of abduction and imprisonment in a basically non-Gothic context; there is also a rescue by a father figure at the dénouement. Charlotte Brontë's *Jane Eyre* (1847), which Aksakov read in translation in 1849, may have suggested the continuing literary potential of the Gothic mode as a model for relations between the sexes.[6]

Aksakov's use of Gothic does not entail the fascination with terror indulged in by Radcliffe and even less the pornography of horror of such works as Lewis's *The Monk* (1796). The historian's detachment prevents sentiment per se from replacing moral judgment, just as the historian's intrusions at the end of chapter 2 of *Family Chronicle* and the historical detachment evident throughout deliberately attenuate the chapter's adherence to a set model. In addition, Aksakov does not give complete allegiance to the Gothic in his characterization; Kurolesov, the villain, can be viewed as a Gothic villain, but he can also be seen in terms of another traditional sort of character, one perhaps more in keeping with the moral sensibility of the historian-narrator. The initial description of Kurolesov as a soldier, a *krasavets*, and *molodets* (a handsome and dashing fellow) might be taken as pointing to a Gothic villain, but also draws on a tradition longer current in Russia, that of the rogue (*plut*), known in Russian literature from the seventeenth century in the character of Frol Skobeev. Thus the second chapter of *Family Chronicle* casts experience in a shape appropriate for the time with which it deals, the late-eighteenth-century form of the Gothic romance, but at the same time it prevents literary form from subsuming life entirely, first through the distancing of experience by use of the historian and

5. A Russian translation appeared in 1794 under the title *Prostaia istoriia*. It is included in a library list in Aksakov's notebook, *Kniga dlia vsiakoi vsiachiny* (1815–ca. 1825), LL, *fond* 3, folder 7, item 1, fol. 82. Aksakov mentions reading the book to his sister, N. T. Kartashevskaia, while visiting her in St. Petersburg in 1840. Letter to his family, 18 October 1840. TsGALI, *fond* 10, inventory 3, storage unit 27, fol. 104v.

6. Incomplete, undated letter of S. T. Aksakov to Ivan Aksakov, c. 1849. LL, *fond* 3, carton 3, item 22g. A Russian translation of *Jane Eyre* appeared in 1849 in the St. Petersburg journal *Notes of the Fatherland* (*Otechestvennye zapiski*), which often published translations of current British fiction.

secondly by offering both a Gothic and a non-Gothic, more traditionally Russian way of viewing the events and persons of the tale.

Kurolesov in particular, with his energetic and destructive mode of behavior, can be seen as the sharpest challenge to the eternal equilibrium, eventless and changeless, at the end of chapter 1. To consider Kurolesov's dual-aspect villainy in further detail, we might point out that Montoni, the evil genius of *Udolpho*, like Kurolesov, is associated with rumors as to his concealed wrongdoing, a military man quite capable of slipping into brigandage. Kurolesov is an officer of obscure origin who plunders other estates at a later point in his career. Both characters are given to drunken carousing and wenching and both indulge in sadistic torture of their victims. Montoni is nearly poisoned by his confederates; Kurolesov is dispatched by arsenic administered by his lackeys. Both use marriage as a means of gaining control over the persons and property—especially the property—of the heroine, and both resort to incarceration when faced with opposition: Montoni murders the heroine's imprisoned aunt and Praskov'ia Ivanovna's death is imminent at the moment of her rescue. Both are asocial and monstrous. Montoni has "no principle of action—but his will,"[7] and Aksakov describes Kurolesov to Pogodin as a "master-tyrant" (*barin-tiran*).[8]

Kurolesov, a typically Aksakovian, unilinear character, adheres more and more fully to the Gothic archetype as his downward motion accelerates, but he also has a side that suggests the rogue. His name, changed from the historical Kuroedov, seems to be based on the verb *kurolesit'*, which originally had implications of sacrilege (pointing toward the demonic Gothic villain) but which has the general meaning of "to make trouble, to play tricks." At first, his marriage to an heiress through trickery, with the hope of material gain and the eventual softening of paternal hostility (Stepan Mikhailovich is Praskov'ia Ivanovna's cousin and guardian), seems to follow the pattern of the rise in respectability typical of rogue literature. But the true rogue, although he is not held up for emulation, is at least granted a certain admiration because he destroys the moral pretensions of a foolish society. The society in which Kurolesov operates is redeemed

7. Ann Radcliffe, *The Mysteries of Udolpho*, p. 394.
8. S. T. Aksakov to M. P. Pogodin, 24 November 1854. LL, Pogodin *fond*, section 2, carton 1, item 60, letter 21.

from folly (abundant enough in its womenfolk), however, by the presence of Stepan Mikhailovich.

Furthermore, the rogue easily becomes an ambivalent character if his victims are granted equal or greater claim to moral sympathy (as is the case with Praskov'ia Ivanovna), and while the pattern of action may remain the same, the uninhibited operation of the rogue's will begins to transform him into something like a Gothic villain. In Kurolesov this deeper capacity for evil is present from the start, for along with his appealingly roguish surface qualities, he is termed, with considerable understatement, "somehow unpleasant" (1:103) and a demonic aspect is suggested metaphorically:

> emu chert ne brat; . . . on lixoi, bedovyi . . . on gus' lapchatyi, zver' polosatyi. (1:104)

> The devil is no match for him; . . . he's wild and daring . . . he's too clever by half [literally, he's a goose with webbed feet, a beast with stripes].

These metaphors are soon reinforced and deepened; in his courting of the childish Parasha (Praskov'ia Ivanovna), he "rassypalsia pered nei melkim besom" ("waited on her every whim"; literally, "fawned on her like a little imp") (1:109), and Stepan Mikhailovich attributes his success in this endeavor to the devil (nechistaia sila) (1:112). After his marriage, which for a more conventional rogue is soon followed by a successful (and concluding) reconciliation with the bride's family, what had been suppressed becomes more and more overt and even flagrant. With all social inequalities overcome and Kurolesov's position in a condition of successful stasis, the remaining moral and psychological barriers and restrictions are also breached. The true rogue, of course, does not go beyond social categories, nor does he desire to, whereas the Gothic villain does as a matter of principle.[9] Kurolesov begins with drink, theft, and highway robbery and eventually comes to reject all authority, both civil and religious, and ultimately commits murder (1:117). Kurolesov's passions, termed "monstrous, inhuman" (1:121), transform him into "a frightful combination of the instinct of the tiger and the rational-

9. It has been noted that the Gothic hero develops "away from dependence for effect on the rigged supernatural and toward a recognition of . . . the 'subnatural,' that is, the irrational, the impulse to evil, the uncontrollable unconscious." Lowry Nelson, Jr., "Night Thoughts on the Gothic Novel," p. 249.

ity of a man" (1:118). They reach their final expression in metaphorical vampirism and actual voyeuristic sadism (its perverse sexuality is clearly implied by Aksakov), accompanied by the classic instrument of the sadist, the cat-of-nine-tails, which Kurolesov prefers for its ability to inflict pain without the danger of serious injury (1:124). Kurolesov's life "led him to even worse, to more frightful development of Mikhaila Maksimovich's natural cruelty, which turned finally into ferocity, the thirst for blood. To torture people became a necessity and pleasure for him" (1:123). Further, "when he approached a man with the intention of amusing himself with the latter's suffering, he spoke quietly and even caressingly: 'Well, dear friend, Grigorii Kuz'mich[10] (instead of the usual Grishka), there's no help for it, you and I must settle accounts.'" (1:124).

Kurolesov's career passes through the various perversions of what Northrop Frye terms the ironic mode[11] and concludes with his murder. As might be expected, Kurolesov's death comes from poison: "Two rascals, from among those most closely attached to the master . . . poisoned him with arsenic, placing the arsenic in the decanter of *kvas* which Mikhaila Maksimovich customarily drank in the course of the night. The poison was administered in such quantity that Kurolesov lived not more than two hours" (1:124). Apart from the treachery subverting whatever minimal society Mikhaila Maksimovich still operated in, the use of poisoned *kvas* represents the final ironic development, in which the most elemental human need, thirst, is perverted and turned against the subject.

If Kurolesov's characterization is that of the rogue combined with that of the Gothic villain, the character of his wife, Praskov'ia Ivanovna (Parasha), is drawn more consistently from the figure of the Gothic heroine. Like the heroine of a rogue tale, she is duped by the villain into marriage, but her blindness results more from the immaturity and the stupidity of her relatives than from her permanent obtuseness. Unlike the rogue's victim, but like the Gothic heroine, she develops a full awareness of the moral dimensions of her situation and suffers because of it. The Gothic heroine's initial infatuation with and submission to the villain proceeds to a peripety, consisting of the discovery

10. Kurolesov addresses the serf by his full name and patronymic because the ironic use of the honorific adds to the piquancy of the situation.

11. Northrop Frye, *Anatomy of Criticism*, p. 149.

of the villain's true nature (he is the embodiment of the passionate and predatory aspects of sex), a radical reevaluation of her relationship with him, imprisonment by the villain (a surrogate death), and resurrection to a new, mature, and independent life, in which sex has been demythologized and its demonic aspect exorcised. With Praskov'ia Ivanovna that new life is celibate, lacking the new, true love of Gothic novels such as *Udolpho.* Here Aksakov is true to fact, but also neatly confounds a literary pattern at a point where it seems to have become dominant.

Praskov'ia Ivanovna's initial immature ignorance is indicated by the combination of advanced physical development and childish behavior, particularly her playing with dolls. Her perception of Kurolesov (prompted by the opinion of all her female relatives) embraces only his appearance, without penetrating to his essence. The infantile nature of the relationship is underscored by the repeated references to the dolls and toys with which Kurolesov woos her, and he also wins over her family with presents, except for Stepan Mikhailovich, who insists that they be returned. Praskov'ia Ivanovna's idea of marriage is of an endless round of games with dolls, "not little ones, but big ones than can walk and bow by themselves" (1:109). At their formal engagement, the boredom of the drawn-out ceremony is relieved by her being allowed to play with her new doll from Moscow. "She declared to all the guests that this was her daughter, and made the doll bow and thank the guests along with herself for the congratulations" (1:120). To Aksakov, for whom all formal ceremonies are potentially of great significance and even mundane actions can take on ritual overtones (as they do at the conclusion of the first chapter of *Family Chronicle*), such incomprehension and mechanical distortion of a rite sums up the utter falsity of the relationship, which is juridically invalid as well, since Parasha's age is changed from fifteen to seventeen (i.e., to the legal age for marriage) in the church records.

Although marriage brings about an apparent maturation, Praskov'ia Ivanovna's new attitude of respect for Stepan Mikhailovich may suggest that her ostensible maturity conceals underlying apprehension about her husband. The inauthenticity of their relationship is indicated by the couple's estates, three of which Kurolesov names Parashino, Ivanovka, and Kurolesovo, for his wife's name, patronymic, and surname; from his point of view, this simply confirms her role as an instrument and his equation of her person with wealth and status. Their permanent residence, Churasovo, presents the fullest expression of the sham nature of the marriage, which lacks an emotional core:

> There he built a manor house, magnificent for its day, with all the appurtenances; he finished it to perfection, furnished it excellently, decorated it with murals both inside and out; the chandeliers, candelabra, bronzes, china, and silver service amazed all; he placed the house on a small rise, from which there burst and bubbled more than twenty marvelous springs. The house, the hill, the springs were all surrounded and enclosed by a rich, fruitful garden. . . . Mikhaila Maksimovich dressed his little Parasha like a doll, fulfilled, foresaw all her wishes, amused her from morn to night, whenever he happened to be home. (1:116–117)

Churasovo, a triumph of conspicuous consumption on Kurolesov's part, constitutes a pseudo-Eden.[12] It is a dollhouse which is ultimately sterile, for the two children that are born there die in infancy, and Praskov'ia Ivanovna, though still young, bears no more children (1:117), perhaps suggesting the end of sexual relations between her and Kurolesov.

Although rumors arise concerning Kurolesov's excesses during his absences from home, Praskov'ia Ivanovna maintains the uneasy equilibrium of her situation until a letter revealing the extent of his vicious criminality prompts her to go to his retreat at Parashino and confront him directly. The three-hundred-mile journey toward discovery ends with the revelation of Kurolesov's true nature (or the end of Praskov'ia Ivanovna's suppression of her awareness of it); the epiphany is literal and graphic, one of Aksakov's most striking visual discovery scenes. The opening of a door discloses a tableau that displays Kurolesov in surroundings totally appropriate to his true nature. Posture and gesture combine with setting to form a perfect emblem of villainous dissolution. Significantly, Kurolesov sports a special costume, which he changes before his subsequent confrontation with his wife:

> She intentionally arrived at Parashino in the evening, left her carriage on the outskirts and she herself with a maid and

12. Historically, the estate was known as Chufarovo. The fictional name Churasovo may suggest *chur*, a syllable used in incantations to ward off evil forces, since the estate is the place where the evil in Kurolesov is suppressed and harmless.

> lackey, unrecognized by anyone (for they hardly knew her),
> proceeded to the manor house, and through the rear gate made
> her way to the annex from which there issued shouts,
> song, and laughter, and with a firm hand she opened the
> door. . . . Fate as if on purpose had assembled everything
> which could in one moment show her the sort of life Mikhaila
> Maksimovich was leading. Drunker than usual, he was
> feasting with some guests. Dressed in a red silk blouse with a
> slant collar, with a glass of punch in one hand, he was
> in the most debauched manner embracing with the other a
> beautiful woman who was kneeling before him; his half-drunk
> lackeys, servants, and peasant women were singing and
> dancing. Praskov'ia Ivanovna nearly fainted at such a spectacle;
> she understood everything . . . shut the door and withdrew
> from the vestibule. (1:125–126)

The entire scene, its moment of illumination and comprehension neatly enclosed between the two actions of opening and closing the door, echoes other such discoveries of the previously concealed sexual violence of the villain.[13] Kurolesov's reaction to discovery recalls the behavior of the Gothic character Montoni: first feigned kindness, that is, an attempt to return to the prior state of equilibrium, then violence, and finally incarceration aimed at the reestablishment by overt force of control over the female, who is now fully aware of the threat to herself implicit in the male's sexuality. Kurolesov, like many of his prototypes, confronts his victim with a dilemma: signing over her property (loss of autonomy and identity, regression to the immature state she is at last breaking out of) or imprisonment (loss of freedom and eventual death). Locked in a cellar, Praskov'ia Ivanovna undergoes a surrogate death that functions as the culmination of the process of initiation that began with her decision to leave the charmed circle of Churasovo and confront her husband. She observes a vigil, praying to the cross on the church at Parashino, until Stepan Mikhailovich, alerted by serfs from Parashino, arrives, breaks down the door of her prison and "carries her out in his own arms" (1:132) in an action suggesting resurrection or the delivery of an infant. This rescue from death by burial symbol-

---

13. Aksakov uses the words *otvorila* and *zatvorila* to describe the action of opening and closing the door; these verbs are more elevated than the more common *otkryla* and *zakryla* and tend to stress the drama and importance of the scene. The unspeakable revels Praskov'ia Ivanovna discovers recall the revelation of Onegin in Tatiana's dream in chap. 5 of Pushkin's *Evgenii Onegin*.

izes a rebirth and the inception of a new life, as indicated by the final image of Parashino, on the seventh day of Praskov'ia Ivanovna's ordeal: "The sun was beginning to rise, and again the cross on the church began to blaze brightly as Praskov'ia Ivanovna rode past it. She had prayed to that cross for six days and nights . . . now she prayed again, thanking God for her deliverance" (1:132).

Kurolesov, his demonic nature revealed and therefore rendered powerless, ceases to have any literary function and is summarily eliminated by the aforementioned arsenic. On the other hand, Praskov'ia Ivanovna undergoes a profound transformation which makes of her a new character. Her initiation ordeal ends with a recapitulation of childhood at Bagrovo and the beginning of a mature existence, reinforced by departure on a new journey: "The next day Praskov'ia Ivanovna left for Churasovo and began to live her own, independent life" (1:138). Aksakov here employs a characteristically "open" ending, closing his chapter with potentialities; he also avoids the clichéd Gothic conclusion of a new, happy marriage for the heroine. Historical fact (as indicated in *Years of Childhood*) and literary needs coincide neatly.

A further dimension of "Mikhaila Maksimovich Kurolesov" is provided by the relationship of Kurolesov to Stepan Mikhailovich, who functions as a moral arbiter, in consonance with the role of lawgiver that is established in the first fragment. His presence prevents (as does that of the historical narrator) the substitution of psychological for ethical values in the reader's perception of the events narrated. Stepan Mikhailovich's innate moral sense takes the measure of Kurolesov at their first meeting; cutting through the favorable attitude of the women of his house, based on rumor, Stepan Mikhailovich brands Kurolesov as a rogue (*plut*) (1:106), refuses to extend Kurolesov the basic hospitality of inviting him to stay the night at Bagrovo, and forbids a second invitation. It is fitting that Aksakov should put into Stepan Mikhailovich's mouth the first mention of the label of one of the literary archetypes Kurolesov approaches; as the individual in *Family Chronicle* least influenced or impressed by Western culture and as a literary character the least dependent on the figures of modern literature as a model, Stepan Mikhailovich naturally emerges as the person most qualified to judge in traditional categories, which tend to be primarily ethical rather than emotional or aesthetic.

The final rescue of Praskov'ia Ivanovna also demonstrates Stepan Mikhailovich's superiority: "Yes, there is a moral power of the just cause, before which the courage of the unjust man gives way. Mikhaila Maksimovich knew the firmness of spirit and the fearless valor of Stepan Mikhailovich, knew the injustice of his own actions, and despite his fury and wild daring— yielded his victim without a contest" (1:133). Aksakov even increased the significance of this paragraph in the final text, through various changes in wording and position, in order to stress the fact that Stepan Mikhailovich operates on a different moral plane from Kurolesov and, like the saint in a hagiography, his presence alone is sufficient to rectify the moral disequilibrium in the world.[14] The avoidance of physical confrontation between the two opponents, which would have made the outcome contingent on factors other than the central, moral one, was deliberate on Aksakov's part, as suggested by an entry in his daughter Vera's diary, which states that Turgenev, after hearing the chapter in January 1855, argued that Stepan Mikhailovich should punish Kurolesov physically.[15]

The contrast between Stepan Mikhailovich and Kurolesov is developed indirectly as well. Broadly, Stepan Mikhailovich is completely identified with his realm, a central expression of the natural world he inhabits. Detailed description of that world is really a veiled form of characterization. Kurolesov, on the other hand, is an enigmatic outsider; the very lack of detail and of integration into society or nature renders him the more sinister. The titles of the first two chapters, "Stepan Mikhailovich Bagrov" and "Mikhaila Maksimovich Kurolesov" suggests this inverse relationship. More specifically, just as his marriage to Praskov'ia Ivanovna travesties both a romantic union and a more traditional marriage such as Stepan Mikhailovich's, Kurolesov's actions in the economic and social spheres imitate and parody Stepan Mikhailovich's mythic civilizing activity in the first chapter. Like Stepan Mikhailovich, Kurolesov, an excellent man-

---

14. In the initial version, this paragraph begins without the assertive "yes" (*da*) and precedes, rather than follows, the paragraph attributing the absence of resistance on the part of Kurolesov's lackeys to their drunken stupor. The paragraph concerning the lackeys is itself presented as an alternative explanation, not as an attendant circumstance, as it is in the final text. LL, *fond* 3, folder 1, no. 2a; the second manuscript version (2b) indicates by numbers the reordering of the paragraphs in question.

15. V. S. Aksakova, *Dnevnik Very Sergeevny Aksakovoi*, p. 45.

ager, acquires new lands and transfers his peasants there (1:115); like Stepan Mikhailovich, he purchases land in the Ufa region. Stepan Mikhailovich grudgingly accepts Kurolesov as a competent manager, but still reserves moral judgment (1:123). Kurolesov's mimicry of the true landowner is underlined by the historian's references in the first and second chapter to the posthumous reputations of the two men among their peasants. Both are recalled as competent masters, but Stepan Mikhailovich's "blagodetel'nyi i strogii obraz" ("beneficent and stern image") (1:89) is virtually canonized. The peasants cross themselves at the mention of him, and the use of *obraz*, which also means "icon," reinforces the characterization. Mention of Kurolesov, however, brings a smile and repetition of his favorite adage, "Be a rogue, thieve, but cover your tracks, only if you get caught, don't cry about it" (1:137), the first word of which (*plutui*) preserves Kurolesov's roguish nature as the "image" of Stepan Mikhailovich preserves his patriarchal virtue.

Perhaps the most telling indication of the difference between the two men lies in their attitudes toward religion. Stepan Mikhailovich makes a vow to build a stone church, but the vow is in fact fulfilled by his son. The outward manifestation of belief is redundant for a man steeped in the values, already inbred with religion, of traditional Russian culture. There is no disparity of inner goodness and outer appearance in Stepan Mikhailovich. With Kurolesov, the construction of a church at Parashino, scene of his revels and ultimately of his murder, becomes a guilty compensation for the evil disorder of his life and personality: "Mikhaila Maksimovich, having attained the highest degree of depravity and ferocity, zealously undertook the construction of a stone church in Parashino" (1:124).

Thus both directly through the plot and indirectly through exposure as a parody, Kurolesov is prevented by Stepan Mikhailovich's presence from accomplishing his ends entirely. He becomes neither an object of admiration for his trickery, like the traditional rogue, nor an object of sympathy in his psychological pathology, as demonic figures, including Gothic villains, tend to do when presented without contrast. Aksakov subjects Kurolesov to an inescapable moral judgment, both through the character who is the work's moral center and through the narrative pose of objectivity and superiority. By recombining traditional elements and devices Aksakov judges and deflates the puffed-up demon of

Gothic, and also of Romantic, literature.[16] Indeed, from this point on, *Family Chronicle* moves further and further away from obvious literary categories. As we move closer to present actuality, the role of literature in shaping events, or at least the narration of them, decreases (though it never ceases to be of some significance in *Family Chronicle*). Like Praskov'ia Ivanovna, with whose departure for a new life the chapter closes, the narrator, and presumably his reader as well, has begun to "outgrow" his too-easy identification with literary models.

The latter three chapters of *Family Chronicle* have as their overall subject the romance and marriage of Aleksei Stepanovich Bagrov and Sofia Nikolavna Zubina. Despite their greater continuity and cohesiveness as compared to the first two chapters, there are still palpable differences among them, justifying the separate consideration of each chapter. As already mentioned, the overt use of literary models decreases, but is still a significant element in the third chapter. Written at approximately the same time (spring and summer of 1854), the third chapter not only employs some methods analogous to those dominant in its immediate predecessor, but also offers a contrasting treatment of the same theme, love and marriage. In the Gothic world of the second chapter, marriage is an ironic travesty of an authentic relationship, based on blind immaturity on one side and pathological viciousness on the other. The third chapter presents, if not true love, then true complementarity, overcoming all obstacles to union. Since *Family Chronicle* consisted of only three chapters in its original version, the fourth and fifth fragments being added after the publication of the first edition in 1856, the work as first conceived ended with a traditional conclusion for comedy or romance, a marriage, thus neutralizing the failure and the indeterminate ending of the second chapter.

The central characters of the third chapter, "The Marriage of Young Bagrov" ("Zhenit'ba molodogo Bagrova"), Aleksei Stepanovich and Sofia Nikolavna (as Aksakov consistently spells her patronymic), are both constructed by looking to literary precedents, although the identity of character and prototype and its determining role in later behavior are not so complete as in the

16. Nelson discusses some of the continuities between Gothic heroes and those of Romanticism, such as Heathcliffe's and Ahab's fusion and confusion of good and evil. See "Night Thoughts," p. 254.

second chapter. In addition, both the characters and the society in which they function seem more aware of literary models, so that any roles they assume are autonomous self-projections rather than the result of authorial fiat. In the case of Aleksei Stepano- vich, the literary models for his behavior are explicit, with direct reference to his taste for second-rate, sentimental adventure novels, such as F. A. Emin's *The Garden of Love* (*Liubovnyi vertograd*) (1:165). (Since the novel was written in 1793, this would strictly speaking be an anachronism, Aleksei Stepanovich having married Sofia Nikolavna in the late 1780s. Aksakov refers to Emin's novel only as a type, but the slip suggests how strong literary patterning is in chapter 3.) Aleksei Stepanovich's assim- ilation of the florid style of such reading is noted (1:175), and a direct sample is provided in his despairing letter to his parents: "I can not long drag the burden of my life without my wor- shipped Sofia Nikolavna, and so in a not distant time a death- bearing bullet will speedily penetrate the skull of your unfortu- nate son" (1:157–158). The historian-narrator provides a footnote designed to limit his responsibility not only for the hackneyed style of the letter, but also for its use as a plot device, affirming its authenticity in both regards by shifting the blame to Aleksei Stepanovich: "I remember this letter almost by heart. Probably it still exists among the old papers of one of my brothers. It is apparent that some expressions were borrowed from novels of that day, of which Aleksei Stepanovich was a great reader" (1:158n.).

Aleksei Stepanovich's behavior throughout conforms with the code of action of the sentimental novel (which coincides with Aksakov's own methods of characterization): total absorption in one emotion, love. As the object of love is elevated, the lover debases himself; *obozhaemaia* ("deified, worshipped)" is used constantly in describing Sofia Nikolavna from Aleksei Stepano- vich's point of view. His response to the dilemma presented by parental opposition to marriage is drastic and self-destructive: sickness and contemplation of suicide in a manner "borrowed from some novel or other" (1:161). Not only does Aleksei Stepa- novich's proposed solution to his romantic difficulties recall sentimental novels, but the entire range of his behavior is consis- tent, particularly in its early stages, with this literary model. The scanty information about him prior to his falling in love illus- trates his immaturity and passivity and the masochistic strain essential to the sentimental lover. At age twenty-eight, Aleksei Stepanovich is described as "a handsome fellow, peaches and cream: 'A woman's blouse and dress, and he would look more like a young miss than any of his sisters do'—thus would his own father speak of him" (1:139).

He undergoes one formative experience, as important for him as such experiences are for other of Aksakov's characters, while in military service; the narrator ironically terms it a "historic event" (*istoricheskoe sobytie*) (1:139), although in fact it more or less eliminates the possibility of any historic event's ever taking place in Aleksei Stepanovich's life. He receives a beating of three hundred strokes at the order of a brutal and obtuse general (of German origin) as punishment for singing in the street while services are being conducted in church (1:140). The beating, though grotesquely comic in its circumstances, can be taken as a rite of passage, one which Aleksei Stepanovich fails. He retires from military service at his parents' insistence, enters the civil service, and remains in a permanently immature, passive state. His behavior is frequently childlike; at his formal engagement, a ceremony presuming adult status, he sobs like a child (1:172) and is overcome by wine. His attitude toward authority is one of fear before the mysteriously omnipotent; he fears his own father more than he loves him, and his prospective father-in-law, a former high official now physically incapacitated, becomes in Aleksei Stepanovich's fantasy an implacable, terrifying figure, ready to subject him to punishment for seeking Sofia Nikolavna's hand.

Other characters predicate their behavior toward Aleksei Stepanovich on the assumption of his immaturity and ignorance. His female relatives, though from varying motives, treat him literally as a child: his mother still considers him an infant (1:152), while his father and the matchmaker Alakaeva assume his adolescent ignorance of social realities and accepted forms. Sofia Nikolavna considers him her social and intellectual inferior (1:165); she specifically and intentionally undertakes to educate him in the social amenities, an enterprise to which she devotes most of the period of their engagement. Her success, in the opinion of the historian-narrator, is at best only apparent and transitory: the couple "afterwards concurred in asserting that a marked change took place in Aleksei Stepanovich, that he had virtually been reborn. I would happily believe this, but I have evidence that Aleksei Stepanovich's advances in the social niceties were not so great" (1:184).

If Aksakov draws on the figure of the sentimental lover in the elaboration of Aleksei Stepanovich's character, the characterization of Sofia Nikolavna also employs literary models, though they are not so explicitly the result of the character's modelling herself on a literary form. Her history up to the point of Aleksei Stepanovich's falling in love with her follows the pattern of a fairy tale.[17] From an initial, idyllic family situation in early childhood, Sofia Nikolavna falls into the clutches of a wicked stepmother, who reduces the young girl to the status of a charwoman (1:141). The stepmother eventually meets appropriate punishment, and her death after childbirth is attributed to divine retribution.

The fairy tale, of course, like Gothic fiction, deals with initiation and maturation, though the role of sexuality is less explicit than in Gothic novels, which deal with the obviously adolescent. Sofia Nikolavna, like Praskov'ia Ivanovna in the second chapter, undergoes a crucial initiatory experience. In despair and on the verge of suicide, Sofia Nikolavna observes a vigil and is reborn with an adult's strength of will, ready to withstand all the trials inflicted by her stepmother. The alteration in her personality is indicated, appropriately enough in a context of the slightly fabulous, by the apparently spontaneous lighting of the candle before Sofia Nikolavna's favorite icon (1:141), recalling the sunlit cross as a source of both physical and spiritual illumination for Praskov'ia Ivanovna in chapter 2. With the stepmother's death, the inner change in Sofia Nikolavna becomes manifest to all. "Death turned everything upside down. . . . The persecuted, tattered miss, whom the cruel servants, especially those who had come as the stepmother's dowry, had insulted as much as they felt like and had trampled in the mud—suddenly became the sovereign mistress of the house, since her sick father entrusted everything to her management" (1:142). The restored daughter, at seventeen, is wise and mature, discharging her father's official duties, managing a household, educating herself along with her

17. The similarities between Sofia Nikolavna and fairy-tale heroines seem to have escaped Russian commentators, who tend to emphasize the historical aspects of the text. V. S. Pritchett, however, has dealt briefly with Sofia Nikolavna as a fairy-tale princess faced with marriage in the real world. See his "A Russian Cinderella" pp. 413–419, esp. pp. 413–414.

younger brothers and even corresponding with such Moscow luminaries as Nikolai Ivanovich Novikov.

Sofia Nikolavna retains the aura of fairy tale in her social life; her acquaintances in society find her enchanting. "Intelligent and educated people, having happened to come to Ufa, were captivated by her and never forgot her" (1:143), verses are composed in which she is addressed as Venus and Minerva, and her appearance at balls is compared to that of a sparkling meteor. Aksakov exploits the richness of the Russian vocabulary dealing with occult powers to emphasize Sofia Nikolavna's exceptional nature. For Aleksei Stepanovich, she is a "marvel of beauty and wit" (*chudo krasoty i uma*) (1:165); she "enchants his tender heart" (*obvorozhila ego miagkoe serdtse*) (1:144); his eyes are charmed by her beauty (*ocharovannye*) (1:145); her father terms her effect on the bashful and tongue-tied Aleksei Stepanovich that of a charmer (*charodeika*) (1:175).

The metaphorical connection of Sofia Nikolavna with magical power is presented not only in a positive light, lest the comparisons be reduced to the polite hyperbole of eighteenth-century salon society or to the excesses of Aleksei Stepanovich's favorite novels, but also in a negative one. The hostility of the Bagrov women to Aleksei Stepanovich's fiancée is focused on what they call her witchcraft, which casts a new light on her power. For them, Sofia Nikolavna is no more than "a witch, who draws all the men to herself by means of [magical] roots; they run after her with their tongues out, and among them she has charmed their poor dear brother" (1:149). The gossip Flena Ivanovna, carefully primed and rehearsed by the Bagrov women, repeats this slander to Stepan Mikhailovich in hopes of setting him against Sofia Nikolavna, although the ploy meets with little success: "'The witch of Ufa has drawn him to herself through evil forces. . . . They say she's such a beauty, she's captured them all, both young and old, trapped them all with potions'" (1:150). In the context of this extreme materialization and primitivization of cause and effect in the description of Sofia Nikolavna's personality, it is interesting to note the literalization of what is metaphorical in polite society, as well as Flena Ivanovna's use of the native Russian doublet *zapolonit'* ("to capture physically," "to take prisoner") of *zaplenit'* ("to capture," "to captivate"), which is of Church Slavonic origin and is used in the more abstract and refined context of enlightened urban society. The difference between the two vocabularies, urban and rural, is systematic and structurally significant in the last three fragments of *Family Chronicle*.

Sofia Nikolavna's status as a fairy-tale heroine undergoes modification at a central event in the third chapter, Aleksei Stepanovich's formal proposal of marriage. Life is beginning to render the patterns of fairy tale inadequate; Aleksei Stepanovich is patently no Prince Charming, and Sofia Nikolavna's acceptance is motivated primarily by practical considerations. The difficulties that in fairy tale are resolved in the concluding marriage are in fact only beginning for Sofia Nikolavna. Aksakov discards literary patterns at a point much earlier than he does in the second chapter, where life's complexity goes beyond formulae only at the conclusion. At the midpoint of the third chapter Sofia Nikolavna's point of view and analytic consciousness replace Aleksei Stepanovich's as the central sensibility of the chapter. With this shift of consciousness and the transition from idle wish to the practicalities of realizing that wish, the imagery linking Sofia Nikolavna with fairy tale and magic all but disappears; the central fact of her power remains, but loses any metaphoric or occult quality. Sofia Nikolavna becomes only too aware of her own power and puts it to use in a deliberate and practical manner. The desire to dominate, devoid of fairy-tale overtones, is expressly isolated as the basic motivating force in her character from this point on: "At the base of her character there already lay the seeds of the craving for power, which at the present time, freed from the heavy oppression of a cruel stepmother, had set out strong shoots; without Sofia Nikolavna's knowledge, love of power was the secret source of her determination" (1:167).

In what is Aksakov's only attempt in *Family Chronicle* to deal with development rather than instantaneous change in a character, Sofia Nikolavna's power is now associated with a new set of terms, stressing not her magical effects but the strength of her will; the key terms of passion (*strastnost'*) and irritability (*pylkost'*) now emerge as constants of her character. The latter term is derived from a root having to do with fire, and the use of numerous cognates and semantically related terms in reference to Sofia Nikolavna underline this side of her personality (*vspyl'chivost'*, *vspykhnula*, *vspyshki*, *goriachnost'*; "combustibility," "flared," "flare-ups," "ardor"). Of telling significance in the internalization of power in Sofia Nikolavna is the change in her attitude toward prayer. Her first, initiatory, religious experience represented a true conversion and maturation, consisting in the emergence of an autonomous will. Subsequent instances of recourse to prayer involve no reordering of the personality and serve primarily as a means of confirming and legitimizing decisions which in fact she has already made. This fact is pointedly stated by the historian in discussing a dream of Sofia Nikolavna's (following prayer), which she "interpreted, as required, in confirmation of her own decision. . . . I have forgotten that dream, but I recall that it was possible to interpret it the opposite way with considerably fewer distortions" (1:168). Finally, prayer becomes for Sofia Nikolavna a certain and repeated method of resolving doubts as to the wisdom of her choice of Aleksei Stepanovich for her husband.

Sofia Nikolavna's attitude toward her fiancé rests on the congruence of their personalities—his submissiveness and her desire for power. Relying on his idolization of her, Sofia Nikolavna uses him as a field for the exercise of power, notably in the scheme of reeducating him in the course of their engagement. Her conscious manipulation of her compliant fiancé is most apparent in her exhortation to him to oppose his sisters for her sake. Stressing her position as a prize to be won through ordeal (perhaps a deliberate echo of her role as a fairy-tale princess), Sofia Nikolavna uses the word "love" (*liubov'*, *liubit'*) frequently, but only to describe Aleksei Stepanovich's attitude toward her. Reciprocity of emotion on her part must be earned, and she goes no further than to speak of her own love as something hypothetical, a possible situation in the future:

> Vy znaete, chto ia ne vliublena v vas, no ia nachinala liubit'
> vas i, konechno, poliubila by sil'nee i postoianee, chem
> vy. (1:181)

> You know that I am not in love with you, but I have begun to
> love you and, of course, would love more strongly and more
> constantly than you.

Aleksei Stepanovich is more than amenable to this superior-inferior relationship, for it is a continuation of what was established at the moment of his initial infatuation. (He is first smitten upon seeing Sofia Nikolavna in church, a standard locus, with overtones of medieval romance.) Since the link between Sofia Nikolavna and Aleksei Stepanovich is virtually assumed in the

third chapter of *Family Chronicle*, the action of the chapter focuses on the overcoming of parental and societal opposition to a
relationship established by authorial fiat in the creation of the
two characters.

Aleksei Stepanovich and Sofia Nikolavna can be seen as prod-
ucts of, and even metonyms for, their respective geographic and
social milieus, and opposition to their match derives from the
basic polarity of the third chapter (as well as the fourth): the
contrast between city and country. The courtship and marriage
are in a sense merely ways of dramatizing and at least partially
resolving this contrast in cultures. The first mention of Ufa—"in
the city of Ufa" (1:140)—shows clearly the categorical difference
between it and Bagrovo. This is the first time that any city enters
the pastoral world of *Family Chronicle*, but withdrawal into the
pastoral world often assumes eventual return to the broader society, and Aksakov accomplishes this rapprochement through marriage in the second generation.

The differences between the two places are underlined by the
elder Bagrovs' decision not to attend their son's wedding in the
city. "The old folk, who had lived too long in the country and
grown unsociable, did not come, it goes without saying: they
pictured the city and city society as something alien and frightening" (1:177). This misperception of the other realm is characteristic of both city and country and is based on their mutually
exclusive systems of values and views of the world. The diver-
gence is clearly seen in the repeated enumerations of the pros
and cons of the contemplated match (the matchmaker Alakaeva,
the Bagrov women, Stepan Mikhailovich, and Sofia Nikolavna
herself all list the advantages and disadvantages at various times).
In each case the same points concerning wealth, status, education, and social etiquette are brought up, but the interpretation of
them can differ considerably, depending on the background of
the speaker. All parties agree that Aleksei Stepanovich's hereditary nobility, with low service rank, outweighs Sofia Nikolavna's
father's high service rank, with nobility earned through service
as provided for by the Petrine reforms, although this fact is felt
to be a major impediment only in the country. Stepan Mikhailovich, the figure who is most archaic in his outlook and values,
posits most of his opposition to the match on this fact. In the
economic sphere, Aleksei Stepanovich, with his family's estate
and prospects of inheritance from Praskov'ia Ivanovna, possess-

es real wealth, which is definitely favored by the country over Sofia Nikolavna's monetary dependence on service unaccompanied by sufficient property; again, property is not a matter of great concern for the city. This distinction between city and country by economic type emerges clearly during the preparations for the wedding: the elder Bagrovs send their son only three hundred roubles in cash instead of the fifteen hundred requested, but dispatch a foursome of horses, a coachman, a cook, and all sorts of foodstuffs, while Sofia Nikolavna uses her own money to purchase a stylish English-made carriage for her fiancé (1:175–177).

However, it is on the question of education and social behavior that city and country diverge most clearly. Alakaeva informs Aleksei Stepanovich that "'You are an unpolished person, countrified, unlearned, and frightfully shy in public as well'" (1:146). Sofia Nikolavna, on the other hand, is "'very intelligent, very proud, very educated'" (1:146). Stepan Mikhailovich repeats this difference even more bluntly, stressing the potential for discord it contains: "'She's a city-dweller, learned, smart, used to giving orders after her stepmother's death and used to living richly, though she herself is poor; but we are simple country people, and you yourself know our way of life; and you should understand yourself: you are a quiet fellow, but even worse than that, she's awfully intelligent. To take a wife smarter than yourself means trouble'" (1:153). For Sofia Nikolavna and her father, of course, the values in this category are reversed, being a question of "an educated, almost a learned young lady" deigning to marry "a complete ignoramus" who has read nothing but stupid novels and is incapable of enlightened conversation (1:165).

The differences of style and educational level between city and country even extend to the ability to express one's self in writing. Aleksei Stepanovich's letters are inept collections of clichés from sentimental novels, and his father sends Sofia Nikolavna's father an awkward letter (1:170–171). On the other hand, Sofia Nikolavna possesses the gift of writing eloquently (1:174), and her first step in the exercise of her power over her fiancé consists precisely in composing a letter to be sent in his name, lest his own clumsy effort offend the addressee: "Difficult was the first step toward disrespecting her future spouse and toward realizing the idea of ordering him about at whim" (1:175). Aleksei Stepanovich, far from opposing the substitution, actually approves it.

The inability to control the medium of cultured self-expression and communication most characteristic of the eighteenth century suggests not only the educational backwardness of the country-side, but also points to deeper differences that deny the premises implicit in such an activity as polite correspondence.

The differences between the city and the country in matters of values, style, behavior, and etiquette are in fact manifestations of mutually exclusive models of the world, which are particularly revealed in their distinctive languages. The country reduces experience insofar as possible to the perceptible and concrete. Hence its preference on the social level for real wealth and its emphasis on hereditary nobility, based on genetic continuity, as the determinant of status and of social relations. Kinship determines not only an individual's position in the family, but also absolutely prescribes his attitudes toward others. Emotions are reduced to and equated with physical conditions; in particular, Aleksei Stepanovich's love is regarded as some sort of outlandish malady by both his parents. He partly confirms their diagnosis by falling sick and being apparently cured of his affliction during a visit to the country, where he hoped to win his parents' approval of his intended marriage.

The countryman's preference for the tangible appears particularly clearly in his language, which tends to avoid abstractions (e.g., the aforementioned use of *zapolonit'*, "to capture physically," in preference to *zaplenit'*, "to captivate") and to employ concrete metaphors and apothegmatic, almost folkloric, constructions. Thus the Bagrov women express their hostility to any sister-in-law and their fear of loss of status in metaphorical terms: "'A young wife will clean out the relatives [of the male line] and our father's house will be an alien place for us'" (1:148). Their perception of Sofia Nikolavna as a witch employing concrete occult roots and potions to gain her ends, as well as the gossip Lupenevskaia's comparing her to a bitch in heat (1:150), is completely consistent with this mode of analyzing, or rather classifying, experience. Stepan Mikhailovich displays a similar style when speaking to his son, although his basic disposition toward Sofia Nikolavna is not hostile: "'Here is my fatherly admonition to you: throw this love out of your head. . . . One must fell a tree appropriate to one's size. . . . After all, my friend, we're not rich [lit. well-feathered out], we have just enough to get by and our income isn't large. . . . So now look, Alesha, let it all slip off you, like water from a goose, and don't let there be a word about Sofia Nikolavna'" (1:154).

Although the country deals with the tangible in so far as possible, this does not imply a great concern for the particular, especially as regards individual experience. In fact, the country's use of fixed metaphor and apothegm implies the assimilation of experience to established, even mythological, categories, in which the individual is entirely defined by a nexus of relations and is assigned a role in which intelligence or any emotion not dictated by the traditional structure is essentially irrelevant. The city, on the other hand, especially the eighteenth-century city, places its emphasis precisely on intelligence, education, and enlightenment, all manifestations of the unique potentialities of the individual; *obrazovannost'* (the state of being educated) is the highest value for a society organized according to a hierarchy of culture rather than of kinship. The urban mentality subjects experience to abstraction and analytic discourse, and its categories, insofar as it resorts to them, are logical and ethical. Sofia Nikolavna exhibits this cast of mind when she weighs her options in arriving at her decision to marry Aleksei Stepanovich (1:164–166) or when she persuades him of the necessity of loyalty either to his sisters or to her: "'Don't make excuses and deny it. That would be dishonorable on your part. I know that you have not stopped loving me, but you are afraid of showing me your love, you are afraid of your sisters and therefore you get embarassed and even avoid remaining alone with me. That is the perfect truth, you know it yourself'" (1:180–181). Such appeals to honor and truth, with their implicit assumption of and appeal to the autonomy of the individual, would be simply inconceivable in the mental world of the country.[18]

Against the background of these differences between city and country, marriage becomes a metaphor for the elimination or neutralization of these differences. However, given the fact of the coherence and strength of each of these two radically different systems, the process can in fact only take the form of the attempted assimilation of a person from one system to the other

18. Aksakov's treatment of the two cultures of village and city is a less well articulated echo of Ivan Kireevskii's distinction between the people (*narod*) and society (*obshchestvo*) or that between community and society (*Gemeinschaft* and *Gesellschaft*) in German thought. See Walicki, *The Slavophile Controversy*, pp. 168–175.

system, in other words, a pseudo-accommodation. In the third chapter, where the action is set primarily in the city, the initiative is on the side of the city; Aleksei Stepanovich is to be reeducated, must write proper letters, acquire a correct carriage, at least try to engage in elevated conversation, and directly confront his family's opposition to an alliance with the consummate expression of the urban culture of the day, Sofia Nikolavna.

The essential failure of these efforts to effect the total reorientation of character (which is precluded by Aksakov's general method of characterization) is reinforced by the dénouement of the third chapter. Here again Aksakov's tendency to end narratives with beginnings and to mark such junctures with rites and ceremonies is at work. In the third chapter, the concluding event in the city is the church wedding and the reception. Despite their importance to the plot as the climax of the entire sequence of events in the chapter, these rites are recorded in a laconic historical tone, perhaps suggesting their implicit failure. "The wedding was in all respects formal and magnificent. . . . Soon after, there began dancing and continued until a rich but early dinner. . . . On the next and following days there took place all that is customary on such occasions, that is a dinner, a ball, visits, again a dinner and again a ball: in a word, as is done now as well, even in the capitals" (1:187).

On those occasions when the city turns to ritual behavior, it is incapable of using such impersonal forms meaningfully, and its desacralized rites (based on the fashions of the ultimate city, the capital) are standardized and sterile—"again a dinner and again a ball." The country, where the third chapter begins and ends, paradoxically asserts the vitality of its traditional and deindividualizing, yet still meaningful forms through the wealth of detail and movement of the concluding paragraph, which describes rites solemnizing the young couple's entrance into Bagrovo:

> "They're coming, they're coming"—resounded through
> the whole house. . . . The old folk with all their family went
> out on the porch: Arina Vasil'evna in a silk dress and
> jacket . . . and Stepan Mikhailovich in some sort of old-
> fashioned frock-coat, shaven and with a cravat on, stood on
> the top step of the porch; he held the icon of the Apparition
> of the Mother of God, she a wedding loaf and silver salt-
> cellar. . . . The carriage rolled up to the porch, the young couple
> emerged, fell at the feet of the old people, received their

> blessing and kissed them and all those surrounding them; the
> young bride had hardly finished this ceremony and turned
> again to her father-in-law, when he took her by the hand, gazed
> fixedly into her eyes, from which tears streamed, began to
> cry himself, embraced her firmly, kissed her and said: "Glory
> to God! Let us go thank Him." He took his daughter-in-law
> by the hand, led her into the main hall through the dense
> throng, stood her next to himself—and the priest, awaiting
> them in full vestments, intoned, "Blessed be our God always, as
> it was in the beginning, is now and ever shall be, world
> without end." (1:190)

The formal arrangements of participants, the specific household
rites of greeting with bread and salt and with the icon specific to
Bagrovo-Znamenskoe, followed by the church blessing—the rit-
ualistic behavior of the last paragraph of the third chapter provides the final counterpoint to the city. Although the form of
action is ceremonial and pointedly views human activity *sub
specie aeternitatis* (note the emphasis on permanence in the
closing benediction and the shift from use of names to use of
terms of relationship, that is, to identification by role), the general animation of the entire passage depicting the young couple's
approach to the house and the inhabitants' outward and encom-
passing movement, coupled with the authenticity of emotion indicated by tears, suggest that the humble ceremonies in Bagrovo
are closer to the sources of human life and feeling than are the
formalities of Ufa.

As he so often does, Aksakov ends the chapter with a situation
of potentiality. In this case, the open ending and its implicit
acceptance of Sofia Nikolavna by her parents-in-law through the
medium of ritual originally concluded the entire work. With the
addition of the later chapters the harmony becomes a possibility
rather than a true resolution, for the third chapter reconciles the
differences of city and country only ceremonially; the larger differences remain. The tension between the two systems continues
in the fourth chapter, "The Young Couple at Bagrovo," which
functions as an inverse of the third chapter, tracing the assimilation of Sofia Nikolavna to the country, a process that ultimately
turns out to be as unsuccessful as Aleksei Stepanovich's assimilation to the city.

The fourth chapter of *Family Chronicle*, "The Young Couple at
Bagrovo ("Molodye v Bagrove")," written, along with the fifth, two

years after the completion of the first three chapters, depends less on established literary modes than do the earlier chapters. Instead it draws on the preceding text of *Family Chronicle* itself; the depiction of the activities and social relations that define life at Bagrovo, with the presentation of which the first chapter closes, is continued in the fourth chapter and its significance deepened. In addition, with its shift of locale back to the country the fourth chapter reverses the treatment of the dichotomy between city and country as it appears in the third chapter. It is now Sofia Nikolavna's turn to find herself in an alien environment and to attempt to seek an accommodation with it. The process of assimilation in the country employs a characteristically rural means, namely, ritual, much as education is the means of transformation in the city.

In "The Young Couple at Bagrovo," Aksakov's tendency to employ rituals reaches its apogee; the entire chapter in fact is constructed as a series of ceremonies, each designed to draw Sofia Nikolavna further and further into the world of Bagrovo and to establish her position in the Bagrov family. Each of these rituals of course forms a stage of the wedding journey to Bagrovo, with its overall ceremonial nature. The use of rituals in the country reflects its dependence on the perceptible and its emphasis on category and role rather than on concepts and the individual.

The rituals in the fourth chapter are arranged in a sequence of constant spatial expansion, which provides a tangible correlative to the progressive broadening of the social context that takes place. The ceremonies of the first day clearly display this order. Because they are the first actions surrounding the new couple's arrival in Bagrovo, and thus the most heavily fraught with implications for the future, they adhere most closely to ritualized patterns and reveal the basic purpose of all the rituals that follow.

The first ceremonially significant event is the entrance of the young couple into the house itself and the presentation of the new member of the family to the family as a whole. The traditional welcoming rites of the *khlebosol'e* end the third chapter, and the fourth begins with the kissing of the cross, blessing with holy water, and formalized speeches, with direct reference to the purpose of the ceremony: "There began again kissing and the speeches usual in such circumstances: 'We beg that you favor us, accept us into your familial regard' and so on" (1:190–191). Then Sofia Nikolavna is led by Stepan Mikhailovich to the drawing

room, the space for formal encounter, where Stepan Mikhailovich never sat and where he entered "only on the most unusual
occasion" (1:191). Official acceptance into Bagrovo is formally
reciprocated when the young couple distribute gifts to their relatives (rich fabrics embroidered, at least in the case of the gift for
Stepan Mikhailovich, by Sofia Nikolavna herself). This initial
stage of the ceremonial process is ratified with a dinner at which
the young couple is toasted, not with champagne from Ufa, but
with home-distilled strawberry cordial, drunk from one goblet by
all, and the couple express their gratitude.

Following her formal introduction to the family and the definition of her place in it, Sofia Nikolavna assumes her role in the
context of the broader social and economic system of the estate.
In a ceremony—Aksakov uses the word *tseremoniia* (1:198) on
this occasion—of presentation as the young mistress (within the
family she has been referred to as *nevestka*, "daughter- or sister-
in-law"), Sofia Nikolavna, once again outside the house, accepts
pledges of fealty from the servants and peasants of the estate,
who kiss her hand. She reciprocates by distributing gifts, as she
did with her new in-laws, as a concrete indication of the bond
that has been formed. Stepan Mikhailovich, as the leader and
lawgiver of the entire area, also presents Sofia Nikolavna to a
delegation of Mordvinians who have arrived from a neighboring
village. The establishment of her social and economic role concludes, as did the inauguration of her kinship role, with an act of
communal feasting as ratification. In this case, the social hierarchy is preserved, even though everything takes place outside, by
using the public space of the estate to indicate rank and degree;
the serfs and Mordvinians are treated to a festive carousal (*po-
poika*) at some distance from the manor house, while the family
takes tea in the shade of the house.

Although the activities of the first day are the most obviously
ritualized in nature, subsequent incidents are also of a ceremonial sort. The young couple undertakes a series of journeys to
the estates of the married Bagrov daughters; at Stepan Mikhailovich's insistence, the trips are taken in order of seniority (1:206).
Stepan Mikhailovich also acquaints his daughter-in-law more
closely with the workings of the estate, showing her his herds of
horses, game preserves, fields and springs, and most importantly,
in light of its role in the first chapter, the mill, the very heart of
Bagrovo. While inspecting the mill, Sofia Nikolavna is dusted

with flour as though for a ball (1:209), suggesting the degree to which she has been removed from her own milieu. The fact that Stepan Mikhailovich is greatly taken with this incident and calls his daughter-in-law his "young miller's wife" (1:209) is another indication that the true focus of the fourth chapter is on a meta-phorical marriage between Stepan Mikhailovich, the personifi-cation of the country, and Sofia Nikolavna, an embodiment of the urban.

The entire sequence of ceremonies is brought to a conclusion with a dinner, attended by immediate family, relatives, friends, and the representatives of civil authority (a judge and the mayor from Buguruslan)—in other words, the society of the area. Even a jester, Afrosin'ia Andrevna, attends. Her preposterous tales of her years in St. Petersburg derive their humor from their presen-tation of the life of the greatest city in the world, the capital of the Russian empire and its ruler, Catherine II, in terms of the speech and customs of the countryside; whatever Catherine did of an evening, she doubtless never accepted Afrosin'ia Andrev-na's invitation to drop in to knit and chat. In actuality, Afrosin'ia Andrevna's tale is appropriate to the occasion, for it consists of a comic variant of the basic theme of the fourth chapter (and in-versely of the third), the relation between city and country and the assimilation of one to the other. The fact that her story meets with the interest and laughter of the entire company, especially Stepan Mikhailovich, suggests a certain awareness by the char-acters of the relation between the story and the ceremonial oc-casion taking place. The comic treatment of the underlying problem may serve an apotropaic function by restricting ludi-crous failure to an incidental narrative. In addition, the motley appearance of the guests, in varied styles of dress and from var-ious social backgrounds from complete rustic to urbane, with a shading off into parody at both ends of the spectrum (the naïve bumpkin Afrosin'ia Andrevna is balanced by the *soi-disant* Vol-tairean, Kal'pinskii, in his frock coat), adds to the sense of fes-tivity accompanying the entire meal. The occasion of course contrasts with the strained solemnity of the young couple's first meal at Bagrovo, when the ceremonial process was only begin-ning. The significance of this dinner as the public acknowledg-ment of the (apparent) success of the ceremonial process is underscored by the device, characteristic of Aksakov at important junctures, of the catalogue: "The story began with cold dishes:

a shank of ham and pork studded with garlic; then followed the hot dishes: fresh cabbage soup and crayfish soup, both accompanied by home-baked turnovers and paté in pastry; immediately after came chilled beet soup, with fresh-salted sturgeon, Urals cured sturgeon, and a whole mound of shelled crayfish on a platter" (1:231).[19] After this public celebration of the young couple's acceptance by the family, the entire chapter closes with a farewell ceremony, which echoes, in reverse order, the arrival ceremonies at the beginning of the chapter: a final meal for the family only, the traditional moment of seated silence before departure, mutual blessings and tears (recalling the tears at arrival), and finally departure itself. As the first chapter ends with Stepan Mikhailovich retiring, so again the curtain falls with the master of Bagrovo beginning his afternoon nap.

The process of assimilation in the country depends not so much on a restructuring of the personality as on a series of reciprocal acts between the newcomer and representatives of the existing society. Specific actions or certain objects, both dictated by tradition, serve as emblems of the process of transforming an outsider; for instance, Sofia Nikolavna distributes gifts to mark her initial reception by both her in-laws and by the serfs who pledge fealty to her. Although many of the ceremonies involve verbal communication, it tends to be of a highly formulaic nature and specific to the given context, the spoken equivalent of the traditionally defined gestures and gifts, and like them intended to establish or confirm a certain new relationship. Set speeches accompany the initial greeting (1:190), and the formal reception of the young couple in the drawing room at Bagrovo also involves formulaic speeches. The conversation accompanying meals, themselves a form of communion ratifying the ceremonies that have preceded them, indicates that the ceremonies have been effective. On the first day, by contrast, the formal dinner lacks general, uninhibited conversation: "There was little conversation, as much because, as Stepan Mikhailovich put it, every one's mouth was hard at work, as because no one knew how to converse, and every one was embarassed as well, each in his own way" (1:192). The second day's dinner is "much more lively and merry" (1:207) and the final, formal meal is "quite merry" (1:232)

19. The catalogue continues for another fifteen lines.

and accompanied by animated and elated conversation, especially on Stepan Mikhailovich's part.

An especially significant situation linking food and communication is the serving of tea (both morning and evening), the importance of which in the daily cycle of life at Bagrovo was established in "A Good Day," and which is of course one of the "privileged moments" in Russian fiction generally. The relationship between Sofia Nikolavna and Stepan Mikhailovich develops most noticeably at these intimate ceremonies. The link between meals and communication operates negatively as well; a character's disinclination to engage in eating or conversation indicates hostility, as pointed out at the initial reception: "Aksin'ia Stepanovna sincerely loved her sister-in-law at first sight and was kind to her, but the others sisters were silent, and it wasn't difficult to guess by their glances what was going on in their minds" (1:121). At the presentation to the peasants and at evening tea, the sisters-in-law whisper, that is, engage in counter-conversation (1:196, 200). Neither the angry Stepan Mikhailovich nor his guilty daughter attend the tea immediately following his outburst of rage over the treatment of the newlyweds at Karataevka, and the faces of those in attendance "doubtless presented a rich and varied mime scene. Conversations did not jell and went along very limply" (1:224). The reference to mime, an axiomatically silent form of theater, stresses the social breakdown and the inhibiting disjunction of expected role and actual emotion. However, things are set right by Sofia Nikolavna at tea the following morning when she takes charge of both tea and conversation and restores equilibrium (note the motif of cheerfulness, *veselost'*):

> She herself poured the tea, she managed to serve first her
> father-in-law and then her mother-in-law and the others. She
> managed to talk with every one, and so cleverly, so to
> the point, and so gaily that her father-in-law was completely
> convinced that she knew nothing of what had happened
> the day before; he was convinced of it and cheered himself up.
> His cheerfulness also had a communicable quality, and
> in an hour not even the traces of yesterday's storm were noticeable. (1:226)

The interdependence of ceremony and communication assumes particular significance with respect to the three figures whose relationships are the chief dramatic element in the fourth chapter: Sofia Nikolavna, Stepan Mikhailovich, and Aleksei Stepanovich. The basic motifs defining both Sofia Nikolavna and Aleksei Stepanovich continue more or less unchanged from the third chapter. Sofia Nikolavna's association with magic is repeated several times—she is "a marvelous, magical being" (1:226); for Stepan Mikhailovich, she is "a sorceress" (1:204). In addition to the association with magic and power, the trait of quickness to anger also continues. Aleksei Stepanovich still worships her and fears his father (1:208); his characteristic response is still passive, although now contemplation of nature rather than an existential dilemma renders him quiescent. This state is correspondingly milder than the lovelorn illnesses of the third chapter.

The relationship between Aleksei Stepanovich and Sofia Nikolavna remains charged with misunderstanding and disharmony; indeed, tendencies which had been latent or ignored during their courtship now become explicit. Their inability to communicate rests on the incongruity of their perceptions, which in turn derive from their differing psychological makeups and backgrounds. While the ceremonial roles imposed on them most of the time tend to keep these differences in the background (since the rituals of the countryside ignore personality), the moments when the young couple are alone are often tense and marred by bickering. These moments usually occur outside the round of ritual, in places such as their room or carriage, where they are isolated from the general society. Their differing outlooks are underscored by their reactions to the natural realm in which Bagrovo exists. Her perceptions conditioned by urban notions of picturesque landscape, Sofia Nikolavna

> sat down at one of the opened windows facing the river, which was densely overgrown with willow and mallow. The night was magnificient. . . . She was used to admiring the magnificent views from the elevated bank of the Belaia River, in the environs of Ufa, and so the little village in a low spot, with its log house, darkened by time and weather, with a millpond surrounded by swamp, and with the constant clatter of the mill even seemed repulsive to her. (1:200–201)

She is of course incapable of a proper response to the country or of perceiving the interrelation between the human and the natural summed up in the mill. Her preference for views rather than for being surrounded by nature recalls the comments on the desiccated urbanite's attitude toward nature in the introduction to *Notes on Fishing*. Aleksei Stepanovich perceives the same summer night entirely differently; he is literally in his element and each aspect of his surroundings is endowed with value arising both from personal association and from a sense of oneness with the natural realm: "He looked out the seven opened windows at the rook grove, sleeping in the murk, at the river brush, grown dark in the distance, the scene of his childhood pleasures and hunts; he lost himself in listening to the hum of the mill, to the trills of the nightingales, to the cries of the nocturnal birds" (1:202).

It is worth noting that Sofia Nikolavna perceives the sound of the mill as clatter or beating (*stuk*), a discontinuous and mechanical noise, whereas Aleksei Stepanovich hears a continuous, steady, and not unpleasant sound (*shum*) more in accord with the quasi-organic central place of the mill in the life of the village. Aleksei Stepanovich, who has heretofore been presented as ludicruously weak and shallow, here first reveals a dimension of his inner life that is in some ways deeper than his wife can imagine. This side of Aleksei Stepanovich is brought out more in *Years of Childhood*, where he is the person who initiates young Sergei (Aksakov himself) into the world of nature.

In addition to the incongruity of their aesthetic perceptions, the young couple disagree in their analysis and evaluation of the motives of others. For instance, Aleksei Stepanovich refuses to see premeditation in his sister's treatment of them at Karataevka, while Sofia Nikolavna sees deliberate malice, a supposition supported by Aksin'ia Stepanovna's statement that Aleksandra Stepanovna purposely left the young couple without bed-curtains and at the mercy of rats (1:218).

Aleksei Stepanovich and Sofia Nikolavna also fail to respond properly to each other's emotional states. In their first conversation on an island in the river, Aleksei Stepanovich becomes lost in nature while his wife discusses her in-laws' reception of her (1:185–186); during the second, Sofia Nikolavna puts words in his mouth (1:208), turning an opportunity for communication into a trite scene. Perhaps the most significant instance of the disharmony between Sofia Nikolavna and Aleksei Stepanovich occurs on the day of the final, solemn dinner, once again on the island that was the scene of their former misunderstanding.

> Sofia Nikolavna recalled her senseless outburst which had
> taken place not long ago at this very spot . . . and her heart
> throbbed; although she saw Aleksei Stepanovich perfectly
> happy and content, laughing loudly, . . . she drew him
> aside, threw herself on his neck and with tears in her eyes
> said: "Forgive me, my dear, and forget forever everything that
> happened here on the day of our arrival!" Aleksei Stepa-
> novich was very unhappy at the sight of tears, but kissed his
> wife, kissed both her hands and saying good-naturedly,
> "My dear, what are you remembering such trifles for? Do you
> have some sort of fancy to get yourself upset?"—hurried
> to hear the end of the amusing anecdote Kal'pinskii was telling
> most entertainingly. . . . Sofia Nikolavna felt sad at that
> moment. (1:233–234)

If the relationship between Sofia Nikolavna and Aleksei Stepanovich lacks reciprocity and true communication (they speak to
each other only of other people), the one between Sofia Nikolavna and her father-in-law, Stepan Mikhailovich, achieves a high
degree of mutual accommodation. Unlike the self-disintegrating,
extra-ritual attempts at understanding between husband and
wife, those between daughter-in-law and father-in-law invariably
take place within the framework of a ceremonial activity and
represent the fullest development of the potential for contact
inherent in these activities. At the first ceremonial meeting, they
are almost the only participants to engage in conversation; at the
first dinner, Stepan Mikhailovich, at Sofia Nikolavna's request
for more of the strawberry cordial used for the toast, "from his
own hands let her drink one sip" (1:193). The interconnection of
food, conversation, and communication at such ceremonies
emerges with particular clarity from Stepan Mikhailovich's animated speech and behavior at the final formal dinner:

> All saw, and he wanted to show, how much he liked his
> daughter-in-law and how satisfied he was with her and how
> she loved and respected her father-in-law. He frequently
> turned to her during the dinner begging various little services:
> "Serve me some of that, pour me some of that, pick me
> out a morsel that suits your taste, because you know my
> daughter-in-law and I have the same taste; remind me, what
> was it I said to you just the other day; do tell us all what
> you were telling me then, it's slipped my mind somehow."
> (1:232–234)

The crucial scene between the two takes place at morning tea on Sofia Nikolavna's first morning at Bagrovo. Again Stepan Mikhailovich specifically connects food (or in this case, tea) with communication: "'Well, if that's so, thank you, dear daughter-in-law. We'll have a talk, chatter a little at your ease, and you can give me some tea to drink'" (1:203). Sofia Nikolavna takes charge of the entire tea ceremony and prepares it precisely to the old man's taste (1:204); he invites her to sit with him, an unusual gesture, since Stepan Mikhailovich invariably took his tea alone, before the rest of the family did. He drinks an unheard-of three cups and insists that Sofia Nikolavna drink a second and eat a special Bagrovo roll. In this encounter the differences between city and country come closest to being resolved. Stepan Mikhailovich and Sofia Nikolavna achieve a harmonious relationship through an empathetic understanding of the other's basic values. He reproaches her for certain aspects of her behavior, specifically for calling her husband simply Aleksei, without using his patronymic; for sending her husband for the gifts she was to distribute and having him carry the tray that held them, as if he were a servant; and finally, "'Now you've just said that you *ordered* him to go back to sleep. A wife shouldn't order her husband; things will turn out badly'" (1:205). All these items are in accord with the country's manner of perception, focusing on specific lexical usage or emblematic details of physical behavior as concrete signs of underlying attitudes. From these characteristically rural perceptions, Stepan Mikhailovich shifts to the normative aspect of the city/country opposition: "'Perhaps, that's the way you do things in the city, but by our way of doing things, the old way, the country way, all that isn't any good at all'" (1:205).

In response, Sofia Nikolavna essentially accepts her father-in-law's insistence that she abandon her city orientation, on the condition that he in turn treat her as his own daughter. Up to this point, Stepan Mikhailovich, despite his delight in and satisfaction with his daughter-in-law, has treated her as an outsider, not as a blood member of his family. For instance, he explains his refusal to let her kiss his hand on the grounds that such an act has a symbolic import and is reserved only for "'*rodnym detiam*'" ("one's own, natural children"), no matter what his feelings toward her (1:194). At the start of his comments to Sofia Nikolavna on her behavior, he allows her the freedom to heed him or not, with the comment, "*'Ty mne ne rodnaia doch'*" ("you're not my own daughter") (1:204). The understanding reached between Sofia Nikolavna and Stepan Mikhailovich involves a reciprocal elimination of the distinction connected with the opposition between city and country and between family and stranger (*rodnoi* and *chuzhoi*).[20] Sofia Nikolavna admits the error of her ways, attributing it to her youth and the improper example of others (1:205), implicitly other inhabitants of the city. She accepts her father-in-law's guidance, forsaking the independence and maturity that her enlightened urban attitudes value, but in return demands a corresponding readjustment of Stepan Mikhailovich's attitudes: "'Always treat me like you own [*rodnaia*] daughter; stop me, upbraid me if I offend in anything, and then pardon me, but don't let dissatisfaction remain in your heart. . . . Remember that I'm in a strange family, that I know no one and no one knows me; don't abandon me.' . . . She threw herself upon her father-in-law's neck; his eyes were also filled with tears; she embraced him as his own [*rodnaia*] daughter and kissed his chest, even his hands" (1:205).

The physical act of kissing her father-in-law's hands, which he now permits, and the mutual tears (tears are always unilateral in the case of the relations between Aleksei Stepanovich and Sofia Nikolavna) indicate the mutual understanding and balance which have been achieved; Stepan Mikhailovich assents to this reinterpretation of their relationship, and as a physical token of their accord, he does not withdraw his hands, adding, "Well, so be it" to his gesture (1:205).

Sofia Nikolavna and Stepan Mikhailovich achieve rapport and the neutralization of divergent values, but they are both clearly presented as individuals who are exceptional in their milieus and capable of transcending the categories that shape their perceptions. Even in their case, accommodation is achieved only on the personal level. Although the bond that is forged between them is probably all the stronger because of the effort each has had to make in effecting it, most characters in the fourth chapter are unable to overcome behavior dictated by their traditional

20. This phrase is lacking in the manuscript, its insertion in the published work suggesting the importance of the word *rodnaia* for the entire passage (LL, *fond* 3, folder 1, item 4, fol. 18). Throughout the discussion between daughter-in-law and father-in-law, the words *rodnoi* and *chuzhoi* ("of one's own lineage" and "alien, not of one's own lineage") occur over and over, indicating verbally the nature of the transaction taking place.

roles. Despite her high estimation of Stepan Mikhailovich's personal qualities, Sofia Nikolavna herself remains indifferent and even hostile to the entire world of Bagrovo to which Stepan Mikhailovich tries to initiate her; she merely affects interest in the fields of the estate and the workings of the mill. A metaphor in the manuscript makes explicit the element of hypocrisy in Sofia Nikolavna's behavior: "It seemed to the old man that all this very much interested his dear daughter-in-law, but the fair side of the medal had a completely different reverse: everything decidedly did not please his daughter-in-law."[21] The final version omits the metaphor entirely (1:228), attenuating but not entirely eliminating the suggestion of duplicity on Sofia Nikolavna's part.

However, the main countercurrent which runs through the fourth chapter and which manifests itself in intermittent conflict is the continued and intensified hostility of most of the Bagrov women, led by Aleksandra and Elizaveta Stepanovna. This ill-will toward an intruder whose higher status is endowed by the males of the family is itself a role dictated by the categorical thinking of the countryside, perhaps echoing residual matrilinear opposition to a brother's wife and certainly reflecting the real economic disadvantage a new wife, with possible heirs, could mean to a family's daughters. The Bagrov women do not overcome their dictated roles, but merely operate on two levels, publicly conforming to the behavior desired by Stepan Mikhailovich and formalized by the various ceremonies, but covertly giving vent to their true attitude: "Sofia Nikolavna's triumphal inauguration as the young mistress . . . irritated, stung their spiteful souls. They suddenly felt their decline in their father's house. 'There's nothing to say about us any more, we're already cut off on our own,' whispered Aleksandra Stepanovna" (1:198).

The eldest Bagrov daugher, Aksin'ia Stepanovna, explicitly rejects her sisters' system of roles and sincerely extends hospitality to Sofia Nikolavna, but she is ostracized by the others and, according to the manuscript, given the nickname *tukhloe miaso* ("carrion," "rotten meat"),[22] consistent in its concreteness with the village mentality. The most overt expression of hostility to Sofia Nikolavna, Aleksandra Stepanovna's subjection of the young couple to the nocturnal forays of rats at Karataevka, also takes a physical form, the rats serving virtually as metonymic exten-

21. LL, *fond* 3, folder 1, item 4, fol. 48.
22. Ibid., fol. 6.

sions of Aleksandra Stepanovna. In a clumsily ironic welcoming speech, which is directed precisely at Sofia Nikolavna, Aleksandra Stepanovna makes it clear that the mistreatment of the young couple is consonant with the conflict of value systems in the third and fourth chapter: "'We're so very, very happy with our dear guests; please do us the honor; dear brother of course will not judge us amiss, but I just don't know how dear sister Sofia Nikolavna will enter our little hut after her father's grand halls in town. You see, we're poor folk, not people with service rank, and we live with what we have; we don't have salaries or income'" (1:215). The speech is of course a parody of a true welcome and of the verbal formulae of the welcoming rituals at Bagrovo; throughout the visit, Aleksandra Stepanovna's treatment of her guest perverts hospitality. The hostess drives home the point by explaining the next morning that the rats only attack "'newish people'" (noven'kikh) (1:216)—gratuitously adding a rather insulting diminutive. Even without his affection for his daughter-in-law, Stepan Mikhailovich's strong sense of the proper fulfillment of roles renders such treatment nearly sacrilegious, and his wrathful punishment of the wrongdoer is not long in coming.

Despite the outward success manifested in the final social gathering, the fourth chapter ends not on a note of achieved and permanent harmony, but rather on one of tenuous equilibrium. The Bagrov sisters demonstrate that the social attitudes of the countryside are not really amenable to change and acceptance. As for Sofia Nikolavna, she values only Stepan Mikhailovich, and for reasons he would probably not understand. Nevertheless, the accommodation that Sofia Nikolavna and her father-in-law arrive at remains a fragile link between their two worlds. Sofia Nikolavna, mainly because of the nobility of character she has discovered in Stepan Mikhailovich, attains a certain degree of sympathetic, if probably transitory, insight into the system of which she has become an element:

> She could . . . recognize and understand the special world in
> which she found herself. She looked more reasonably,
> more kindly on her mother-in-law and youngest sister-in-law,
> both foreign to her in all respects; she looked upon her
> father-in-law with less partiality and understood from what
> background her husband had come; understood in part
> that he could not be otherwise and that for long, often, and
> perhaps always, they would have moments of not under-
> standing each other. (1:235)

This understanding instills a degree of forbearance and wisdom in Sofia Nikolavna, and the newlyweds' final days at Bagrovo are marked by moments of mutual communication with each other and with Stepan Mikhailovich. Although this is the purpose of the ceremony of the wedding trip as a whole, the usual forms of communication typical of the countryside break down under the excess weight of feeling they are called upon to bear. This inadequacy is particularly apparent in the case of Stepan Mikhailovich, whose efforts collide against the basic problem of the thought and language patterns of his ethos. He is unable to find "the fitting word" (1:236) for the particular moment of emotion and falls back upon timeless truisms. In form, his advice consists of bare imperatives and constantly threatens to revert entirely to the proverbial and metaphorical style characteristic of country speech:

> "Chti ego i postupai s uvazhen'em. Ne stanesh' pochitat'
> muzha—puti ne budet. Chto on skazhet ili sdelaet ne tak, ne
> po-tvoemu,—promolchi, ne vsiako lyko v stroku, ne vsiaka
> vina vinovata. . . . Radi boga, ne perelivai cherez krai,
> vse khorosho v mere, dazhe laski i ugozhden'ia." (1:236)

> "Honor him and treat him with respect. if you begin to lack
> respect for your husband—there will be no getting on. If he
> says or does something not in the way you want—keep silent;
> not everything should be counted against him, not every
> offense is deliberate. . . . For God's sake, don't overdo, every-
> thing is good in measure, even caresses and kindnesses."

Stepan Mikhailovich uses proverbial patterns, with numerous sound repetitions and syntactic parallels: "'ne vsiako lyko v stroku, ne vsiaka vina vinovata'"; "'ne perelivai cherez krai,'" as well as concrete metaphors: "' not every strip of bark can be used'"; "'don't pour over the rim.'"

Thus the third and fourth chapters of *Family Chronicle* make up a diptych, using the ostensible plot of the romance and marriage of Aleksei Stepanovich and Sofia Nikolavna, in which the mental paradigms of the two sides of Russian culture in the eighteenth century are depicted. Similar contrasts underlie another major work of the period, Goncharov's *Oblomov*, which is set in the mid-nineteenth century. Although one can view the two realms historically, as two successive layers of Russian culture, or spatially, as urban and rural societies, the considerable differences in type of mental operation (abstract conceptualization as opposed to concrete metaphorization) and values (accomplishment versus security) suggest that Aksakov is also dealing with two constant poles of the mind itself. We might consider in this respect Aksakov's own fluctuations between extremely urbane pursuits such as the theater and pastoral, even atavistic activities like hunting and fishing. Seen in this light, the central chapters of *Family Chronicle* transcend a simple family drama, and the tenuous balance at the end of the fourth chapter may indicate the tentative resolution, through art, of a basic human tension.

The fifth and concluding chapter of *Family Chronicle*, "Life in Ufa" ("Zhizn' v Ufe"), is primarily concerned, as the title suggests, not with individuals, their characters, and emotional lives, nor with romance and marriage, as were the preceding three chapters, but rather with the totality of human existence and particularly its two termini, birth and death. The interplay of spatial and social categories that loomed so large in the preceding chapters is relegated to a relatively minor role in the fifth; any return to the theme after the near stasis at the conclusion of the fourth chapter would perhaps have been redundant. Instead, the major dynamic of the final chapter is provided by time; the entire work thus closes with a clear emphasis on the continuity and passage of time, as is appropriate to a work at least partly presented as history. A conclusion stressing time also balances the first chapter, creating an overall symmetry to *Family Chronicle* which would otherwise be lacking (the first chapter opens and the last chapter closes with Stepan Mikhailovich at the narrative's focus). Although it echoes the theme of time of the first chapter, the fifth chapter also presents a new beginning, the continuation of the special Bagrovo time, the inception of which was the central event of the first chapter, beyond the confines of the narrative.

Although the basic concern of the fifth chapter is time and continuity of human society, its structure seems to depend on discontinuities, with more noticeable shifts in subject than is the case in the three preceding chapters (the looser narrative may also be a reprise of the episodic first chapter). Situations in the fifth chapter lack development, just as characters throughout the work lack it. Instead, change is dialectical, one condition giving way to its complete opposite, with little or no real transition. The first part of "Life in Ufa" is dominated by death; the second, relatively shorter part, is concerned with life.

The aura of death pervading the first half of the chapter is focused on the moribund figure of Sofia Nikolavna's father, Nikolai Fedorovich Zubin, whose paralytic condition symbolizes the blight that affects the entire physical and social environment. Given the dynamic nature of Aksakov's narrative in general and the emphasis on time in the fifth chapter, it would seem that Nikolai Fedorovich's illness is really a metaphor for lack of change, for a stasis in which no real event occurs and new beginnings are blighted. This buildup of inertia functions as a sort of reverse suspense, increasing the significance and the impact of the events of the latter part of the chapter, as we shall see. At this stage, however, all innovation is thwarted, and the entire brief life, from conception to death at the age of four months, of Parasha, the young Bagrovs' first child, is attended by images of ill health. Morning sickness, naturally enough, provides the first sign of Sofia Nikolavna's pregnancy, but the motif of illness persists; she is described as being among "those women who pay for the happiness of being a mother with a constantly sickly condition, more painful and agonizing than any illness" (1:245). In addition to her primary physical illness, Sofia Nikolavna temporarily loses her beauty, and neurotically engages in a hypochondriacal consultation of medical books (1:254). When her daughter is born, although the delivery is uncomplicated, the child is puny and weak (1:257), as well as overprotected by its mother, who now makes her child the object of her hypochondria. Parasha soon dies of an infantile convulsion (1:259). Her departure from life without a struggle concludes the pattern of illness associated with her; the final reference to her, ending with the word *dead* (*mertvaia*), sums up her brief life, which was really a sort of protracted death: "Sitting by the cradle and noticing that Parasha suddenly trembled and that her little face was distorted, Sofia Nikolavna quickly picked up her daughter: she was already dead" (1:259).

In the first part of the fifth chapter, death and illness extend without limit and are echoed metaphorically on the social level, where discord and dysfunction reign. Sofia Nikolavna comes into conflict with her father over his Kalmyk servant, who exploits his position as Nikolai Fedorovich's nurse to alienate father from daughter and to usurp Sofia Nikolavna's place. The Kalmyk's rise in status and his desire to replace Sofia Nikolavna is vividly revealed to her on her return from Bagrovo, when, in a scene reminiscent of Praskov'ia Ivanovna's discovery of Kurolesov in chapter 2, she opens the door to her father's room to find the Kalmyk sitting in her chair. By his behavior, the Kalmyk, who had been raised by Nikolai Fedorovich in a benevolent way but had joined the Pugachev rebellion, only to be pardoned afterward by Nikolai Fedorovich, not only seeks to reverse the relationship between master and servant by gaining control over the physically helpless man, but also perverts parental bonds, both by having rebelled against his foster father and now by seeking to displace Sofia Nikolavna and turning her father against her. Finally the Kalmyk forces Sofia Nikolavna into presenting her father with an ultimatum; he chooses the Kalmyk over his daughter and gives her money to purchase a separate house (1:245). He then becomes indifferent to his daughter and shows no interest in his granddaughter when she is presented to him (1:257). Relations between Sofia Nikolavna and Aleksei Stepanovich also deteriorate; Sofia Nikolavna focuses all her attention on her sickly daughter and curtails contact with her closest friends. Aleksei Stepanovich is cast aside and seeks refuge in card-playing, while his wife, once the toast of Ufa society, becomes the victim of its gossip.

Since geographical boundaries and distinctions are not so strong in the fifth chapter as they are in the other chapters of *Family Chronicle*, social discord easily extends beyond the boundaries of Ufa to include Bagrovo and its master, Stepan Mikhailovich, although there is some attenuation of the seriousness of the dysfunction. Upon learning of his daughter-in-law's pregnancy, Stepan Mikhailovich, in misdirected elation, misuses his power (the only incident of the sort in *Family Chronicle*, for even when he goes to extremes, Stepan Mikhailovich is always shown as being in the right); by marrying off his tea-server, the ugly, thirtyish, and vituperative Aksiutka to a much younger and handsome man out of a desire to enhance his own jubilation, Stepan Mikhailovich brings about the permanent unhappiness of both parties. The narrator, in a deliberate departure from the earlier idealization of Stepan Mikhailovich, directly condemns his insistence on this obvious mismatch: "A pity, a great pity! Stepan Mikhailovich committed a sin and fashioned woe for others from his own joy" (1:244). Stepan Mikhailovich later blames his daughter-in-law for her break with her father, causing a breach in his own previously warm relationship with her. Finally, he displays rather comic anger at the birth of a granddaughter, who he hoped would be a grandson, and vetoes his daughter Aksin'ia Stepanovna's planned trip to Ufa to stand as godmother (1:256).

Having reached a necessarily static situation of universal discord and illness, Aksakov can only resort to an absolute and total reversal of affairs. It is in this respect that the structure of the fifth chapter echoes the manner in which Aksakov constructs his characters. The reversal in the balance of power between life and death, harmony and discord, begins in paradoxical fashion at the moment of death's seemingly utter hegemony; Sofia Nikolavna undergoes a surrogate death following her daughter's actual death, and, as is often the case in Aksakov's works, this leads to a rebirth and ultimately to a new order. Semiconscious for four days, Sofia Nikolavna first recognizes Aleksei Stepanovich, shrieks, and then regains her hold on existence:

> When on the fourth night Sofia Nikolavna came to her senses, looked consciously at the objects around her, recognized Aleksei Stepanovich, whom it was difficult to recognize, so much had he changed, recognized her constant friend, Katerina Aleksevna,—a frightful shriek tore itself from her breast, and healing streams of tears burst from her eyes: she had not as yet cried even once. She embraced Aleksei Stepanovich and long and silently sobbed on his breast; he himself sobbed like a child. (1:259)

Once again, progress forward in life is made possible only by an ending of the old self and the emergence of a new personality, although the present change is not so radical as her previous one, or the change in Praskov'ia Ivanovna. The mutual tears, as is common in Aksakov, mark the brief attainment of community of feeling, so tenuous between Aleksei Stepanovich and Sofia Nikolavna, while the presence of her friend suggests the reestablishment of social relationships. As was the case in earlier incidents of rebirth, there are suggestions of a miracle in which an icon plays a prominent role (1:260). Of course, a miracle of sorts is also demanded structurally in order to change the static situation, so Aksakov could be said to be turning a possible defect into an advantage.

Once the principle of renewed or reaffirmed life is liberated, it begins to extend as the forces of death had done previously; death, the weight of the past, is now powerless to affect the living, and the symbolic focus of death is soon eliminated: "Old Zubin was already very badly off, and the miraculous restoration of his daughter's health made no impression whatever on him. Everything was finished for him on earth, all links broken, all the threads of life torn, and only his soul scarcely tarried in his ruined body" (1:265). But reconciliation soon takes place on the social level; Nikolai Fedorovich's last days are eased by Sofia Nikolavna's solicitude, and even the Kalmyk retreats, respecting Sofia Nikolavna's rights as a daughter. Nikolai Fedorovich's last words to his daughter are "I thank you," and his death is a model of joyful resignation (1:267).

Inserted in the midst of the account of her father's last days, in fact between his expression of gratitude and his actual death, there occurs the first mention of Sofia Nikolavna's second pregnancy. The location of this information makes explicit the new ascendancy of life over death and also suggests their complementarity; in fact, there seems to be a certain economy of life and death operating; Parasha's death is balanced by her mother's metaphorical rebirth and Nikolai Fedorovich's death by the conception and birth of a second child, with birth following death in each case, as one would expect in Aksakov's basically open-ended and optimistic universe.

The actual birth of the second child (historically, Aksakov himself) is deliberately isolated from the rest of the narrative, both in order to enhance its importance by increasing still more the inertia that must be overcome before it is reached, and also to avoid too evident a clash between the tone of the first part of the chapter, dominated by death, and that of its conclusion, which approaches comedy in tone. Aksakov separates these two parts of the chapter by inserting a subnarrative concerning a romance between a Russian officer and a Tatar princess. Connected to the main narrative only by the historian-narrator's assertion of its contemporaneity and contiguity with the primary plot, this rather obvious exercise in the oriental romantic tale à la Lermontov, beyond its function as a retarding device at a crucial juncture, also may echo the quasi-literary romances of preceding chapters. The tale of Timashev and Sal'me, despite the narrator's insistence on historicity, is in fact the most blatantly literary narrative in the whole of *Family Chronicle*, and serves to enhance by counterexample the actuality of events in the main narrative of the chapter and to suggest that experience has begun to develop beyond the forms and formulae of literary plots.[23] The digressive narrative also conceals a sharp reduction in the time scale; whereas the first part of the chapter covers some three years, the concluding section, dealing only with the birth of Sergei, treats a span of merely several days. The conclusion continues the pattern of health established at the time of Sofia Nikolavna's recovery, but elaborates the potential of this image, culminating in the doctor's comment on the newborn Sergei: "'What a fine, healthy fellow'" (1:277).

On the social level, an atmosphere of comedy, of social relations so harmonious that they almost become play, replaces the discord of the first part; the aura of comedy focuses primarily on the German Doctor Klous, who begins to function as the chief doctor only after the Timashev-Sal'me story.[24] Klous is described as an "extremely kind, intelligent German, at the same time extremely comical in appearance. Though not yet an old man, he wore a yellow wig. Everyone wondered where he could have gotten human hair of such an extraordinary color; his brows and the whites of his small hazel eyes were also yellowish, while his small round face was as red as a coal" (1:272–273). His name fortuitously suggests the Russian *kloun* (clown), and he is termed "quite a character" (*bol'shoi original*) (1:273). He is devoted to his patients and to children, addicted to the terms *varvar* and *varvarka* (literally, "barbarian") as expressions of endearment, and is comically, rather than viciously, tight with money, using second-hand cards when he is not playing for stakes. In addition to his appearance and behavior, Klous is also the center of comic suspense concerning the date of Sergei's entry into the world. First Klous's scheduled departure for Moscow is delayed by Sofia Nikolavna's failure to give birth on the anticipated date (15 September); then the birth occurs on the twentieth, while Klous is

23. Tolstoi, to whom the fifth chapter was read in the spring of 1856, readily perceived that in and of itself the tale resembled an exercise in an established form and advised Aksakov to omit it. Mashinskii, *S. T. Aksakov*, p. 391. Not being the foe of established forms that Tolstoi was, Aksakov kept the tale for his own artistic purposes.

24. We are moving closer to the present and to the larger world. In an 1818 letter, Aksakov's mother, Maria Nikolaevna, mentions consulting the actual Klous while she was in Moscow. Pavlov, ed., "Iz semeinoi perepiski starikov Aksakovykh," p. 104.

absent for a few hours. He returns to find Sofia Nikolavna in bed amidst all the accoutrements of a new mother, which he at first takes as some sort of joke at his expense:

> "Congratulate me, our friend," she said in a firm and resonant voice. "I am a mother. I have given birth to a son." The German, looking at Sofia Nikolavna's face, hearing her healthy voice, took the whole situation for a joke, a comedy. "That's enough joking with me, barbarian; I'm an old fox, you can't fool me," he said laughing. "Come get up; I've brought some new cards." (1:276–277)

On learning the truth and seeing the new baby, he reacts with a brief fit of comic rage:

> Klous lost his temper, became enraged, sprang away from the bed as if he were burnt, and began to shout: "What? Without me? I've stayed here an extra week and paid for it every day, and I'm not summoned!" . . . His red face turned crimson, his wig slipped to one side, his entire plump little figure was so funny that the new mother began to laugh. (1:277)

The comedy and health extend spatially, as had the disharmony that characterized Parasha's birth.[25] Stepan Mikhailovich, during Sofia Nikolavna's second pregnancy, had expected the worst (a girl) and gruffly dismissed Klous's predictions of a boy (1:273), lest speaking of it preclude such an outcome. He does have services conducted for Sofia Nikolavna's health, and selects the name for a possible grandson: Sergei, because Stepan Mikhailovich has heard that Saint Sergei of Radonezh' intercedes for mothers desiring sons and also because there has never been a Sergei in the Bagrov line (1:274). With the birth itself, joy and celebration spread in an ever-widening circle with the parents at its center. "Aleksei Stepanovich almost smothered the still damp doctor in his embraces; he had already embraced all the household and cried with all of them. Sofia Nikolavna . . . but I don't dare even to think of expressing her feelings in words. The were ecstasy, bliss which is given to few on earth and then only for a short time" (1:278). The elation spreads to the neighbors, who

25. The laughter surrounding the birth of Sergei and the general atmosphere of joy in the second part of chap. 5, contrasting so strongly with the dominance of death in the first part, may constitute a muted echo of an ancient pattern. In myth, laughter is often forbidden in the realm of death and sometimes accompanies actual birth and symbolic rebirth in initiation ceremonies. V. Ia. Propp, "Ritual'nyi smekh v fol'klore: Po povodu skazki o Nesmeiane," pp. 174–204.

"for some reason became joyful" (1:278), and to the servants, whose singing, dancing, and drinking in the courtyard form a chorus of celebration, which willingly falls silent at Klous's regretful request for quiet for the new mother. The moment of harmony extends as far as the environment, and "even the autumn day was as warm as summer" (1:279).

Finally and climactically, the circle of celebration widens to include Stepan Mikhailovich, informed by courier of the birth of a grandson. His reaction is in keeping with his characteristic mode of thinking; Sergei's name is immediately entered in the family tree. "Stepan Mikhailovich's first action was to cross himself. Then he nimbly sprang from his bed, went barefoot to the cabinet, quickly pulled out the family tree, familiar to us, took the quill from the inkwell, extended a line from the circle with the name 'Aleksei,' drew a circle at the end of the line, and in the center of it wrote: 'Sergei'" (1:297). Placed at the conclusion of the entire narrative (only the non-narrative *envoi* follows it), Stepan Mikhailovich's action stresses the importance of Sergei's birth both by position and by structure, which continues the expanding relay of the good news originating in Ufa and transmitted by courier to Stepan Mikhailovich. In what is for Aksakov a typical manner of rendering significant action, Stepan Mikhailovich's actions are broken down into microsegments, with the inscription of Sergei's name as their culmination.

Stepan Mikhailovich's predilection for the palpable and concrete dictates the registration of the birth in the family tree as the act necessary to make it real; without this visible representation of relationships, Sergei's contiguity with his ancestors and his continuation of their line would remain a pointlessly abstract metaphor. By representing relationships graphically through lines and circles, Stepan Mikhailovich immediately incorporates Sergei into a meaningful system. (Stepan Mikhailovich did not inscribe Parasha's name, out of male chauvinism no doubt, but the absence of any mention of her link with the family's continuity seems to contribute to the inevitable quality of her death.) Given the blurring of the distinctions between persons and things and between signifier and signified in Stepan Mikhailovich's act, and in his thinking in general, his tracing of Sergei's name is an affirmation of his grandson's existence and, more importantly, a definition of Sergei as a being who participates in and sums up those with whom he is linked.

Stepan Mikhailovich also defines time in terms of its relation to actual persons rather than abstractly. In his eyes, time is not indifferent, but like everything else in the traditional universe is organically linked with a specific group and place—the Bagrovs and Bagrovo. Without someone to continue it as a humanly meaningful category, Bagrovan time would simply cease. Sergei's birth and particularly its visual representation on paper means that the special category of time which began with Stepan Mikhailovich's founding of the Bagrovo mill in chapter 1 has avoided the danger of annihilation.

In using lines and words to construct a model of reality, Stepan Mikhailovich is making a schematic version of a chronicle, so his action is homologous to the author's. Thus *Family Chronicle* closes with a figuration of its construction. This concluding harmony is reinforced by the focus on both "authors" and on the final word, *Sergei*. At this moment the boundaries between the two authors are effaced, as their motives merge in designating Sergei as the end to which all things have been tending and the new beginning from which all things will proceed. Sergei is the end only in a relative sense, and the word which concludes the final action, the fifth chapter, and the entire text constitutes a supreme instance of Aksakov's avoidance of an absolute terminus to action, which can only begin, never really end.[26]

Sergei culminates one chronicle but contains *in potentia* an entire further narrative. The open-endedness of *Family Chronicle* (and of the majority of Aksakov's narratives) recalls the *letopis'* ("chronicle") of medieval Russia, which may only begin and never, in principle at least, conclude, for its entries are always causally connected with the present state of the polity and form an organic and meaningful history.[27] In Aksakov's narratives as well, such a link is always present, whether connected to the present state of the narrator (Aksakov himself, in those works where he does not conceal himself behind a pseudonymous narrator) or with the present condition of Russian culture as a whole (the literary biographies and memoirs). The assertion of this link of causality reciprocally enhances the fictive reality of both the

26. There had originally been a short epilogue relating the birth of a second grandson, Nikolai, and mentioning the old Bagrovs' deaths, but this was omitted, possibly on Tolstoi's advice, perhaps because Aksakov was already planning to treat these events in what would become *Years of Childhood*. See Mashinskii, *S. T. Aksakov*, p. 392.

27. Iu. M. Lotman, *Struktura khudozhestvennogo teksta*, pp. 259–260.

narrative and its narrator, the interplay of fact and fiction in Aksakov's works.

The further chronicle that the word *Sergei* implied was to become Aksakov's last major work, *Years of Childhood*, the link that would connect *Family Chronicle* with *Reminiscences,* which were published together in 1856. *Years of Childhood* was not to be a mere extension of *Family Chronicle,* however; rather, it was to become a work of a very different sort, in which Aksakov's fiction meets and solves new challenges.

6

The Worlds of Childhood: Growth and Perception

Aksakov's final major work, *Years of Childhood of Young Bagrov* (*Detskie gody Bagrova-vnuka*) (1857), which traces Sergei Bagrov's life from earliest perceptions to the eve of separation from his family and the start of study in Kazan, fills the chronological gap between the two major works published in 1856, *Family Chronicle* and *Reminiscences* (*Vospominaniia*). The three works form a sequence, but they are by no means merely convenient segments of a uniform narrative. *Reminiscences* represents a new departure for Aksakov in that it attempts to deal with character dynamically rather than statically. Both works on childhood focus on psychological change and development, that is, gradual modification of a single character, which was generally lacking in Aksakov's earlier works. Spatial oppositions, with contrasting social patterns, still play a role in *Reminiscences*, but these elements are now reduced to secondary importance, contingent on the capacity of a specific consciousness to perceive them; in *Years of Childhood* they play even less of a structural role. Subjective perception now becomes central, and the basic movement of the two works, especially *Reminiscences*, consists in the demythologizing of reality, as manifest in certain places.

The works on childhood represent an innovation in Aksakov's narration. Both are first-person narratives, thus bringing the narrated world and the narrator himself much closer in existential status; the interplay between the self who experienced the narrated events and the self-reflective persona of the narrative present tends to take the place of *Family Chronicle*'s tension between fiction and history, with its obvious allusions to prior forms.[1] Literary patterns play a reduced role in the childhood works, although their structural importance for *Reminiscences* is still considerable.

From the point of view of overall structure, *Reminiscences* and *Years of Childhood* can be seen as successive experiments with the same apparatus, but the two works differ considerably in specifics, as considering them by order of composition rather than their internal chronology makes apparent. As its title suggests, *Reminiscences* presents Aksakov's own experiences (his school days) as a more or less faithful record of the past. It has an affinity with Aksakov's literary memoirs and, like them, it is concerned in part with recording an aspect of an earlier period of Russian cultural life. Although *Reminiscences* gives much more relative weight to the observer than to the observed, Aksakov's use of actual names in *Reminiscences* suggests that the work is the closest of the trilogy to the particularity of historical fact. Aksakov's displeasure over critics' public identification of the Aksakovs in *Reminiscences* with the Bagrovs in *Family Chronicle* (an identification facilitated by the publication of the two works in a single volume in 1856) points to this essential difference. *Reminiscences*, unlike its companion works, was intended primarily as a record of a specific life, with less overt universal significance. Nevertheless, it does rely on patterns that could be called universal to provide a shape for individual experience.

Whether Aksakov chose to present a work on childhood as memoir or as something closer to fiction, there was ample precedent at the time for either approach; autobiographies such as those of A. T. Bolotov and S. P. Zhikharev included extensive treatment of childhood and education,[2] and on the more literary end of the spectrum, there were such works as *David Copperfield* and *Jane Eyre*, and Goncharov's fable of childhood, "Oblomov's Dream" ("Son Oblomova"), 1849, later incorporated into *Oblomov*. Tolstoi's *Childhood* (*Detstvo*), which appeared in the *Contemporary* (*Sovremennik*) in 1852, may have provided the most intriguing indication of the possibilities latent in the subject of childhood; in June 1854, with *Reminiscences* in progress,

1. See Stanzel, *Narrative Situations in the Novel*, pp. 60, 70, on the distinction between the experiencing and the narrating self in the first-person novel.

2. In 1853 and 1854 the *Muscovite* published Zhikharev's *A Student's Diary* (*Dnevnik studenta*) and excerpts from M. A. Dmitriev's *Bits from the Store of My Memory* (*Melochi iz zapasa moei pamiati*). Both are concerned with childhood, education, and cultural life in the early nineteenth century.

Aksakov informed Turgenev, "I am impatient to read Tolstoi's *Boyhood* (*Otrochestvo*) and I hope to have the pleasure soon."[3] The final volume of Tolstoi's trilogy, *Youth* (*Iunost'*), appeared in 1857, when Aksakov was at work on *Years of Childhood*. In the literature of the period dealing with childhood, the degree of fictionality was in large measure up to the author; Aksakov, while apparently seldom intentionally violating facts (unfortunately, his works are the only source on many matters pertaining to his childhood), is closer to the memoir in *Reminiscences* and to fiction in *Years of Childhood*, though in neither does he totally eliminate the link either with fact or with fiction.

Aksakov composed *Reminiscences* in the period from late 1853 to January 1855, approximately the same period in which he was writing the first three chapters of *Family Chronicle*; he intended that the two works be published in one volume.[4] The first chapter, "The Gymnasium" ("Gimnaziia"), was completed in early 1854, before he turned to *The History of My Acquaintance with Gogol*. "The Gymnasium" marked the first time that Aksakov had directed his memory and imagination to his own childhood, and the experience was not altogether pleasant; "The Gymnasium," he wrote his son Ivan, "I must confess, not only strongly occupies me, but even upsets me; the remembrance of childhood has so revived in me that its old vessel is on the point of bursting."[5] According to a letter to A. I. Panaev, Aksakov's childhood friend, who figures in *Reminiscences* and with whom Aksakov renewed friendship in 1855 after a forty-year hiatus, Aksakov completed his re-creation of "the golden age of our youth" on 15 January 1855;[6] the complete text appeared a year later together with *Family Chronicle* and several shorter works ("Memoir of A. S. Shishkov," "Acquaintance with Derzhavin"), which suggest both the terminus toward which *Reminiscences* tends—full integration into the cultural life of the city, St. Petersburg—and the work's affinity with memoir as a genre.

3. S. T. Aksakov to I. S. Turgenev, 11 June 1854. Maikov, ed., "Pis'ma Aksakovykh," no. 11, p. 16.
4. S. T. Aksakov to M. P. Pogodin, 29 November 1853. LL, Pogodin *fond*, section II, carton 1, storage unit 59, letter 8.
5. S. T. Aksakov to Ivan Aksakov, 13 December 1853. PD, *fond* 3, inventory 3, item 14, fol. 4.
6. S. T. Aksakov to A. I. Panaev, 29 January 1855. PD, *Razriad* I, inventory 1, item 10, fols. 13v and 15.

As a work concerned primarily with education, *Reminiscences* employs the traditional pattern of such works, whether fictional or memoiristic, namely, the incorporation of the self into society. When such incorporation is unsuccessful, the reason may be the psychological peculiarities or defects of the individual in question (as is the case with Oblomov, whose failure is so protracted it lasts his whole life), or the failure may be due to the shortcomings of a basically oppressive society to which the child is forced to conform to his detriment, as it is in Tolstoi's *Boyhood* and *Youth*. In *Reminiscences*, this process of integration is ultimately successful, but failure is at first a distinct possibility.

With the first sentence of *Reminiscences*, Sergei (I will refer to the central figure of both *Reminiscences* and *Years of Childhood* as Sergei, whether Aksakov or Bagrov, to distinguish the literary character from the mature Aksakov himself) arrives in Kazan in 1799, and the story of his education ends on the eve of his departure from Aksakovo for St. Petersburg some seven years later. The structure of *Reminiscences* is that of the cyclical journey, with change and development in the self rendered tangible by the hero's recurrent visits to places that remain constant. Sergei's development may be divided into two phases, each consisting of two chapters of the text. The first two chapters, "Gymnasium: First Period" and "A Year in the Country" ("Gimnaziia: Period pervyi" and "God v derevne") involve two journeys between Aksakovo and Kazan, while the last two chapters, "Gymnasium: Second Period" and "University" ("Gimnaziia: Period vtoroi"; "Universitet"), mainly set in Kazan, are also framed by journeys to Aksakovo. The first two chapters recount Sergei's near failure to begin the process of acculturation; the second two record his ultimately successful incorporation into student life, and by implication into the larger society of the adult, educated, and Europeanized Russian gentry, for which his education is the necessary preparation.

In the first half of *Reminiscences* the childhood world of Aksakovo contrasts with the city of Kazan as heaven contrasts with hell. Aksakov employs more emphatic and consistent poetic or literary imagery in the first two chapters than in the concluding two; as might be expected, given Sergei's level of development, the imagery of the first two chapters often suggests a fairy tale, with Sergei the helpless and abandoned victim of overwhelmingly powerful hostile forces. Sergei's subsequent maturation is in part signaled by the disappearance of these infantile categories of perception.

As Aksakov frequently does in his works, he begins *Reminiscences* with incidents which, *in parvis*, serve as emblems of the entire work, adumbrating the themes and patterns of the rest of the narrative. In this instance, Sergei's initial trip to Kazan with his parents, a trip that the narrator says "determined my whole future,"[7] serves this function. Just as the entire text is built around the two foci of Aksakovo and Kazan, the bipolar nature of Sergei's experiences throughout the book is suggested by two contrasting incidents. Upon arrival in Kazan in the dead of winter, Sergei gets a severe chill and is put to bed next to his mother, where "snuggled up to my mother's heart and covered . . . with a fox and satin cape [*salop*] which had been part of my mother's dowry, I became warm, fell asleep, and awoke the next day quite hale" (2:7). This world of warmth, sleep, and maternal proximity, with its suggestions of birth and infancy is rudely, if only temporarily, shattered by an irruption of the adult world and Sergei's first, unwilling entrance into urban society. Sergei is "plucked from the bliss of childish sleep" (2:8) by the servants, dressed, and taken in the dark to a destination unknown to him (actually to the home of the Kniazheviches, friends of his parents). There Sergei is thrust into the archetypically adult space, the drawing room:

> The blaze of candles and the loud talk so confused me that I stopped at the door petrified. My father saw me first and said: "Well, here's the recruit." I became even more confused. "Forehead!" uttered someone's thundering voice and a man of enormous height rose from a chair and started toward me. I took such fright, for I understood the awful meaning of that word, that, almost beside myself, I began to run away. (2:8–9)

The apparent aggression with which Sergei is met is completely unrelated to his prior experience, as is the danger of sudden and inappropriate maturation: the command, "Forehead" (*lob*), was given to military recruits, whose forelocks were shaven, and since Sergei is a *dvorianin*, and such a command was reserved for

---

7. Aksakov, *Reminiscences* (*Vospominaniia*), in *Sobranie sochinenii*, 2:8.

peasant conscripts, it is doubly inappropriate. The shock of this threatening experience at the threshold of an adult space is dispelled only by his parents' explanation that the man is a family friend, and the incident a joke. Once Sergei can relate the present situation to prior experience, he begins to overcome his fear; he even recalls that his host's children had once taught him how to crack walnuts with his forehead, so that even the physical aspect of the recent threat is assimilated to childhood experiences and neutralized. Nevertheless, the process of education and maturation is set in motion on this trip to Kazan, for enrollment in the Kazan gymnasium is first discussed by Sergei's parents at this time.

With the second journey to Kazan in the winter of the following year, the easily dispelled fears of the first trip are transformed into a more painful and permanent reality. Examined and accepted by the gymnasium, Sergei experiences the trauma of separation from the central figure of his life to this point, his mother. On his first day as a state-supported student (viewed by the service-oriented Russian educational bureaucracy as a category analogous to military service) Sergei undergoes the external forms of initiation, being dressed in a quasi-military uniform and having his hair, if not shaven off, at least well cropped, in partial fulfillment of Kniazhevich's prophetic threat (2:18). The sight of her transformed son, whom she at first does not recognize, causes Sergei's mother to faint. The separation of mother and son is prolonged and painful for both, with a surreptitious departure and sudden, repentant return by Maria Nikolavna (as she is called in *Reminiscences*) before her final withdrawal. With her ultimate departure, the gymnasium assumes for Sergei its final configuration of a fearsome fairy-tale castle in which he will be a helpless prisoner, overwhelmed by the scale of the building:

> Standing on a hill, the enormous white building of the gymnasium, with its bright green roof and its cupola, now struck my eyes and affected me as if I had never seen it before. It seemed to me a terrible enchanted castle (of which I had read in books), a prison, in which I would be a prisoner in fetters. The enormous door between columns on the high porch was opened by an old veteran and, it seemed, swallowed me up; two broad stairways . . . the shouts and bustle of confused voices . . .—all this I saw, heard, and understood for the first time. (2:24)

The enormous size of the building, like Kniazhevich's height in the recruitment incident, expresses and inversely projects Sergei's sense of his own smallness and helplessness. In the world of a child, large size is easily equated with hostility and hyperbolic disparities in size and power, like the contrast between the hero and villains in a fairy tale. Every castle requires an ogre, and every jail a jailer; this function is assumed by the chief inspector (*glavnyi nadziratel'*), Kamashev, who becomes Sergei's persecutor and takes on features of an omnipotent and omnipresent demon in Sergei's eyes.

Sergei's response to his infernal environment is in perfect accord with his initial perception. As a powerless victim of obscure and inhuman forces, he can escape only through the self-annihilation of psychosomatic illness or through nostalgia, specifically for Aksakovo, which Sergei recalls as "a promised land" (*obetovannyi krai*) (2:31). Both of these defenses (and they are at times combined) seek to repeal the present and abolish the future; the interrelation of these two patterns of defense is made clear by the causal role of his memories of Aksakovo in Sergei's illnesses (2:33). Although this seems at first glance to be the inverse of Aksakov's partiality for physical stimuli as causes of emotional states and changes of condition, memory (and a physical attack) depends on Sergei's realization of the identity of some facet of the present and a perception in the past, which is then evoked with such strength and detail that the present is obliterated and the change in his situation denied:

> Some tone of a voice, probably similar to one I had heard before, a band of sunlight in the window or on the wall, just like one that had at one time illuminated objects known and dear to me, a fly buzzing and beating on the window glass, which I had often absorbed myself in watching as a child— suddenly, for a moment imperceptible to the consciousness, such things would summon forth the forgotten past and shake my strained nerves. . . . There caught my eye a simple wooden table, which previously I had probably seen many times without noticing it, but now it was newly scraped and appeared unusually clean and white: in one second there appeared before me a lindenwood table of the same type, always sparkling white and smooth, which belonged at one time to my grandmother and later stood in my aunt's room; in it were kept various trifles valuable for a child: packets

of pumpkin, watermelon, and melon seeds, from which my
aunt made marvelous little baskets and trays; little sacks of
carob seeds, of crayfish gizzard-stones, and most of all,
a large needle-case, in which, along with needles, there were
kept fishhooks, once in a great while issued to me by Grandmother; all this, I used at one time to inspect with excitement, with intense curiosity, hardly taking a breath. . . . I was
struck by the similarity of these tables, the past flashed
brightly, came to life before me—my heart stopped, and a strong
attack ensued. (2:34)

The objects of memory are present to Sergei in greater immediacy, abundance, and richness of detail than are the features of
his current environment, which seems to lack any qualities not
pertinent to its role as a prison. The suppression of detail in
regard to the gymnasium depends on its unequivocal definition
as a prison (what else need one know about it?) and is of course a
projection of Sergei's emotional state of depression; in contrast,
the variety and vitality of the remembered objects suggest where
Sergei's inner life still has its focus. The use of catalogue and
retardation, of richness of detail, is a characteristically Aksakovian means of creating value. Sergei's eventual deliverance from
the gymnasium also suggests a fairy-tale rescue; his mother, upon
learning of his illness, sets out for Kazan during the spring thaws.
The famous passage describing her crossing of the Kama hours
before the breakup of the ice suggests the perilous rescues of
fairy tale or melodrama. Upon arrival in Kazan she engages in
"open warfare" (2:43) with Kamashev over her son and finally
obtains Sergei's leave for a year on grounds of illness (in part
feigned). Sergei views withdrawal from the gymnasium as "liberation from a stone prison" (2:48).

Sergei's escape from the gymnasium and return to the village
takes the form of a wish-fulfilling regression, a journey backward
in time in which the phantasms of memory that had sustained
Sergei in Kazan are resurrected in ever greater numbers and with
ever greater strength. Thus Sergei's first sight upon leaving the
infirmary is of the means of conveyance back to Aksakovo, a metonymic link with his promised land: "I cried out with joyful
surprise: at the door stood our country carriage, hitched to four
of our home-bred horses; on the box sat a familiar coachman, and
on a saddle horse, a postilion even better known, who also used
to get me worms for fishing" (2:51). The actual journey home

begins on 19 May with spring in full flower; Sergei's two trips to Kazan both took place in winter, the time of death. The trip is bathed in an aura of beauty, joy, freedom, and bliss at reunion with Maria Nikolavna. The approach to Aksakovo comes in the early morning, the time of daily reawakening and rebirth; Sergei awakens at the edge of the estate (reversing the unpleasant arousal he experienced at the beginning of his life in Kazan). The first sight of Aksakovo overwhelms him:

> Four versts from Aksakovo, on the very boundary of our property, I awoke, just as if someone had awakened me. . . . I constantly asked the coachman: "Can you see the village?" And when at last he said . . . "There's our Aksakovo, as if on the palm of your hand"—I began to beg my mother so urgently that she could not refuse and permitted me to sit on the box with the coachman. I will not attempt to transmit what my heart felt when I caught sight of my dear Aksakovo! There are no words in human language for the expression of such feelings! (2:35–36)

The sight of Aksakovo is followed by Sergei's return to the fold of his family and the entire household, completing his reentry into the resurrected past.

In the second chapter of *Reminiscences*, "A Year in the Country," Sergei's life in his paradise regained is devoted to the timeless pursuits (*okhoty*) of country life, notably fishing, hunting (as an observer), falconry, mushrooming. Without the knowledge and even against the orders of his mother, who, city born and bred, disapproves, Sergei listens to the fairy tales at the heart of country life and observes the peasants' year-end festivities (*sviatki*), with mummery, song, dance, and even theatricals of a sort (2: 70–71).

However, in the cyclical structure of *Reminiscences*, the past in the final analysis remains the past. Sergei eventually begins to perceive the mutability even in Aksakovo and to become aware both of conflicts within his family and of the limitations of country existence. Consequently, returning to school in Kazan no longer seems a fate worse than death: "I . . . began to look into my surroundings with greater attention, began to understand things I had not noticed before; . . . after several months, life in Aksakovo no longer seemed to me to be the former bright paradise, and a second entrance into the gymnasium—especially as a tuition-paying student—did not seem a terrifying event" (2:73).

"A Year in the Country" closes with Sergei's departure for Kazan, and the concluding paragraph reverses the ceremony of arrival at the conclusion of the first chapter: "The same capacious carriage, hitched to the same six-in-hand, with the same coachman and postilion, stood at the porch; the same crowd of house servants and peasants assembled to see the masters off; . . . I leaned out of the window and looked at dear Aksakovo until it disappeared from view, and quiet tears trickled down my cheeks" (2:78). The lexical insistence on identity (in Russian: *ta zhe prostornaia kareta, tem zhe shesterikom, s tem zhe kucherom*, etc.) and the inversion of Sergei's approach of Aksakovo a year earlier underlines the cyclical nature of experience throughout *Reminiscences*, as well as his growth through this very cycle. The tone of quiet resignation suggests a realization on Sergei's part that the past is indeed the past, that it has its value as memory but that the nostalgic reversal of time is ultimately impossible—a theme that would later become central in the works of Vladimir Nabokov.

Upon his return to Kazan, Sergei, now eleven, is ready to accept a new life; the gymnasium becomes a new society into which he enters, rather than a prison from which he seeks only to escape: "At last I saw the gymnasium, at one time frightening and repulsive to me, and I looked at it without fear and without any unpleasant feeling. I was very encouraged by this" (2:81). The third and fourth chapters of *Reminiscences*, "Gymnasium; Second Period" and "University," are almost entirely concerned with Sergei's socialization and acculturation and are much closer to Aksakov's memoirs of literary figures. As might be expected from Aksakov's method of delineating character in his literary memoirs and in *Family Chronicle*, this process is described primarily in terms of the inception of lifelong passions, specifically those passions which are most explicitly social and most intimately connected with the urban, Europeanized life of the Russian nobility, particularly literature and theater. In "Gymnasium: Second Period," these passions receive formal confirmation. Sergei's taste in literature undergoes molding by his teacher of Russian literature, N. M. Ibragimov, whom Aksakov accords great significance in the formation of his literary outlook (2:86), and by his tutor and guardian (later brother-in-law) G. I. Kartashevskii, who orders books for Sergei and directs his reading both in Russian and French (2:100). Sergei's interest in the theater is abetted by his first attendance at a real theater; a moment of initiation similar to those in Aksakov's literary memoirs, especially of Shchepkin, takes place. "These two productions had almost the same effect on me as hunting with a gun . . . reality far exceeded my previous notions. I dreamed both night and day of the performances I had seen and became so distracted that I absolutely could not apply myself to my studies" (2:119). In the final chapter, "University" (the Kazan gymnasium was in part reorganized as a university in 1804), these nascent interests find expression on the plane of action, marking Sergei's attainment of full development (if not complete adulthood) within the context of his schooling. Sergei and his friends the Panaev brothers start amateur theatricals (2:136). In the field of literature, Sergei's passion meets with general success; becoming a confirmed Shishkovite after a brief attraction to Karamzinian Sentimentalism, Sergei, in collaboration with Aleksandr Panaev, begins issuing a handwritten journal, *Journal of Our Activities* (*Zhurnal nashikh zaniatii*). In addition, a circle (*kruzhok*), the other sine qua non of expressions of Russian literary and cultural solidarity, is founded, headed by Ibragimov, with Sergei, the Panaevs, and others attending the Saturday meetings. Aksakov still considered himself a member of the Society of Lovers of Russian Letters of Kazan University (*Obshchestvo liubitelei rossiiskoi slovesnosti pri Kazanskom universitete*) at the time of the writing of *Reminiscences*.

Sergei attains independence during his second stay in the Kazan gymnasium in social terms as well. At first he rooms with and is looked after by Kartashevskii, a mathematics teacher at Kazan, who functions in loco parentis in the full sense of the term, undertaking Sergei's mental and moral training. In the final chapter, however, dissension between tutor and pupil breaks out; Sergei, preferring his age-mates and his own interests over the claims of his surrogate parent, elects to remain in town to work on a model theater rather than to accompany Kartashevskii on an excursion to the countryside, an obvious withdrawal from pastoral. Finally, Sergei rents quarters for himself and "for the first time began to live an independent and personal life" (2:147). This new, independent life serves as a prelude to his final break with the university and (after a brief return to Aksakovo) his departure for an adult existence in the center of social and cultural life, St. Petersburg; *Reminiscences* ends, in a typically Ak-

sakovian manner, on the eve of this new journey. With the pros-
pect of the assumption of a truly adult role imminent, the years
of schooling become an exemplary time, a "golden time" of fond
memory set off from subsequent experience and constituting an
ideal microcosmic society closer to perfection than the social
reality encountered outside the gymnasium in later years:

> Farewell, first, unreturnable years of ardent, mistaken, sense-
> less, yet pure and noble youth! Neither the world nor fam-
> ily life with all their petty cares have yet dulled your clarity!
> The walls of the gymnasium and university, my comrades—
> this formed for me a complete world. . . . There reigned utter
> contempt for everything low and base, for all self-profiting
> calculations and advantages, for all worldly wisdom—and deep
> respect for everything honest and lofty, even if it be sense-
> less. (2:162)

As an indication of the level of maturity attained by Sergei at
the conclusion of his school years, we might refer back briefly to
a passage in chapter 1, in which nostalgia for childhood, that is,
early childhood, is expressed: "Oh, where are you, magical world,
the Sheherazade of human life, which adults often treat so un-
kindly and crudely, destroying its enchantment with jokes and
premature words. You, golden age of childish happiness, the
memory of which so sweetly and so sadly excites the soul of an
old man!" (2:12–13). Aksakov uses the term *magical* (*volsheb-
nyi*), which also denotes the largest and most typical category
(*volshebnye skazki*) of Russian fairy tales.[8] The reference to
Sheherazade also emphasizes the function of early childhood for
later life: a realm of enchantment, the source of innumerable
narratives or scenarios which provide a perpetually available escape from the stultifying round of adult existence. Given Aksakov's own retreat into nostalgic narrative in his later years, the
emphasis on the "tale" of childhood in this passage has implications beyond the immediate context. This magical world is of
course located in the village, and the suggestions of fairy tale
echo Sergei's perceptions of the world in his early years. The two
passages apostrophizing two stages of childhood are presented
from the point of view of the mature author and suggest both the

---

8. The allusion to Sheherazade is particularly apt. The *Arabian Nights*, like
Sheherazade's life, depends on endless narration; the remembered "tales" of
childhood are for Aksakov necessary to real life. See Tzvetan Todorov, "Narrative
Men," pp. 66–79.

stages of development the individual goes through and their significance as constituents of the personality; each is necessary,
yet neither can be a complete end in itself, as the personality,
like life itself, constantly progresses.

Reminiscences is Aksakov's most overtly nostalgic work, bor-
dering at time on the sentimental in its treatment of the personal
past. Aksakov's next (and last) major work, Years of Childhood,
continues the exploration of childhood experience begun in
Reminiscences, but paradoxically generalizes such experience
into a universally valid "prehistory" of the self.

Aksakov first mentions what would develop into Years of
Childhood in his programmatic letter to Pogodin in the autumn
of 1853. However, nothing treating Aksakov's early childhood
was written until after the completion of both Reminiscences
and Family Chronicle in 1856. According to Aksakov's letters,
Years of Childhood was composed between 18 October 1856 and
19 June 1857, a remarkably short interval of time, considering
both the length of the work (it is Aksakov's longest) and the
usually lengthy gestation period that most of Aksakov's works
required.[9] Aksakov doubtless had a more definite and unified
concept of the work as a whole before he began dictation than
was the case with many previous works, and one might also
suspect that because it was Aksakov's most personal and intimate work, it had a more insistent claim on its author's attention
and creative powers. The writing also was hastened by the fact
that he was not engaged in several projects simultaneously during the composition of Years of Childhood, as had often been
true in previous years. This coherence of conception and concentration of effort are reflected in the text itself, which is much
less clearly segmented than its two immediate predecessors and
which approaches a continuum in its imagery and themes.

Information on the writing of Years of Childhood from Aksakov's letters or other sources is scanty, even for Aksakov; references to it date mainly from the initial period (late 1856) or from
the late spring and early summer of 1857, when the text was
virtually completed and one section (the three chapters dealing
with Stepan Mikhailovich's death) had already been earmarked

9. S. T. Aksakov to I. Aksakov, 17 June 1857. PD, fond 3, inventory 3, item 14,
fol. 144v. Also S. T. Aksakov to M. P. Pogodin, 22 June 1857. LL, Pogodin fond,
section II, carton 1, item 63, letter 10.

for publication in *Russian Conversation* (*Russkaia beseda*). However, Aksakov's statements on his work give some indication of his intentions and attitudes toward his final and perhaps most ambitious undertaking.

From the start, Aksakov saw his work as a new departure and also his crowning achievement; as he wrote Ivan, "If strength and talent suffice, a remarkable and new book may result."[10] These inner hopes were balanced by proportional apprehension, probably stronger than with any earlier work, both over his own ability to achieve his ends and over the reception of the book by a public which might fail to perceive it in the way the author intended. Perhaps in part to allay his misgivings, Aksakov refers to his new work in its early stages as a children's book (the dedication to his granddaughter Olga remains as a reflection of this). However, given Aksakov's penchant for creative fusion of genres and for distinguishing a fictive and a real audience, one might wonder to what degree *Years of Childhood* was ever meant to be a work exclusively addressed to children and to what degree it presupposed a reader who could adopt the point of view of a child. In a letter to Turgenev from November 1856 (while the work was still in its early stages), Aksakov puts even his child-reader fairly close to adulthood, and matters of structure and style loom as large as those pertaining directly to audience:

> I am occupied at present with a project on which I would like your opinion. I'm afraid—have I hit the right tone or is it necessary to change the devices: I'm writing a book for children, not little ones of course, but those around twelve. I couldn't think of anything better than to write the history of a child, beginning with the fabulous through to the historical, and taking him through all the impressions of life and nature, primarily country life. . . . Of course, there's no shamming to suit a child and no moralizing. I feel that it's possible to accomplish something significant, but I don't dare hope for a successful outcome.[11]

Even while characterizing his new work as a book for children, Aksakov clearly has an investigation of human development, and an audience beyond children, in mind.

10. S. T. Aksakov to I. Aksakov, 29 October 1856. LL, *fond* 3, carton 3, item 22d.
11. S. T. Aksakov to I. S. Turgenev, 16 November 1856. Maikov, ed., "Pis'ma Aksakovykh," no. 12, pp. 590–591.

Although in his comments to Turgenev Aksakov treats his plan somewhat impersonally, focusing on "devices" and audience, that is, on the rhetorical aspects of the work, the exemplary childhood in question was of course his own, and the process of "rummaging about in the storeroom of childhood memories"[12] did not always lead smoothly to the embodiment of those memories in a verbal medium. The frequent disparity between the evanescent, mute brilliance of things remembered and their expression in words seems to have disturbed Aksakov considerably during the composition of Years of Childhood, attesting to the greater psychological intimacy the work had for its author compared to his previous works:

> The picture of the past has just arisen in my mind's eye with all its details and vitality of hue, when guests start to arrive and often a sentence breaks off in the middle of a word. One day I'll write a few lines, another day there is time, but nothing comes. Furthermore, a picture, summoned up from the depths of inmost recollections, and not cloaked at once in words, definitely loses unity, wholeness, and originality of presentation; others, perhaps, wouldn't notice this, but I know it very well.[13]

Although the comparison of writing and painting may in part be suggested in this case by the profession of Aksakov's correspondent (Trutovskii was an artist), the idea of the presentation of the past as pictures, visually perceptible constructs, occurs at the beginning of Years of Childhood, where earliest impressions are referred to as a series of old, faded paintings.[14] It may well have been the case that Aksakov's memory was primarily visual. In Years of Childhood, the act of perception, particularly visual perception, becomes a central concern.

Although we know from entries in Tolstoi's diary that parts of Years of Childhood were read to him at the Aksakovs' in January of 1857 (by Sergei Timofeevich himself or by Konstantin, who often read for his father),[15] Aksakov scarcely mentions his book

12. S. T. Aksakov to I. Aksakov, 15 October 1856. LL, *fond* 3, carton 3, item 22d.

13. Letter of S. T. Aksakov to K. A. Trutovskii, 7 January 1857. Trutovskii, "Vospominaniia o S. T. Aksakove," no. 3, p. 134.

14. A possible parodic echo of this device, with slides substituted for paintings in the metaphor, may be seen in Vladimir Nabokov's *Speak, Memory*, p. 153.

15. L. N. Tolstoi, *Polnoe sobranie sochinenii*, 47:112. The diary entry for 20–25 January 1857 includes the comment: "A reading at S. T. Aksakov's. Childhood, charming."

again in extant letters until the spring of 1857, when it was nearly completed. In a May letter to his friend M. A. Maksimovich, Aksakov still expresses misgivings over the existence of an audience properly disposed for his new work, but now clearly shifts his attention to his real audience, the adult reader receptive to a work dealing with the life of a child in large part from the point of view of the child:

> I read some to all of our friends and acquaintances, and they assure me that this is better than everything else I've written. I think that's so in some parts, but I am still not entirely convinced of the quality of the whole composition, and quite sure that it cannot elicit the general sympathy that *Chronicle* and *Reminiscences* elicited. The life of man in a child will not be intelligible to all, and the details of the narrative will seem petty and insignificant to many.[16]

Finally, Aksakov announced to his son Ivan and to others that his work was complete. Although he still felt the need for revisions because his conception of the work had changed somewhat in the course of writing it, Aksakov felt the end of his efforts keenly, as he reported to Iurii Samarin:

> I finished my work the nineteenth of June—and since then I haven't stopped grieving over it. Something has gone, something is missing! This is my last *intimate* work. I don't know whether there has been expressed in it that intimacy which disposes readers of *Chronicle* to me; but much of my soul has been placed, so to speak, in the stories of my childhood. If the readers don't sense that, it means that the expression has not transmitted the feeling.[17]

This sense of intimacy may have been what Aksakov had in mind in his earlier references to his work as a children's book, and he sought in several ways to ensure that his readers would be disposed to intimacy; in particular, he stresses the actuality and authenticity of the text in order to establish the reality of the narrating self. As with the *envoi* to *Family Chronicle*, Aksakov resorts to "definitions" of the text as a means of guaranteeing the proper perception and response. Instead of the deliberate and pronounced ambiguities that surrounded the status of the text of *Family Chronicle*, however, Aksakov strives to efface the

16. S. T. Aksakov to M. A. Maksimovich, 3 May 1856. In S. Ponomarev, ed., "Iz pisem k M. A. Maksimovichu: Pis'ma S. T. Aksakova," p. 840.

17. S. T. Aksakov to Iu. F. Samarin, 5 July 1857. PD, *fond* 3, inventory 11, item 15, fol. 31–31v.

authorial presence in *Years of Childhood*, increasing the immediacy between the reader and the central character/narrator.

In the forward to the three chapters published in *Russian Conversation* in 1857—the three chapters were the pivotal ones concerning Stepan Mikhailovich's death: "Return to City Life in Ufa," "Trip to Bagrovo in Winter," and "Bagrovo in Winter"— and also in the notice to readers preceding the complete edition, Aksakov notes that *Years of Childhood* continues the events of the narrative of *Family Chronicle* but differs from the preceding text in important ways. He reports that he wrote *Family Chronicle* "in accord with the accounts of the Bagrov family" ("napisal po rasskazam gg. Bagrovykh") (1:285), suggesting simultaneously the use of historical sources (*rasskazam*) and the presence of an author who has selected and shaped this raw material (*napisal*). With *Years of Childhood* the scope for creative authorial activity is considerably reduced:

> Zapisal ego rasskazy s vozmozhnoiu tochnost'iu. (1:285)
> (Notice in first edition of *Years of Childhood*)
>
> I wrote down his tales with all possible exactitude.
>
> Rasskazy zapisany mnoiu s sovershennoiu tochnost'iu. (1:625)
> (Notice in *Russian Conversation*)
>
> The tales have been written down by me with complete exactitude.

The author is now little more than a stenographer, directly recording an individual's account; both notices use forms of *zapisat'* ("to write down," "copy down"), suggesting the mechanical taking of notes, a shade of meaning which the neutral perfective *napisat'*, used to describe authorial activity in *Family Chronicle*, lacks. (Note also the use of the past passive participle in the *Russian Conversation* version, reducing authorial activity even further). Thus Aksakov tries to link the narrative as much as possible with the "real" person who experienced it and has related it—not the writer Aksakov, but Bagrov.

For similar purposes, metaphors of literary artifice, with their implication of authorial control, are reduced and relegated to a single sentence; even this sentence refers to the elder Bagrovs, suggesting that the literary modes of organizing and relating experience, familiar from *Family Chronicle* and adequate to its world of time past, recede irrevocably into that past along with its actors or characters. "The former persons of *Chronicle* appear again on the stage, and the older ones, that is Grandfather and Grandmother, quit it forever in the course of the tale" (1:285). The experience of childhood in *Years of Childhood* is "new" (even if universal) and free from any preexisting literary schema or pattern. The reader must discard any ready-made expectations of a certain sort of order; in fact, as we shall see, *Years of Childhood* does use definite literary patterns, but the reader has been carefully prepared to ignore this.

All of Aksakov's preliminary definitions of the text seek to persuade the reader that *Years of Childhood* has undergone minimal shaping by the author, and the text itself seems to verify this. Aksakov's "priming" of the reader of *Years of Childhood* comes before the text opens, the only possible point, given the extreme open-endedness of an account of childhood, while *Family Chronicle* has both preceding and concluding statements, suggesting a greater degree of historical "boundedness."

In place of the fragmented world of *Family Chronicle*, with its multiplicity of genres or approximated genres and its interplay of history and fiction, *Years of Childhood* presents a uniform and continuous narrative reflecting the psychological unity and continuity of the central figure—the few discontinuities that do occur are psychologically motivated. The first-person recollection of individual development and the mode of narration are thus complementary; the creation of a single, coherent universe depends on and expresses a single voice.

This sustaining narrative voice in *Years of Childhood* is established in the Introduction (Vstuplenie), the function of which is to guarantee the reliability of the narrator's memory, since all events in the text must be contained by that memory. Aksakov achieves this through the illogical but artistically effective means of intensification by repetition, namely, by the presentation of remembering the act of remembering (1:287). The reader is led to accept the act of memory on the primary level of discourse because the act remembered is itself of the same structure. That this double memory as such is more important than its content at this point in the text is indicated by the omission from the final text of various details which are included in the manuscript; Sergei recalls communicating memories of even earlier events: "At three or four, I would recount to those around me that I remembered how I would be taken from my wet nurse, how she would worry about me, how she would watch me, having hidden behind the door or the bedcurtains of my bed, how one time she quietly crept up to me, thinking that I was asleep, and kissed my hands."[18] In the final text, in a move hardly typical of Aksakov, the sentence is ended after "wet nurse" (1:287). Since the content of the memory is deleted, we may suppose that Aksakov is concerned with establishing only the validity of the faculty of memory itself.

Having affirmed the reliability of the basic mechanism of the text, Aksakov can elaborate the world in all its detail. However, he does not merely record facts or indulge in nostalgia for its own sake, but shapes experience according to a structure that underlies *Years of Childhood*. It is here that the literary aspects of the work assert themselves, despite the careful camouflage and subterfuge. In *Reminiscences*, Aksakov had already experimented with the basic pattern of progress from a state of inadequacy or immaturity to one of sufficiency, that is, from nonbeing to being; there his pattern of movement was presented primarily in social terms, in terms of growth from the inferiority of childhood to the equality of adulthood. *Years of Childhood* focuses on an earlier and more basic variant of the same process, the progress from infancy to childhood, which involves profound perceptual and psychological changes.

Thus both of Aksakov's books on childhood involve what may in a very broad sense be termed education, or enlightenment. Perhaps adhering to his eighteenth-century background, Aksakov sees the process of mental and social development as inevitable, and its end, the attainment of a more mature state, as basically desirable. In both works Aksakov gives little indication of total subscription to the Rousseauistic or Romantic view of childhood as a condition inherently superior to adulthood, as is the case in Tolstoi's trilogy or (perhaps ironically) in Goncharov. Childhood for Aksakov may have its advantages, such as innocence and freshness of perception, and may assume at times the status of a golden age from the viewpoint of the later adult, but it has its compensating disadvantages, such as ignorance, susceptibility to fear and anguish, and dependence, as well.

Unlike *Reminiscences*, which is concerned almost exclusively with its central character's maturation into an adult of a given

18. LL, *fond* 3, carton 2, storage unit 2, fol. 1.

historical society, *Years of Childhood* is multidimensional, dealing with several interrelated aspects of the development of the personality. As Aksakov stated to Turgenev, he desired to trace the process of growth from the "prehistoric" infant into a full, though not mature, human being; *Years of Childhood* ends at the point when the "historic," the accommodation of the individual to a specific time and society, begins to become dominant; specifically, it ends on the eve of the trip to Kazan with which *Reminiscences* opens. The diversity of aspects of development makes *Years of Childhood* a more varied work, but by the same token renders it less amenable to summary and discussion, both because of the implicit interdependence of various components of the personality at different stages of development and because of the importance of the context of a given incident and its place in the overall sequence of the narrative. The importance of narrative order as a function of personal development can also be seen in the role of space in the work; not only are places in *Years of Childhood* dependent, to a greater degree than was the case in *Reminiscences*, on Sergei's consciousness for their meaning and value, but the very process of travel, of movement from one space to another, assumes much greater significance, and it is often in the process of travel itself that Sergei undergoes change.

Although he does not often make explicit connections between a given incident in Sergei's experience and later ones that are thematically related to it (to do so would tend to destroy the immediacy of narration), Aksakov deals in the main with three primary factors in Sergei's personal development. Most incidents in the text are relevant to at least one of these factors, and occasionally to more than one. Without drawing overly strict boundaries, we can distinguish the following principal areas of concern: (1) perceptual development, the object of which is physical reality per se, the constants of time and space, or later on, the world of nature; (2) social or human development, involving awareness of the constants of human reality, in particular, time, as it is pertinent to human existence and manifest in birth and death; and (3) ethical development, the elaboration of moral concepts and precepts which are the necessary precondition for life in a given society. Obviously, these areas are successively more restricted in domain and also successively more complex and sophisticated, so that even though these various aspects of growth are integrated into a continuous spectrum of development, a certain predominance of one aspect or another in different sections of the text is discernible.

Perceptual development, the sine qua non, is most prominent at the beginning of the text, while ethical development becomes increasingly important toward the end; however, neither is completely restricted to one period of Sergei's life. The second area, awareness of the givens of human existence, is perhaps the most problematical for the child, and for that reason is perhaps the most complex and pervasive theme; it receives its fullest treatment at the center of the text, implying its crucial role in humanization, but it figures significantly at other points as well. Although in the following, we shall discuss perception and then turn to an examination of moral development in chapter 7, it should be stressed that this is an artificial, if heuristically necessary procedure; in the actual text, since themes are interwoven, the effect is much more one of diffuse and gradual increment, even geological accretion. This is of course one of Aksakov's principal points—human growth is just that, growth, a slow process with episodes of more intense change in a given area, but with no total breaks or discontinuities. Even a crucial incident, such as contact with death, can be comprehended only if the personality is sufficiently developed to be receptive to the situation; part of the function of Sergei's little sister throughout the text, most notably in the presence of death, is to serve as a personality who is *not* ready to grasp what Sergei comprehends.

Years of Childhood begins with a chapter that is in principle opposed to all the others, as suggested by its title "Fragmentary Recollections" ("Otryvochnye vospominaniia") and its internal discontinuities—temporal, spatial, and psychological. The chapter serves as the starting point of the overall process of development or journey to awareness and focuses on the first steps: spatial and temporal organization of reality by the subjective consciousness. It does not begin with the subject's birth (with which *Family Chronicle* concluded and which presumably is below the lower threshold of personal memory); instead it begins with an analogue of birth, the inception of consciousness, without which, given the status of *Years of Childhood* as a narrative of remembered experience, the text itself could not exist. The notion of an initial primordial condition, of a state of chaos and inertia from which the previously nonreflective individual begins to construct order and impose it on his environment, is suggested by the dominant metaphor of the first chapter, that of pictures or paintings (*kartiny*) which reduce reality to a series of discrete and disjunct surfaces, one-dimensional, bounded in space and lacking any real sequence, that is, unconnected in time. Needless to say, these pictures are also alien to the passive observer, who remains aloof and uninvolved. Aksakov had equated memory and painting in his letter to Trutovskii, and the idea is repeated in the introduction (1:287). "Fragmentary Recollections" opens with a fuller statement of the same metaphor: "The very first objects preserved in the antique picture of the distant past, a picture much faded in some places from time and the course of sixty years . . ." (1:288). Aksakov stresses that in this "prehistoric" chaos time itself is reduced to a nonexistential category, leaving only a nonsequential arrangement of unrelated events, like paintings on display: "Here there follows a long interval, that is a dark spot or faded area in the picture of the distant past, and I begin again to recall myself as already very sick" (1:289).

In keeping with the notion of old, faded pictures, the first two "fragmentary reminiscences" are completely devoid of any description of physical objects and lack virtually any mention of objects whatever; only toys, clothing, and food (*igrushki, plat'itse, kushan'e*) are mentioned (1:288), without further specification. The avoidance of objects by a writer who is as given to extensive presentation of the precise details of the physical environment as Aksakov of course serves a definite end; Sergei's earliest recollections are dominated by, in fact consist almost entirely of, persons who constitute his universe (his wet nurse, little sister, and mother), but who are by the same token scarcely distinguished from the self or from things. In fact, they are referred to as objects (*predmety*), a fact which is obscured and attenuated somewhat by the separation of subject and complement in the first sentence of the text: "The very first objects which remain in the ancient picture of the distant past, a picture much faded in places from time and the course of sixty years, the objects and images which still remain in my memory are my wet nurse, little sister, and mother; then they did not have any definite meaning for me and were only nameless images" (1:288).

Since no other "objects" are mentioned, the three people indicated must be considered the equivalent of things in Sergei's consciousness at this time; they are also referred to as images (*obrazy*), suggesting figures in a painting rather than persons in any full sense of the term. Aksakov's use of this word in the *envoi* of *Family Chronicle* to refer to his personages specifically as literary characters lacking existential reality confirms that for Aksakov the term denotes something less than real life. Sergei's relations with these vague entities operate on a commensurately primitive level. The wet nurse, "at first some mysterious, nearly invisible being" (1:288), is an indistinct source of comfort and gratification: "With sobs and cries I would repeat one and the same word, summoning someone, and someone would appear in the murk of the weakly lit room, take me in her hands, put me to her breast . . . and I would be content" (1:288). The vagueness of the "someone" involved and the crepuscular lighting are matched by uncertainty over whether the person who appears is identical to the person summoned, or whether either of these are the same on different occasions, since the situation is a repeated one. In addition, the basically paratactic construction ("I would repeat . . . and someone would appear . . . and I would be content") suggests a marginal awareness of cause and effect and by implication of temporal sequentiality. Even the trauma of weaning is not recalled as a single event which might serve as a temporal marking post, but rather as the contrast between two states, both of which are described with imperfective verbs, with no mention of the cause of the change in condition.

The figure of Sergei's sister is somewhat more distinct. His constant companion throughout the text, Sergei's "dear little sister," never named in *Years of Childhood*, is of course Aksakov's own sister Nadezhda. In *Years of Childhood* she functions as an alter ego for Sergei, a sort of confidante and living symbol of his own receding childhood. At this stage vagueness still reigns; Sergei loves his sister "more than all my toys, more than my mother" (1:288), suggesting a difference only of degree, not of kind, in his attitudes toward people and things. His emotional attitude toward his sister finds expression in an appropriately primitive way, through a reversal of the inward-directed act of nursing, as he constantly attempts to "dress her in my own frock and feed her with my food; of course I was not allowed to do this, and I would cry" (1:288). Sergei's attentions to his sister merely reverse his role in the only interpersonal exchanges he knows at this stage.

Progressive differentiation from his sister, and more importantly from his mother, along with the development of a more complex repertoire of responses, marks Sergei's gradual expansion of consciousness. At the earliest stages, Sergei's awareness of his mother is so little distinguished from his awareness of self that "her image is inseparably joined with my existence, and therefore it hardly stands out in the fragmentary pictures of the first period of my childhood, although it constantly participates in them" (1:289).

The change from this totally infantile stage of passive, minimal perception begins immediately. The transformation from initial solipsistic ignorance to the start of knowledge is accompanied by, or accomplished through, repeated images of death and rebirth: illness and recovery, darkness and illumination, and, as a spatial concomitant, travel from one place to another. Thus, on a journey to Zubovka, his mother's small estate near Ufa, Sergei awakes in an unfamiliar room, for the first time clearly aware of all dimensions of his immediate environment. His physical awakening at this moment serves as a metaphor for the inception of an organized perception of the world, a sense of one's place in it and the distinction between self and others. Sergei now acquires these interrelated categories of perception, without which further advancement in dealing with reality is impossible. Objects and details suddenly intrude in all their variety, vivid in their specific qualities. This sense of new, striking perception is reinforced by the switch from past perfective to historical present: *prosnulsia* ("I awoke"), *ochnulsia* ("I came to my senses"), *ne uznaiu* ("I don't recognize"); this sequence of verbs, by grammatical shift and by meaning, provides a figure of the passage as a whole. After a sixty-year interval this moment of vision still retains its power and immediacy for the narrating self.

> Odin raz, rano utrom, ia prosnulsia ili ochnulsia, i ne uznaiu,
> gde ia. Vse bylo neznakomo mne: vysokaia, bol'shaia komnata, golye steny iz pretolstykh sosnovykh breven, sil'nyi smolistyi zapakh; iarkoe, kazhetsia letnee, solntse tol'ko chto
> vskhodit i skvoz' okno s pravoi storony, poverkh redinnogo
> pologa, kotoryi byl nado mnoiu opushchen, iarko otrazhaetsia
> na protivopolozhnoi stene. . . . Podle menia trevozhno spit,
> bez podushek i nerazdetaia, moia mat'. (1:289)

> Once, early in the morning, I awoke or came to my senses,
> and I didn't recognize where I was. Everything was unfamiliar

> to me: a high, large room of very thick new pine logs, a
> strong smell of pitch; a bright, apparently summer, sun was
> just rising and through a window, from the right side, above
> the loose-woven bedcurtain that had been lowered around
> me, was brightly reflected on the opposite wall. . . . By
> my side, my mother fitfully slept, without pillows and fully
> dressed.

The passage provides a good example of Aksakov's careful and subtle marshalling of poetic resources to intensify the effects of his prose. The three key verbs mentioned are not only significant in their meaning and tense, but their repeated stressed vowel (u) both links them and calls attention to the contrast of the third element with the first two. In the next several phrases, the continuous consonants s, n, v, and l become more and more frequent in a series of balanced phrases that culminate in the key word solntse ("sun"), which contains three of them and provides the source of the real and metaphorical illumination which floods the passage. Solntse is also the first noun to have a verb, vskhodit ("is rising"), in a series of asyndetic nouns arranged in a catalogue; thus the sun also animates the scene, providing the first action. All of these understated devices serve to intensify the sense of the sudden dawn of mental life. The suggestions of birth and rebirth in the final image of Sergei lying beside his mother provides another metaphoric perspective on this crucial moment.

At this instant of sudden lucidity, Sergei for the first time elaborates a true space which is inhabited by distinct and definite objects; indeed, the fact that he is in a three-dimensional space is underscored by repetition (he is within a bedstead draped with netting which is in turn within a room) to stress the revolutionary nature of the occurrence. Not only does Sergei perceive the room as a coherent space, but the shafts of sunlight provide both an axis of orientation in the world at large (Sergei is presumably lying supine with his head more or less to the south) and a point of reference in time, both of the day and of the year. His new relationship with his environment is emphasized by his reaction to the new objects filling the universe of which he is now consciously the center: "I felt good and was happy, so that for several minutes with curiosity and pleasure I inspected through the bed curtain the new objects that surrounded me" (1:289).

The revelation Sergei has experienced is confirmed by his perception of a bottle from which he is given some wine: "They poured me the Rhine wine from an odd sort of bottle, with a flattened, wide, round bottom and a long, narrow neck. I have not seen such bottles since that time" (1:289). This description is lacking in the manuscript; its inclusion in the final text suggests the importance at this point of presenting objects as unique, perceived in the fullness of their individuality and preserved permanently by memory. The deliberate and conspicuous shift back to the narrating self at this point underlines the fact that this old-fashioned wine bottle has remained as an emblem of Sergei's attainment of consciousness and has been preserved from the flux of time. It serves to verify the content of memory, much as the double memory in the introduction does; if a unique object can be exactly recalled, the whole moment at which precise perception and a sense of personal continuum began can also be summoned forth. Sergei's first moment at this new level of consciousness soon dissolves into repetitious motor play and indistinct awareness of the protective female figure (his mother), but this regression is only a temporary relapse, and even a regression implies an order and sequence heretofore lacking.

The link between travel (even only simulated travel in a carriage in the courtyard) and recovery from illness dominates the first chapter even after the first, decisive awakening. On another occasion, when Sergei is ill, he is more directly in contact with the natural world (he is placed on the earth, an archaic mode of healing);[19] he also perceives, but is unable to react to, an emblematic image of social relations in their most elementary form. Prior to this Sergei lacked any notion of the emotional links within the family as a whole, perceiving only those between himself and other individuals:

> Once, we made a long journey, I don't know where to; Father was with us. . . . They took me out of the carriage, placed bedding in the tall grass of a forest meadow, in the shade of the trees, and placed me there almost lifeless. . . . I heard how my father wept and comforted my desperate mother, how ardently she prayed, raised her hands to heaven. I heard everything and saw it clearly, but could not say a word or make the slightest movement—and suddenly it was as if I awoke and I felt better, stronger than usual. (1:292)

19. Eliade, *Patterns in Comparative Religion*, pp. 251, 255.

However, this hint of the complexities of social relations remains only a hint for the time being; the world of nature is of more immediate concern. The chapter concludes with the beginning of clear, chronologically connected memories—"from that moment I remember everything clearly" (1:293). Instead of the discontinuities and isolated episodes, linked by similarity of structure, which were prevalent in the first chapter, the second chapter, "Connected Memories" ("Posledovatel'nye vospominaniia"), and those that follow are at least overtly structured by temporal sequentiality.

Sergei's first journey to a definite place occupies three chapters: "The Trip to Parashino," "Parashino," and "The Trip from Parashino to Bagrovo" ("Doroga do Parashina," "Parashino," "Doroga iz Parashina v Bagrovo"). The process of travel itself (though not the stay at Bagrovo at the end of the journey) involves constant discovery, and the words *new* and *first* (*novyi* and *pervyi*) are the most frequent and important terms in Sergei's discovery of the larger physical environment. The journey begins with the crossing of a river (the Belaia, on which Ufa is located), and the river forms a clear boundary between two realms—that of the human world, which up to now has been the only reality in which Sergei has lived, and the world of nature. Sergei is at first frightened by the crossing, but his fear is balanced by a wealth of new perceptions;[20] for the first time, Sergei is aware of the distinction between the human and the natural orders and also of the beauty of nature: "I fell completely silent. . . . Everyone laughed, saying that the cat had gotten my tongue out of fear, but that was not entirely fair; I was struck not so much by fear as by the novelty of objects and the grandeur of the scene, the beauty of which I sensed, although of course I could not explain it" (1:302).

Once he arrives in this new world on the other side, Sergei begins to assimilate, organize, and make sense of it. "We all stepped off onto the dock quite calmly. So many new things, so many new words! Here my tongue became untied, and with great curiosity I began to interrogate our boatmen about everything" (1:303). In an echo of the Creation itself, he seeks to understand things through learning their names, frequently equating the two. "I ceaselessly cried out, 'Oh, what kind of tree is that? What is it called?'" (1:304). This fixation on names is of course a rather

20. In a letter to his wife (24 June 1835), Aksakov comments, "I hate large rivers! They're graves!" and describes his terror while crossing the Volga by ferry. PD, *fond* 3, inventory 15, item 26, fols. 5–5v.

primitive form of knowing, and has analogues in Sergei's moral thinking at this period.

In addition to the naming of things, Sergei's initial encounter with the world of nature involves two other almost mythic methods of integrating the human and the natural: fishing and the starting of a campfire. Fishing, as we know from Aksakov's hunting books, involves human interaction with a particularly obscure part of the natural environment. But perhaps even more important is Sergei's first observation of the starting of a campfire, an action that suggests the foundations of culture and mastery of the natural world. The importance of this incident is suggested in two ways. The description of the starting of the fire retards the action considerably, as Aksakov often does for emphasis; in fact this description is expanded considerably from manuscript to final version. In the manuscript, the entire action is described in two words: "They lit a fire" (*razveli ogon'*).[21] In the printed text, this brief statement is expanded into an Aksakovian segmentation of actions and things, with great precision of description and vocabulary, in proportion to the importance of the event:

> The servants undertook to start a fire: one man brought some dry wood from nearby, chopped it into lengths, planed off some shavings, and chopped some kindling to feed the fire; another dragged up a whole pile of dry brush from the river; and a third, namely Makei the cook, took a flint and steel, struck a spark into a large piece of tinder, wrapped this up in dry tow (we brought it with us just for such occasions), took it in his hand and began to swing it vigorously back and forth and up and down until the tow caught; then they set fire with it to the ready pile of logs, shavings and kindling—and the flame flared up. (1:305)

Secondly, the significance of the starting of the fire is underlined by Sergei's request for permission to start a small fire of his own, his first imitation of adult action and his first attempt to humanize and transform the environment. Both fishing and the building of his own fire have the same effect on him: "I quite forgot myself for joy" (*ne pomnil sebia ot radosti*) (1:309).[22] As Aksakov's hunting books attest, such a state is the highest degree of happiness man can attain in his relation with nature.

21. LL, *fond* 3, carton 2, storage unit 1, fol. 28.
22. The participial form, *ne pomnia sebia ot radosti*, is found at 1:305.

At Parashino, Sergei has a further encounter with an emblem of man's interaction with nature, namely, a mill, something he had never conceived of before (1:319). The mill, the importance of which for Aksakov is apparent from the prominence accorded to mills in *Notes on Fishing* and in *Family Chronicle*, is described in the detail that is typical for an important object (1:319). Sergei's reaction to his new discovery underlines the mill's role as a summation of human culture: "This decrepit mill seemed to me a marvel of human artifice" (1:319). The investigation of the mill by Sergei and his father recalls similar scenes in the first and fourth chapters of *Family Chronicle*, where Stepan Mikhailovich conducts first his daughter and then his new daughter-in-law through the mill at Bagrovo. Here, as then, Sergei and his father emerge dusted with flour in token of Sergei's initiation into the central activity of the estate, the humanizing of the natural. Given Sergei's position as a member of the landowning gentry, this initiation is important not only for his knowledge of the world, but also for his future social role.

The next significant period of interaction between Sergei and the natural environment occurs in the chapter "Sergeevka." Sergei has by this time become aware of the differences between the city and the world of nature, and Sergeevka, a parcel of land near Ufa acquired by his parents and named specifically for him, functions as a Garden of Eden for him. "Sergeevka occupies one of the very brightest spots in the earliest memories of my childhood. . . . The entire time spent by me in Sergeevka that year seems to me a merry holiday" (1:378). The journey to Sergeevka is a penetration of nature "into the river growth, into the green, flowering, and fragrant river growth" (1:378), recalling in motion and vocabulary certain passages devoted to perception of nature in the hunting books.

"Sergeevka" tends to contrast and polarize the world of the urban and that of the rural and natural in a manner that was absent in Sergei's earlier experience of nature, when mere acquaintance and man's culturizing interaction with the natural realm were most important; the incipient, conscious opposition of society and nature in "Sergeevka" already points toward adult attitudes such as Aksakov's own. Many of the details and incidents in "Sergeevka" reinforce this sense of the otherness of the nonurban. For instance, the family lives in a modified peasant cottage (*izba*) and uses a type of cart with a cloth roof that can be raised for shade, characteristic of the nomadic Kalmyks (1:387). They are visited by one of the denizens of this chaotic area, the titanic Maliutka, who seems to Sergei to be an archaic survival out of Xenophon and who urges in broken Russian that the land be properly surveyed (Aksakov notes that even in 1856 title was still unclear [1:387n.]). In short, Sergeevka sums up the natural world in its disorganized state, lacking a human civilizing presence. Sergeevka may be an Eden, but it is an Eden in want of a gardener.

Perhaps the clearest indication of the tenuousness of the human (or at least the Russian) presence in this land occurs when Sergei, his father, and Evseich, Sergei's nurse, inspect an enormous oak and an even larger stump that stand at the shore of the lake (the importance of the conjunction of tree and water as an image of the world, which appeared in *Notes on Fishing*, should be borne in mind here). Just as the Russian family summering in the countryside is somewhat lost in the formless space of the unsettled plain, so is their significance in time reduced to its true scale by measurement against the great trees:

> Beyond the dock stood a most enormous oak several spans in
> girth; alongside it there had once grown another oak, of
> which there remained only quite a high stump, much thicker
> than the oak still standing; out of curiosity all three of us
> climbed on this huge stump and of course took up only a small
> corner of it. . . . [Father] pointed out slashes on the stump
> and on the growing oak and said that the Bashkirs, the
> true owners of the land, make such marks on large oaks every
> hundred years. . . . There were only two such slashes on
> the stump, and five on the growing oak, but since the stump
> was much thicker and therefore older than the growing
> oak, it was evident that the other slashes had been on the cut-
> off trunk of the tree. (1:381)

Thus at the very start of his summer at Sergeevka, Sergei now senses the dimension of infinity implicit in all of nature. Despite the fact that nature and time in "Sergeevka" assume some of their inhuman enormity, the place is still important in the development of Sergei's relation with nature. Perhaps in response to the more complete revelation of nature, it is at Sergeevka that Sergei becomes a serious fisherman, developing a lasting bond with nature through a form of the hunt. Sergei had previously only been an observer, making the first steps toward interaction with nature. Now he has been fully initiated, and it is appropriate that nature, with which he has formed a lifetime bond, should be revealed as a partner sufficiently complex and awesome to occupy man for a lifetime. Sergei leaves Sergeevka as though leaving Eden, with the memory of his first full contact with nature to sustain him. "With regret I left behind Sergeevka and bade farewell to its marvelous lake, the dock, from which I fished, to which I had become accustomed and of which the image lives till now in my grateful memory; I parted with the magnificent oaks, beneath whose shade I would sometimes sit and which I always marveled at. I bid farewell—for a very long time" (1:398). Later, after he moves with his family to Bagrovo, Sergei renews his acquaintance with nature, but in many respects he is already the hunter, for whom the first realization of his insignificance vis-à-vis nature has already passed.

The polarity of man and nature presented in "Sergeevka" is to some degree resolved later in the text with the family's move to Bagrovo. This is only to be expected, given Bagrovo's role (not its only one in Years of Childhood) as the locus of the harmonious integration of man and nature, a function familiar from Family Chronicle. Bagrovo's function is suggested by the first sight of the estate as the Bagrovs approach it to take up permanent residence: "I noticed that he [Father] could not look without pleasure at the reedy ponds, green groves, the village and the house, which all were opening out before our eyes" (1:442). Ending a paragraph, a chapter ("Ufa") and also the first half of the book, this sentence, progressing almost cinematically through the features of Bagrovo and concluding with its center, the house, suggests the world of which the manor house at Bagrovo will be the focus. It is also an Aksakovian conclusion in its suggestion of new possibilities.

The move to Bagrovo is structurally important to Years of Childhood and marks the achievement of a certain maturity in Sergei in many respects. I shall have occasion to refer to the move in other contexts, but with regard to Sergei's relation with nature, his years at Bagrovo depict the emergence of the passionate hunter and lover of nature. That depiction culminates with the chapter "First Spring in the Country" ("Pervaia vesna v derevne"), wherein for the first time Sergei experiences the entire sequence of the annual renewal of life. "The approach of spring in the country produced an unusual, unsettling effect in me. I felt a special form of excitement, never before experienced by me" (1:491). Sergei engages in the central Aksakovian act of man's relation with nature, observation: "Shut up in the house, since I was not allowed even on the porch in wet weather, I nevertheless followed every step of spring. In every room, almost at every window, I had marked out special objects or places on the basis of which I made my observations. . . . Everything was noted by me precisely and attentively, and every step of spring was celebrated like a victory!" (1:491–492).

The passage of migratory birds forms the high point of these observations; Sergei is finally let out of the house for a brief period with Evseich and his father, and is "staggered, driven out of my mind by such a sight" (1:493)—the loss of self is typical for Aksakov's attitude to nature. The correlative, active phase of the hunter's mentality makes its appearance at once; although Sergei still lacks the knowledge or skill (*opytnost'*), he already begins to learn from the running commentary provided by his father and Evseich (1:494), and experiences the excitement of the hunt vicariously from the house. "Suddenly a shot thundered beneath the very windows; I dashed to the window and saw a puff of smoke dissipating in the air, Filipp the old falconer standing with a shotgun, and the poodle Triton . . . who, holding some sort of bird by the wing, was coming out of the water onto the bank. Filipp soon came with his prize: it was a mallard drake, as I was told, and with plumage so beautiful that I admired it for a long time" (1:494).

The combination of desire to possess the prey and admiration for its beauty (bestowed in part by its desirability as prey) is of course typical for the Aksakovian hunter; though still only an observer, Sergei has become a hunter in spirit. Thus as the period of childhood draws to a close, Sergei's relations with the natural environment conform more and more closely to the model elaborated by Aksakov in his hunting books. The activity of hunting is already assuming the features of a pursuit distinct from and even inimical to the concerns of society, particularly urban society. Sergei's father, always more a man of the village than of the city, serves, along with various serfs, as Sergei's mentor as he learns how to hunt, while his mother, in one of the rare instances in *Years of Childhood* of failure of sympathy between mother and son, finds such pursuits uncultured and repulsive. She even insists on sitting on leather cushions rather than directly on the ground on her one excursion to the island in the river flowing past the manor house (1:517). In the course of *Years of Childhood*, Sergei's relation with the physical world has progressed from the beginning of perception itself through awareness of nature, to a relation with nature based on a distinction of the natural and the human, which approaches the adult configuration. In the process, the aesthetic element of perception has become more and more localized in nature as the things of man have become more familiar; at the conclusion, nature alone, and particularly hunting, retains aesthetic potential. Sergei has matured in regard to the world around him.

7

The Worlds of Childhood:
Mortality and Morality

Organized perception of the physical world and awareness of the natural environment is of course the foundation on which the development of other levels of the personality rests; other dimensions of Sergei's awareness of reality expand in rough proportion to his increased awareness of the natural order. The most important of these is his recognition of the constants of human existence per se, in particular (and as a symbol of them all) of the role of time in human life and of the fact of death. That this awareness is as important as the perception of nature is suggested by the organization of the first half of *Years of Childhood* (up to the permanent move to Bagrovo) in which each contact with nature (the first journey to Bagrovo, the stay at Sergeevka) is followed and complemented by an episode involving some sort of contact with mortality; in both cases this episode is set at Bagrovo, which, as the locus most directly connected with the past, seems the appropriate setting for Sergei's initiations into the human meaning of time. Unlike the more or less inevitable and automatic development of physical perception and awareness of nature, the realization of the human dimension of time is a painful process involving emotional suffering; human time must be mastered by the child, as is suggested by the contrast between the scene with the oak trees at Sergeevka and the sequence which follows it in which Sergei's grandfather, Stepan Mikhailovich Bagrov, dies. In the oak scene Sergei is a curious but unaffected observer of an impersonal and immense sort of time, existing separately from people and their concerns; in the death scene he suffers intensely as human time impinges on his life and that of his entire family. Death is the central riddle of human time which the child must solve, and his grappling with the problem involves two distinct stages: ignorance of the full implications of time and death, with death serving really as a metaphor for an emotional state and realization of the universality of human mortality, mitigated by a qualified resignation to the fact. The second of these phases is the critical one; it takes place on Sergei's second trip to Bagrovo and indeed constitutes the crisis of the entire work. Sergei's successful passage through it really marks the end of childhood—at least of childhood conceived as a period of ignorance and bliss—and the beginning of Sergei's transformation into an adult. Aksakov's view of the child in *Years of Childhood* is hardly that of the Romantics; contact with death is presented as essential and ultimately beneficial for a dynamically developing and constantly more complex personality. The loss of innocence is but the beginning of wisdom.

Sergei's earliest imaginings concerning death begin shortly after the inception of continuous memory, but they are of an infantile nature. Prompted by the tales of his nurse, he fancies he sees the ghost of his grandfather Zubin sitting at a table in an unused part of the house. Sergei's trivial fantasies are quickly dispelled by his mother and play only a small part in his life at this time, but they do suggest his complete ignorance concerning the realities of death, for he perceives no difference between death and life and imagines a dead person as if alive. Death in fact does not exist for Sergei at this time.

A more complex though still inadequate notion emerges during Sergei's first stay at Bagrovo, recorded in the chapters "Bagrovo" and "Staying at Bagrovo without Father and Mother" ("Bagrovo"; "Prebyvanie v Bagrove bez ottsa i materi"). Although the journey to Bagrovo is connected with the discovery of the natural world, the journey's end has a decidedly different significance for Sergei. Throughout *Years of Childhood* the estate of Bagrovo, whenever it is the goal of travel, is associated with anxiety, fear, illness, and ultimately death; it is there that Sergei faces his most severe tests. If the most frequent word during the journey to Bagrovo is *new* (*novyi*), the key words in the two chapters set in Bagrovo are *fear* and *horror* (*strakh* and *uzhas*). While traveling to Bagrovo, Sergei was a willing recipient of new impressions of nature; now he is an unwilling participant in events over which he has no control and of which he has little understanding.

The association of Bagrovo with illness begins at the moment that the boundary of the estate is reached; the travelers learn that Stepan Mikhailovich is ill. At first sight of Bagrovo, Sofia Niko-lavna's eyes fill with tears, Aleksei Stepanovich becomes somber, and Sergei readily accommodates himself to the emotional at-mosphere surrounding the adults, without comprehending their motives. "I became sad, and in great confusion I sat down in the carriage" (1:332). Sofia Nikolavna is also ill; indeed the purpose of the trip to Bagrovo has been to leave the children there while she consults a doctor in Orenburg. At Bagrovo her condition worsens, adding to Sergei's apprehensions concerning Bagrovo. "I had never before seen her so ill . . . fear and anxiety possessed me" (1:335). Throughout the chapter entitled "Bagrovo," Sergei is haunted by fear of separation from his parents; at the moment of their departure, he attempts to run after their carriage and is brought back to the house by force (1:342). With motion arrested and escape cut off, Sergei abandons himself to despair and then falls asleep. The aura of death becomes pervasive in the follow-ing chapter, but, like Sergei's falling asleep, it is only an emo-tionally determined reaction to a situation of stress.

Aksakov draws on his experiment in *Reminiscences* in de-scribing Sergei's perception of his surroundings at Bagrovo. He and his sister, he feels, are prisoners (1:343), shut up in a converted drawing room which constitutes their "own world" (1:344). In fact, the siblings are rather neglected by the household and are cared for only by Evseich. In this state of confinement, itself a metaphorical death, the subject of death becomes Sergei's principal preoccupation, although he is not aware of the full import of the notion. As he did when he feared the ghost of his grandfather Zubin, Sergei derives the material for most of his fantasies from the accounts of others. He reads Evseich a story about a family who live under the snow (1:347); Evseich responds with an account of a peasant buried by a blizzard. Both stories of course recall the association of snow and death in Aksakov's own "The Blizzard." Later Sergei sees the peasant who figures in Evseich's story, but it is clear that these tales concerning snow and death are only metaphors for Sergei's own situation, and their literary shape and articulation increase their appeal as equivalents of Sergei's emotional state while at the same time reducing their immediacy.

As his depressed withdrawal proceeds, he becomes increasingly explicit in his fantasies, replacing peripheral stories with scenarios that directly express his fears in his immediate situation—in particular, separation from his parents and a stay in an unfamiliar place: "Often, having opened my *Child's Reading*, I would become lost in thought, and my child's imagination would sketch for me sad and then terrifying scenes. I would imagine that Mother was dying, had died, that my father had also died and that we would remain in Bagrovo, that we would be punished, dressed in peasant clothes, banished to the scullery (I had heard of such punishments) and that, at last, my sister and I would also die" (1:349). In their vagueness and in the universality of their consequences, Sergei's fears suggest fairy tale. His foreboding for himself and his family evokes a proportional dislike and even fear of his grandfather Stepan Mikhailovich, the dominant figure at Bagrovo, whom Sergei finds "very frightening" (1:333) and who becomes a sort of ogre, ever more ominous in Sergei's perception as his depression and anxiety deepen. Sergei is also aware that the Bagrovo women, in accord with the mental outlook of the village, consider Sergei and his sister as extensions of Sofia Nikolavna, and transfer their dislike of her to her children.

In keeping both with the conceptual and behavioral modes of the countryside and with Sergei's limited perception, much of this hostility is manifested in matters pertaining to food. The differences between city and country in this respect are suggested when Sofia Nikolavna inadvertently asks for a lemon and is pointedly told that lemons are unheard of in Bagrovo (1:337). Discussion of the proper food for the children reveals the antagonism between the two systems (1:333), while Sergei's obvious and overtly expressed distaste for country food displeases Stepan Mikhailovich, to the delight of the Bagrovo women (1:339). In this respect food functions as a tangible indication of affection. Aksin'ia Stepanovna, Sergei's kind godmother, gives him raisins and prunes, but tells him to eat them secretly; Sergei, however, obeying his mother's ban on Bagrovo food, hides the fruit altogether (1:346). Sergei's cousins are given tea sweeter than his and his sister's as a sign that the children from the city have not been accepted (1:346). The transactions involving food indicate that, although Sergei does not fully comprehend it, the assignment of roles typical of the country has continued, and he and his sister have been allotted roles appropriate to their parentage.

Deliverance from this mock imprisonment and metaphorical death, as well as from the more real distress deriving from the imposition of strictly defined roles, comes only with Sofia Niko-lavna's return, which brings about a rebirth in Sergei. The de-scription of his first glimpse of his mother employs the term *image* (*obraz*) which Aksakov often uses at such crucial junc-tures. That first glimpse of course precipitates a total emotional transformation in Sergei: "The carriage rolled up, in its window there flickered the image of my mother—and from that moment I remember nothing. . . . I woke up or came to my senses on my mother's knees; she was sitting on a couch, having placed my head on her breast. This was joy, this was happiness indeed" (1:351). The suddenness and totality of this transformation in Sergei accords with his use of death as a metaphor for his situa-tion at Bagrovo, although he has no real comprehension of the significance of the term.

With the return of Sergei's parents, the ominous quality that all of Bagrovo, and particularly Stepan Mikhailovich, had for Sergei quickly dissipates, and the relation between Sergei and his grandfather undergoes a polar transformation. The motifs of fear and anxiety are replaced by love and caresses (*liubit'* and *laskat'*), although Sergei is not able to assess accurately the sin-cerity of such demonstrations of affection.[1] "My timidity sud-denly passed, and sad Bagrovo seemed to become more cheerful. It even seemed to me, and perhaps it really was so, that every one became kinder, more attentive and more concerned about us. I thought, because of my childishness, that everyone had come to like us. . . . In a few days I had been reborn, as it were" (1:353). Sergei's former fear of Stepan Mikhailovich is replaced by ac-commodation and mutual esteem not unlike that achieved be-tween Sofia Nikolavna and Stepan Mikhailovich in the fourth chapter of *Family Chronicle:*

> Even now I think that in that last week of our stay in Bagrovo Grandfather really took a liking to me, and took it precisely from the moment when he himself saw that I was deeply attached to my father. He even told me that he had considered me a spoiled darling, a mama's boy, who did not love his

1. *Laskat'* and *liubit'* and their cognates occur in combination in various works by Aksakov, but with particular frequency in *Years of Childhood*. The equivalence of the emotional and the physical is appropriate for the perception of a child.

father, never mind his father's relatives, and scorned every
one at Bagrovo; obviously this had been suggested to him,
but my shyness, sorry look, and timidity, even fear, instilled
by his presence, confirmed such opinions. But now, when
he caressed me, when my fear and anguish for my mother had
passed, when my heart had become light, and I myself
began to caress him, it was quite natural that he began to like
me. (1:353)

Sergei's second trip to Bagrovo divests the concept of death of
any potential as a facile and essentially infantile metaphor for
vague apprehensions; instead, the horrifying reality of death is
revealed, and metaphoric possibilities based on ignorance are
eliminated. This demythologizing of death and the realization of
its true significance forms the central event in *Years of Childhood*, as suggested by Aksakov's decision to publish separately
(in *Russian Conversation*) the three chapters that deal with it:
"Return to City Life in Ufa," "Trip to Bagrovo in Winter," and
"Bagrovo in Winter" ("Vozvrashchenie v Ufu k gorodskoi zhizni,"
"Zimniaia doroga v Bagrovo," "Bagrovo zimoi"). The subject of
the three chapters, the breach through contact with the reality of
death in the charmed circle of childhood ignorance and innocence, is one of the central events in fiction depicting childhood
(cf. the death of the mother in Tolstoi's *Childhood*). Such a traumatic experience necessarily entails both suffering and growth,
and this journey to Bagrovo does not end, as its predecessor did,
in an emotionally satisfying restoration of the status quo and
resolution of difficulties, but rather leads to a new, more valid
insight on Sergei's part into the human condition.

At the initial point of this journey, Sergei's conception of death
is still at the rudimentary level of his first trip to Bagrovo; any
emotional detachment he evinces with regard to the subject
merely masks ignorance, and the instances of death of which he
is cognizant are either literary or remote.

He relishes the bloody battle scenes in M. M. Kheraskov's *Ros-
siada*, while the significance of an event in the macrocosm, the
death of Catherine II and the accession of Paul I (termed a *sobytie*, often Aksakov's term for an event on the plane of history),
is quite beyond Sergei's grasp. Sergei resents being told that children can not swear allegiance to the new emperor as adults do
(1:402), and his fantasies of the dead empress and her successor
equate superlatives (*great* becomes *big*) in typically childish

fashion, indicating his lack of comprehension of the reality involved.

> My imagination presented me a striking picture: the dead
> empress, of immense size, lying beneath a black baldacchino,
> in a black church (I had heard much talk of this) and along-
> side her, on his knees, the new emperor, also some sort
> of giant, who was weeping, and behind him there sobbed
> aloud the entire populace, gathered in such a mass that it
> could stretch from Ufa to Zubovka, that is, ten versts. (1:403)

Sergei's fantasies of death, drawing on distant events, are soon displaced by the more ominous news from Bagrovo that Stepan Mikhailovich is dying. Death is no longer a fictional device or a distant event, but something which has inexplicably entered the universe of his own family. Sergei now begins to experience fear of death, which he objectifies and considers a threat not only to his grandfather but to everyone he loves, and to himself as well. Drawing on the stories he heard on his first trip to Bagrovo, he immediately equates death with cold, snow, and darkness; these become constant motifs, both subjective and objective, of the following two chapters.[2] Previously death served Sergei as a metaphor for his emotions, but now snow and cold stand in a metaphorical relation with death, emphasizing the centrality of its mystery and also, through their objective presence, its immediacy and actuality.

> "Well, Serezha, we will all go to Bagrovo; Grandfather is
> dying." I listened to such words with woeful amazement. I
> already knew that everyone dies, and death, which I understood
> in my own fashion, seemed to be such a frightful thing
> and evil spirit that I was afraid even to think of it. I was sorry
> for Grandfather, but I in no way wanted to see his death
> or to be in the next room when he, dying, began to cry and
> shriek. The thought that Mother might get sick from it

2. The association of winter and death was quite strong for Aksakov personally, as indicated in a letter to his distant relative, the young artist K. A. Trutovskii: "I hate the cold and therefore don't like autumn frosts. All the fine phrases about fields *silvered with a frosty dust* have no meaning for me. I see only death, a white shroud and nothing more." S. T. Aksakov to K. A. Trutovskii, 18 September 1852; in Trutovskii, "Vospominaniia o S. T. Aksakove," no. 2, p. 53. Aksakov's poetic citation may be an inaccurate quotation of Pushkin's Lycée anniversary ode "19 oktiabria," 1825, the second line of which is "Srebrit moroz uvianushee pole" ("Frost silvers the faded field"). Or he may be thinking of *Evgenii Onegin*, chap. 4, stanza 42: "I vot uzhe treshchat morozy / I serebriatsia sred' polei" ("And lo the frosts already crackle and turn silver 'midst the fields").

also upset me. "But how can we go in winter," I thought,
"aren't Sister and I little, won't we freeze to death?" (1:405)

Although in Sergei's conception death is still a being, a *strashi-lishche* or bogeyman, it is no longer a distant object of curiosity and fantastic speculation, but an intrusion threatening to destroy the entire world Sergei inhabits; for the first time he would rather not travel, and sees the trip as exposure to the death pervading all of nature.

This journey to Bagrovo, unlike Sergei's previous trips to various places, all of which were undertaken in warm weather, is not a voyage of immediate discovery for Sergei. Rather unusually for Aksakov, physical motion is for once not correlated with perceptual and psychological expansion, but instead involves constantly greater constriction and contraction, which are parallel to Sergei's increasingly closer approach to death and his more intense awareness of it. The family departs in darkness and Sergei perceives the carriage in which he rides as a sort of coffin. "As soon as we went out to get in the carriage, I became completely frightened by the low leather cab with its little door, through which it was difficult to clamber. . . . I begged to be allowed in the *kibitka* with my mother, but the frost was terrible and I was sternly ordered into the cab" (1:405–406). Contact with the world is restricted and soon shut off completely by the cold. Sergei turns to thoughts of Bagrovo, which bring out even more clearly his subjective apprehension of the symbolic link of snow and death:

> In both doors of the cab there was a small rectangular window
> with glass that was sealed shut. I somehow crept to the
> window and with pleasure looked out; the night was moonlit,
> bright; the thick milestones and occasional trees flickered
> past, but alas! even this pleasure disappeared; the panes
> became foggy, traced with snowy patterns and, finally, covered
> with a thick layer of impenetrable frost. The unhappy fu-
> ture arose before my eyes: the sad house at Bagrovo, all in
> snowdrifts, and Grandfather dying. (1:406)

The loss of contact with the landscape deprives travel of its customary value of new experience and forces Sergei into introverted and fearful fantasies, a degeneration of travel's psychological significance paralleled by a slowdown of physical motion; the travelers soon turn off the highway. At a stop, a filthy and drafty Mordvinian hut, the cold increases and invades the carriage, which had been relatively warm, when a door is left open by mistake (1:407). Progress stops altogether in order to revive a Chuvash postilion who has nearly frozen to death (recalling Evseich's tale of the peasant Arefii). Finally, on approaching Bagrovo, once again at night, the carriage in which Sergei is riding overturns, temporarily halting the journey altogether. In the confusion, Sergei is hurt, hitting his brow against an exposed nailhead, and is nearly smothered under the cushions (1:409). His bruise remains as an emblem of the psychological experience of death he is soon to undergo as his grandfather experiences it physically. Sergei's fantasies of death during his first stay at Bagrovo, like the stories of near-death in the snow, now become terrifying realities.

During this stay at Bagrovo, Sergei's entire experience divides into two phases, diurnal and nocturnal. During the diurnal phase, Sergei is relatively open to his environment and capable of observation, in particular, of scrutinizing the customs of Bagrovo connected with death. Although his days are not free of fears, Sergei can succeed in overcoming them, either by himself or with the help of his mother or other adults. At night, however, he is a helpless victim of his fears; it is at night, moreover, that the most fearful external events take place, culminating in Stepan Mikhailovich's death.

Night and its attendant fears at first dominate Sergei's consciousness; his apprehensions about once again meeting his grandfather stem from the premise that death is universal (as the entire journey has been suggesting symbolically) and that contact with death is tantamount to one's own death. "I knew that he wished to see us, and must confess that this unavoidable meeting brought indescribable fear into my heart. Most of all I feared that Grandfather would begin to say farewell to me, embrace me and die, that it would be impossible to extricate me from his arms, because they would *starken*, and that it would be necessary to bury me along with him in the ground" (1:411). Sergei's fantasy expresses visually and metonymically his incipient realization of the universality of death; although he has foreshortened time, his insight is basically valid: death is universal, but it is not simultaneous. His night of terror ends only when his mother awakes and tends his swollen eye.

The climax of Sergei's fears occurs on the second night at

Bagrovo, during which Stepan Mikhailovich dies. Sergei himself undergoes a surrogate death, the most protracted and explicit in all of Aksakov's works. As night approaches, Sergei is left alone, and Stepan Mikhailovich's imminent death, mentioned during the day in a relatively neutral manner, begins to assert its nocturnal control over Sergei's psyche. He begins to perceive and to react with greater intensity to reminders both of what is happening elsewhere in the house and of his own mortality. His first hint of death is also an indication of the difference between Sergei's stage of development and a less mature stage as his sister, still too small to comprehend the real nature of the events taking place, expresses pity for Stepan Mikhailovich in infantile terms. "She kept saying: 'Grandfather won't be able to eat. They'll bury Grandfather in the snow. I feel sorry for him.'" (1:413). Her statement shares the symbolism which is obsessing Sergei and which Aksakov develops throughout the chapter, but she lacks any awareness of the tormenting pertinence of that symbolism to the self; her uncomprehending words provide a transition for Sergei from the safe world of the day to that of the night, where the full import of these "natural" symbols emerges for him.[3] Possessed by the "new, ever more frightening image" of his dying grandfather, who is motionless and unable to speak, Sergei clutches his nurse in panic and refuses to let the candle go out, lest he be entirely abandoned to darkness (1:414). The candle of course is a traditional metaphor for human life, and its tenuous battle against engulfing darkness reverses the copious light attending the scene of the inception of consciousness in the first chapter; it also recalls the lamp of the icon and the illuminated cross of other moments of existential crisis in Family Chronicle.

Sofia Nikolavna returns and Sergei is lulled to sleep by her presence, but later on he awakes alone, with the light again on the verge of failing. His intimations of death are even stronger, and he again visualizes Stepan Mikhailovich, who is now even more vividly present to him. Previously Sergei had imagined his grandfather's image (obraz), but now he is referred to directly as Grandfather (dedushka), suggesting the immediacy and intensity of Sergei's experience.

---

3. Such symbolism is particularly apt for works in a pastoral mode, as has been pointed out with regard to Robert Frost. Lynen, The Pastoral Art of Robert Frost, pp. 51–53.

> Opening my eyes, I saw that neither Mother nor Parasha was
> in the room; the candle was out, the nightlight was burning
> down, and the fiery tongue of the guttering wick, tossing in all
> directions at the bottom of a little crock of burned-out
> tallow, now and again lit the room with a flickering uncertain
> light, threatening at any moment to leave me in total dark-
> ness. There are no words to express my fear! It was as though
> boiling water was dashed on my heart, and at the same time
> a chill raced over my whole body. . . . In vain did I keep shut-
> ting my eyes—Grandfather stood before me, looking into
> my eyes and moving his lips, as Parasha had said. (1:414)

Sergei is at the point of imagined death, the dichotomy of his
inner and outer sensations suggesting the sundering of death. At
this moment, Stepan Mikhailovich does in fact die and general
lamentation begins throughout the house. Sergei and his sister,
influenced by her brother's fears, begin to shriek and first their
nurse Parasha and then Sofia Nikolavna enter to calm them. The
candle is relit, and daylight soon appears at the window, ending
but not entirely resolving Sergei's night of crisis (1:415).

Alternating with his nocturnal agonies, endured in darkness
and isolation suggestive of the grave, Sergei's daytime experiences are of quite a different quality. While not entirely free of
the subjective terror predicated on identification with his grandfather, during the daytime Sergei observes and finally participates in various rituals. These socially established mechanisms
integrate the fact of death into the human continuum rather than
allowing it to destroy the isolated individual.

Even before Stepan Mikhailovich's death, the events of the
first day at Bagrovo set in motion the chain of rituals by which
death is neutralized. Stepan Mikhailovich himself, bringing his
role in Aksakov's works to a fitting close, conducts the initial
ceremony, the bestowing of his blessing on his family, including
his grandchildren; Sergei responds to this with a total reversal of
the fear of contact with his grandfather that he had experienced
in imagination the night before:

> Grandfather opened his eyes, not saying a word, with a
> trembling hand blessed us and touched his fingers to our heads;
> we kissed his withered hand and began to cry; everyone
> in the room began to weep, even sob, and only now did I
> notice, that there stood around us all my aunts, uncles, old

> women, and my grandfather's servants. My fright was com-
> pletely gone, and at that moment I fully felt both love and pity
> for my dying grandfather. (1:412)

During the day, the contact Sergei so feared at night forms the
nucleus of a ceremony which cancels the terror of death; the fear
of contact is replaced by a realization of belonging to a community connected by a bond of love and sympathy. The fact that
Sergei senses his love for his grandfather only after he becomes
aware of the presence of the entire household underscores the
role that established social mechanisms play in reducing the
anxiety surrounding death.[4]

On the second day at Bagrovo, immediately after Stepan Mikhailovich's death, Sergei's fears begin to subside. He first reacts
with fear to the ceremonies connected with death, such as the
laying out of the body in the main hall, the reading of the psalter,
and the traditional lamenting, and seeks refuge in his cousins'
room, the most distant from the corpse. However, although his
fear is still strong, the narrator terms it ridiculous (1:416). Sergei
begins to take an interest in the ceremonies taking place around
him, starting with the first meal (an exceptionally hearty one, as
dictated by tradition) after Stepan Mikhailovich's death (1:417–
418). The meal combines mourning for the old master with
recognition of Aleksei Stepanovich's assumption of the master's
role; all wait for him before the meal begins, as they once waited
for Stepan Mikhailovich. Significantly, after this meal, whose
full ceremonial importance of course Sergei does not fully understand, the link of snow and death is broken for the first time.
The winter landscape suddenly becomes an object of aesthetic
contemplation for Sergei, who once again looks out a window
(though a stationary one) as he had tried to do on the journey to
Bagrovo. "The view of the swiftly flowing river in the snow, the
summer kitchen on the island and the high crossways to it, the
other island with its large and graceful trees, dusted with frost,
and in the distance the swelling cliffs of Cheliaev mountain—all
this picture produced on me a pleasant, calming impression. For
the first time I felt that the sight of nature in winter had its own

---

4. In the course of the same day, Sergei comes upon the workroom and watches
women servants spinning; the work is broken up by the outbreak of lamentation in his grandfather's room (1:413). The suggestions of links between spinning and life and death may echo ancient metaphors. Mircea Eliade, *Images and
Symbols*, pp. 110–119.

beauty" (1:418). Sergei's aesthetic perception of the dead time of the year suggests that he is beginning to gain perspective and equilibrium and to realize that each death is not a universal or cataclysmic event, although each of us is subject to death.

The third night passes quietly, as Sergei's fears continue to subside. At dawn he overhears his parents and learns that his mother is pregnant, which, according to the excluded final paragraph of *Family Chronicle* (1:616), is a chronological inaccuracy, Aksakov's brother Nikolai having been born in June of 1796, six months before their grandfather's death. Aksakov seems seldom to depart from fact, and it is less likely that he would do so in a brief statement at the conclusion of *Family Chronicle* than he would in the midst of a narrative, where artistic reasons may supersede. The inversion of events in *Years of Childhood* may well have been deliberate and for a symbolic purpose; the mention of new life in the midst of death recalls the similar juxtaposition of Nikolai Fedorovich's death and Sergei's conception in the final fragment of *Family Chronicle*.

Immediately after the mention of new life, the procedures of the physical and psychological removal of the presence of death begin. Sergei first hears, then sees the funeral procession (1:420–421); as it did on the occasion of his grandfather's final blessing, the performance of a ritual in the presence of the entire society once again prompts Sergei to a positive attitude toward his grandfather. "Every one went to bid farewell to the deceased, then in the hall there arose a wail, resounding through the entire house; I felt strong emotion, but not any longer from fear, but from an obscure comprehension of the importance of the event" (1:720). As the funeral procession carries the still uncovered coffin to the waiting sleigh, Sergei, seeing that his grandfather is the focus of general concern, desires contact with him. "Standing on a chair and looking out the window, I wept from the depths of my soul, which was filled with a sincere feeling of love and kindness toward my grandfather, who was so warmly loved by everyone. For one moment I even wanted to see him again and kiss his withered hand" (1:421). Stepan Mikhailovich's hand, which during his first night Sergei feared would clutch him, now becomes the passive object of Sergei's desired action, suggesting both the reversal of attitudes in Sergei and the end of his victimization by events. Although fears return at night and Sergei dreams of the funeral procession with the corpse in its shroud lying in the coffin, the content of his imaginings repeats the general motion of separation of the dead from the living (1:422).

The diurnal, ceremonial neutralization of death concludes with Sergei's direct participation in a rite. He returns to the room in which Stepan Mikhailovich died, now empty except for an icon and the bed frame, and observes the reading of the psalter, which continues day and night until the ninth day after the death. "I stood a long time in silence, experiencing a feeling of sorrowing pity. Suddenly I wanted to read the psalter for Grandfather myself. . . . Making me first pray to God, Myseich [one of the two lectors] placed me on Grandfather's low side-chair and I, standing, began to read. . . . I felt . . . an inexpressible satisfaction" (1:424–425).

On the ninth day, a day marked by special requiem services in the Russian Orthodox Church, Sergei again reads the psalter, participating by proxy in the requiem rites being held at the graveyard. This time Sergei intentionally goes to his grandfather's room to read the psalter. The significance of his action, his first deliberate participation in a rite, is pointed out by Evseich: "I read with even greater satisfaction than the first time. . . . When we were leaving the room, Evseich said to me: 'See how well things turned out! In Nekliudovo they said a requiem for Grandfather on his grave, and you, little falcon, have been reading the psalter for him in his chamber'" (1:425). Sergei has not only put an end to his own fears, but also begun to assume a certain role in the ceremonially structured life of the country. The fact that he instinctively desired to read the psalter suggests that, at least in the context of death and its aftermath, Aksakov sees the country way as the only humanly meaningful approach.

The religious rites are followed by the traditional popular rite of the funeral meal, which concludes with pancakes (bliny) and obligatory mourning (1:426). Sergei's last contact with the physical presence of death comes when he learns that the meal was served, in accordance with custom, on the table on which the corpse had been laid. "These words so struck me that I myself felt a certain aversion to the dishes I had eaten. I even felt nauseous" (1:426). His reaction might suggest that he has not entirely accepted death, but the more likely explanation is that he is uncomfortable with the archaic, probably pre-Christian nature of the ritual, which in part represents the darker side of village life. It is the women who mourn on this occasion, and Sofia Nikolavna, the embodiment of urban sensibility, also is disgusted by the use of the table for the funeral meal. Sergei has, after all, reacted positively to the other rites he witnessed, which are traditional, but Christian or thoroughly assimilated to Christianity.

When the rituals have all been concluded, Sergei, having more or less successfully incorporated the experience of mortality into the development of his personality, leaves with his family for Ufa, although Bagrovo is soon to become the center of his life. As if to point out by contrast the symbolic weight of the environment throughout the journey to Bagrovo and the stay there, contact with the world outside is maintained during the return trip, which "was completed more quickly and more comfortably: the cold moderated, the windows in our cab did not become completely covered with snow, and the cab did not overturn" (1:426–427).

The following chapter, "Ufa," is set in an environment contrasting sharply with the village where Sergei has undergone his traumatic experience with death. It also complements his new awareness of mortality with a confirmation of life and the continuity of life, as symbolized in the birth of a younger brother. The cold and snow, emblematic of death, which dominated the midwinter scene of the preceding three chapters, are replaced by midsummer heat.

Birth, of which he has been ignorant until now, involves vicarious suffering, as did death, but to a lesser degree. Sergei bruises his leg (1:432), as he had his forehead at Bagrovo, and Sofia Nikolavna undergoes a surrogate death recalling the fifth chapter of *Family Chronicle*. Sergei parallels her suffering with nocturnal fears like the ones he felt at Bagrovo (1:434–435), which again subside in the daytime, and are finally replaced with joy. The moment of new life is bathed in the light of dawn. "My convulsive sobs and gasps, my inner and outer tremors did not soon subside. Finally, everything little by little calmed down, and first of all I saw that the room was bright from the dawn's light, and then I realized that Mother was alive, and would be all right— and a feeling of inexpressible happiness filled my heart!" (1:435). That the birth of his younger brother represents for Sergei an experience analogous to the one he underwent at Bagrovo is underlined by his comment to his mother that he would have died if she had (1:438). As on the prior occasion, Sergei completes and ratifies his acceptance of a previously unacknowledged fact of life by participating in a rite; he insists on standing as godfather to his new brother, although in fact he is deceived and simply allowed to come forward with the actual godparents (1:438).

With his first encounter with the mystery of birth, Sergei's initiation into the ultimate facts of human life is more or less accomplished. Like his development with regard to the natural world, this initiation is relatively complete, since he has undergone the essential crisis that marks the boundary between the ignorance of childhood and the knowledge characteristic of full human existence, even if adulthood has not been achieved in other respects. Even after the family moves to Bagrovo the estate retains its association with death, but there is a significant alteration in Sergei's relationship with this aspect of the estate. He does not participate in the event as he did at the time of his grandfather's death, but is rather an observer. The two incidents which involve death, one of them a premature death, serve as codas of sorts to the crucial death of Stepan Mikhailovich and indicate how far Sergei has progressed beyond that point.

In the first incident, the miller Boltunenok drowns in the Buguruslan on Easter Sunday in full view of the entire household, including Sergei, as if to assert Bagrovo's connection to death even at the moment of the celebration of the renewal of life in all its forms. Although Sergei for the first time actually witnesses a death, his role is strictly that of an observer, and his fears are easily overcome. "But I had the fortitude to overcome my fear and not wake Mother and Father up. The horrible night passed, it grew light and at sunrise my inflamed imagination grew quiet and I fell sweetly asleep" (1:502).

The second death, that of Sergei's grandmother Arina Vasil'evna, is treated in more detail, but Sergei accommodates himself to her passing even more easily than he did to the miller's, although the death is most difficult for his father. Arina Vasil'evna's final illness occurs while Sergei and his family are visiting Praskov'ia Ivanovna, and their trip back to Bagrovo is once again a trip which concludes with a confrontation with death; however, as the chapter title, "Autumn Journey to Bagrovo" ("Osenniaia doroga v Bagrovo"), suggests, the atmosphere is autumnal rather than wintry. Rain, water, and mud attend the journey, suggesting a final resigned dissolution into the all-embracing elements rather than a struggle of darkness and light, life and death; Arina Vasil'evna's steady decline has been mentioned several times previously. Nevertheless, the journey is fraught with difficulties and delays caused by bad roads and rain. The crossing of the Volga is particularly difficult (1:558), recalling the use of rivers as boundaries on other occasions in Aksakov's works, although it is Aleksei Stepanovich who is most affected: "Fate desired to test my father's patience. While his heart raced ahead to Bagrovo, to his dying mother, hindrances sprang up at every step. Our entire journey was the most unlucky, wearying, and sorrowful" (1:559). As a final confirmation of the funereal nature of the trip, snow falls, although it is quickly dissolved in the rain and mud (1:560).

If Sergei feels more sympathy for his father than he does real sorrow over his grandmother's death, his first perception of Bagrovo, to which he had desired to return, nevertheless suggests his inner harmony with events. The sight in particular of the millpond in a storm, recalling the Volga, where the family had come close to perishing, suggests this correlation: "I threw myself to the window in order to look at our broad millpond. My God! How sad it appeared to me! A cruel wind was blowing, dull waves coursed the whole pond, so that they recalled the Volga to me; the leaden sky was reflected in them; the reeds had withered, turned yellow, the waves and the wind tossed them in all directions, and they rustled hollowly and sadly. The green banks, the green trees—all had disappeared. The trees, the mill, and the peasant huts—all was wet, black and muddy." (1:563) The elements that had been the constituents of the vital world of the spring and summer (and are the constant realities in various microcosms Aksakov creates in his works) now reflect universal decay.

His grandmother had died and been buried before his family arrived at Bagrovo. Although Sergei's reaction to her death lacks the dimension of existential struggle that characterized his response to his grandfather's death, nevertheless he is not entirely free of a certain vague unease. As he did in the case of the death of Stepan Mikhailovich, Sergei resorts to ritual to neutralize the effects of death. He reads the psalter on the ninth day after burial, but "I did not get through a page—every word resounded painfully in my head" (1:566). He participates in the ritual commemorative meal, but falls sick and remains semiconscious for three days. His psychosomatic reactions to his grandmother's death suggest that there is still some residual fear, much less intense or explicit, that must be overcome. The reduction of the level of response to the physical indicates that death is no longer the catalyst of a crisis, but only the occasion for an indefinite apprehension. Sergei's illness on this occasion, while recalling in milder form the surrogate death he undergoes at the death of Stepan Mikhailovich in the central chapters, seems also to provide a concluding balance to the illness that characterized the opening of the text, and thus signals the end of childhood, both with regard to cognitive development and with regard to the awareness of human limitation. The final chapter of the text, "Life in Bagrovo after Grandmother's Death" ("Zhizn' v Bagrove posle konchiny babushki") is concerned primarily with Sergei's moral development.

Sergei's moral development in *Years of Childhood* forms a much less prominent strand in the total narration of the work, but nevertheless constitutes a significant theme, linking incidents that at first seem isolated but which are in fact manifestations of a single process, the growth of ethical awareness. This facet of Sergei's development complements the growth on the levels already discussed and presupposes a degree of perceptual and social consciousness. However, unlike his perceptual or social maturation, Sergei's moral growth, since it pertains to a more abstract faculty, is not directly associated with an obvious set or system of images, but depends instead on the inference of principles from individual acts. Sergei's moral development is not closely linked with a specific place, as mortality is with Bagrovo; significant steps in this development occur in Ufa, during travel, and at Bagrovo. However, the crucial step of the attainment of ethical autonomy does occur at Ufa, the primary locus of abstract thought and self-determination.

In its initial stages, Sergei's moral consciousness resembles the opening period of fragmentary memories on the perceptual level, in that any moral question is vague and simplified in the extreme; more importantly, there is virtually no distinction between self and other—specifically, his mother. Sergei feels a certain amount of guilt over his mother's illness, but she quickly dispels his obscure sense of unjustified responsibility (1:300). As the episode of his fear of the ghost of Grandfather Zubin indicates, Sergei is so lacking in autonomy that parental authority

is sufficient to sway his opinions. In his most primitive perceptions of self and environment Sergei does not identify this external authority as emanating from another, and it is not until he
encounters enigmatic social relationships, different from those to
which he is accustomed, that moral questions, though not yet
specifically pertaining to authority or autonomy, begin to arise.
Sergei's first journey, so pregnant with significance on other levels, also inaugurates the sequence of moral development.

His initial ethical problems center on Parashino, one of Praskov'ia Ivanovna's estates (historically, the estate is Nadezhdino,
where Aksakov himself lived in the 1820s). Sergei's first attempt
to deal with Parashino involves seeking a definition, recalling
his nomenclative approach to new phenomena throughout this
journey, which is Sergei's first. "Hearing the word *Parashino*
often, I asked what it was and they explained to me that it was a
large and rich village" (1:313). However, Parashino is not the
same sort of thing as other places Sergei encounters on this trip,
since it involves a system of social relations, and its name is
inadequate to the reality. The actual encounter with Parashino
(the conclusion of "The Trip to Parashino" and "Parashino") involves social and ethical facts that elude Sergei's still fairly primitive notions of morality. It is also perhaps worth noting that, like
Sergei's early notions of death, which is either remote or metaphorical for him until the decisive incident of Stepan Mikhailovich's demise, questions involving morality are at first remote,
having no great immediate significance for the self, and focusing
on a place called Parashino and on people whom he knows only
slightly.

At the boundary of the estate, the Bagrovs are met by reapers,
who call Sergei, for the first time in his life, by his name and
patronymic (1:314), as a mark of respect to the relatives (and
presumed heirs) of their mistress. Sergei immediately attempts to
assimilate this fact to his previously held model of human behavior, which divides the world into kind and unkind people
and defines all relationships by the presence or absence of love.
"I . . . very much liked these kind people, who loved us all so
much" (1:314). However, his father's brief conversation with the
peasants on the condition of the estate engenders a whole set of
questions on the social realities of the estate—how do they know
our names? what is *courvée* (*barshchina*)? who is Mironych (the
overseer)? Sergei grasps some of the answers his parents provide,

but others escape him; he understands who Mironych is, since it involves a personal relation, but *barshchina*, an impersonal juridical notion, remains unclear (1:314–315). In the face of uncertainty, Sergei resolves problems in a manner consistent with his lexicographical bent at this time, engaging in a verbal fetishism, accepting and using words without full awareness of their meaning; in fact, as the narrator points out, Sergei even endows them with a private significance:

> On this occasion, as in many other cases, not having understood several answers to my questions, I did not leave them obscure and undecided for myself, and always interpreted them in my own fashion, as children usually do. Such explanations remain in their minds for a long time, and afterwards it often happened that, calling an object by its proper name, which made in and of itself perfect sense, I would not at all understand it. (1:315)

This automatic use of words, analogous with his moral impressionability at this stage, is particularly clear in Sergei's repetition, apparently without comprehension, of his father's expression of concern over the harvesting. "My father, watching them, often said with sympathy: 'They won't have time to cope with the grain before bad weather.' . . . Not understanding how and why, nevertheless I felt sorry that they wouldn't be able to cope with the grain" (1:315).

Parashino presents Sergei with a challenge to his previously unquestioned ethic of sympathy based on love among all individuals. Sergei is confronted with the mysterious and repulsive figure of the overseer Mironych, whose behavior suggests that the universal applicability of the model of the relations within the family, which Sergei has merely extended to all of humanity, may in fact not be valid. Mironych, himself a serf, is contemptuous of the other peasants, mistreating the old Grigorii by a petty and vindictive display of power, disrespectfully calling him "Grishka," though Aleksei Stepanovich himself pays him the courtesy of using his full name, all because he wants to revenge himself on the old man's grandson. Sergei, vaguely aware of Mironych's injustice, expresses his sympathy for Grigorii in physical terms, asking his father that the old man be put to bed and given tea (1:320). Aleksei Stepanovich concurs to the extent of insisting that the old man be retired from any sort of labor, but

Mironych's manifestations of suppressed hostility elicit another burst of questions from Sergei.

For the first time he comes into contact with some of the negative aspects of serfdom and absentee ownership, with the power and status on which the system rests and which clearly run counter to Sergei's premise of universal kindness. Mironych is secure as overseer at Parashino because he is a relative of Praskov'ia Ivanovna's general manager; Sergei's own family are deferred to because of his father's delicate position as Praskov'ia Ivanovna's presumed but undeclared heir. However, these practical realities and the behavior (including his parents') predicated on them remain incomprehensible to Sergei, to whom it seems that the codes in effect at Parashino condone cruelty and inhibit justice, a conclusion he reaches when his parents reluctantly decide not to report Mironych's behavior for fear of exacerbating the situation. Sergei's ethic takes no account of ultimate result, limitations on the efficacy of one's actions, the legitimate spheres of action of others, or the realities of power. "Why did Father not allow Mother to drive Mironych out at once? It must be that Father could do it? Then why doesn't he? Such questions swarmed in my child's mind, and I decided them for myself by concluding that Mikhailushka [the general overseer] and Grandaunt were bad people and that my father was afraid of them" (1:321).

Although Sergei's quandary at Parashino has been exploited by socially minded critics since Dobroliubov,[5] any revelation of the evils of serfdom at Parashino is incidental to the child's moral dilemma in the face of a system which is divergent from the norms he entertains at the time. Any inferred criticism of serfdom in the chapters set at Parashino should be qualified by consideration of the fact that the place is run by a peasant overseer (doubtless an upstart in Aksakov's eyes) and owned by a distant, somewhat frivolous woman unconcerned with the proper management of her estate. Stepan Mikhailovich at Bagrovo is obviously much closer to the model of the serf-owner for Aksakov. Aksakov is not, either here or elsewhere in *Years of Childhood*, using a child's putatively purer and more sensitive consciousness to point out failings of adults or of society as a whole, but

5. N. A. Dobroliubov, "Derevenskaia zhizn' pomeshchika v starye gody," 2:290–326. Mashinskii basically repeats this canonical interpretation in S. T. *Aksakov*, pp. 484–485.

rather is showing how a child's unformed and immature personality gradually comes to grasp the complexity of life, in its physical, social, or moral aspect. In any case, a work whose purpose
is to expose serfdom as a current social evil hardly gains suasive
power by being set sixty years in the past, particularly when
emancipation was already under discussion in Russia in the late
1850s.

Although Sergei's questions at Parashino reveal that his faith
in his parents' omnipotence is somewhat shaken, the full consequences of his discoveries at Parashino are not worked out at
this time. Sergei tends to continue his simplistic moral schema
after the stop at Parashino, and while he is beginning to learn
that the world contains not only kind but unkind persons as
well, the latter tend to be relegated to the distant and unknown,
while the former are known and have a direct bearing on his life.
The understanding that people run the gamut of the moral spectrum rather than being clustered on either end of it is still as far
beyond Sergei's capability as is any recognition that circumstances alter cases. The village elders' contention that any other
overseer would be worse leaves him unconvinced: "Worldly
wisdom can not be understood by a child; voluntary concessions
are incompatible with the purity of his soul, and I could in no
way reconcile myself with the thought that Mironych could fight
with people without ceasing to be a good person" (1:327).

The next major stage in his moral growth occurs after his first
trip to Bagrovo and the return to Ufa. "Winter in Ufa" ("Zima v
Ufe"), set in the city, involves Sergei's uncles, who have been
studying in the larger city of Moscow. In many respects this is
the most important stage in the process of coming to ethical
awareness, for Sergei emerges as morally autonomous, basing his
actions on principles which he himself elaborates rather than on
the authority of others. After this point, Sergei may modify or
change his principles as he becomes more mature, but they are
his own principles. Thus the incidents in Ufa, though occurring
much later, are the equivalent on the ethical plane of the inception of awareness on the perceptual level with which continuous
growth began.

Sergei's moral faculties develop primarily through a seemingly
trivial conflict with his uncles and their friend Volkov, but his
quarrels with the three young men lead to the formulation of
rules of conduct that are valid beyond the confines of the family

and depend on principles other than that of kindness and un-kindness—in other words, principles independent of affective bonds and also of socially defined roles such as those within the family.

The entire conflict with his uncles begins with a single prob-lem, Sergei's inability to gauge motivations or to take them into account. For him, idle trickery is the equivalent of seriously and maliciously intended falsehood because their formal expressions are similar. However, even this new emphasis on the formal moral aspects of an act represents progress; at Parashino, Sergei had dealt in essences, conceiving of Mironych and Praskov'ia Ivanovna as intrinsically evil beings. Similarly, the tenacity with which Sergei holds to his convictions indicates movement for-ward. We can see how far he has come by noting that at the end of his stay at Bagrovo, while clearly recognizing a lie in his nurse's assertions of constant care of the children in Sofia Nikolavna's absence, Sergei remained incapable of resisting the heteronomous moral authority of adults, even to the point of doubting the validity of his own observations in the face of the nurse's protestations to the contrary (1:354).[6] Sergei's susceptibil-ity to adult suggestion is repeated at the beginning of the present chapter; he believes and becomes frightened by the joking of a friend of the family, Col. L. N. Engelhardt, who threatens to recruit him; the incident is similar to the imposition of an adult role at the opening of *Reminiscences*. Sergei's older playmate, Andriusha, repeats the threat and is also believed, although doubt later creeps in, perhaps because of Andriusha's lack of adult status in either biological or social terms: "He was older than I and I believed him. Later, it seemed to me that he was scaring me on purpose." (1:359).

His uncles' first joke on Sergei capitalizes both on his uncrit-ical acceptance of an adult's statement and on the fear of pre-mature assignment of adult status. They and Volkov threaten military conscription, citing a ukase of their own devising re-quiring military service of eldest sons. Sergei is content to call the order "falsehood" and "inventions" (*nepravda* and *vydumki*)

6. Jean Piaget discusses the child's lack of moral autonomy in *The Moral Judgment of the Child*, p. 111ff. He points out (p. 121) that young children often judge the gravity of a lie by its degree of departure from the truth, not by the intention of the liar or the effect of the lie. This is Sergei's approach to his uncles' deceptions.

until they present him with a counterfeit copy, complete with seal, of the supposed ukase. However, even when confronted with the purported physical evidence, Sergei continues to resist (unlike his easy assent to his nurse's arguments at Bagrovo) and resorts to attacks on his persecutors when he feels himself on the verge of believing them. His reaction suggests the beginnings of a sense of moral realism, of law that is superior to and binding on all individuals, including adults, in whom Sergei had previously placed moral authority. As Piaget points out,[7] children's notions of justice at this stage of development tend to stress expiation, with little or no congruence of crime and punishment or sense of equity in the operation of punishment. Thus, when Volkov receives a black eye from the Bagrov cabinetmaker, Mikhei, in a scuffle totally unconnected with Sergei's problems, Sergei interprets this as divine retribution for Volkov's participation in the young men's second joke, a supposed attempt to marry Volkov to Sergei's sister. This fulfillment of Sergei's desires—"I wanted to shoot Volkov with a cannon" (1:364)—is particularly sweet because it prevents Volkov's attendance at a ball, a consequence perceived by Sergei as an eminently appropriate part of the punishment. "With this gentleman just at this time there occurred a ludicrous and unpleasant event, as if in punishment for his pastime of perstering people; I, out of my stupidity, greatly rejoiced at this, and would say: 'See, God has punished him for wanting to take my sister away'" (1:364). The appeal to God represents the full development of moral realism: the law is transcendent and absolute; punishment, though swift and sure, is meted out in a form that surpasses human understanding because of its complete lack of logical connection with the crime.

Sergei's new sense of the absolutism of moral law is even more forcefully brought out in his response to his uncles' and Volkov's third endeavor, an attempt to convince Sergei that Sergeevka, toward which Sergei feels a strong proprietary sense, has been made part of the dowry set aside for his sister, who is to be married to Volkov. Again a document, a purported deed of the transaction, is produced, this time complete with forgeries of the signatures of Sergei's parents and of one of his uncles, the latter attesting to Sergei's agreement. Sergei at one and the same time believes in the validity and efficacy of the document (reflecting

7. Ibid., p. 228.

his new conviction of the moral efficacy of acts) and is outraged at the deception, while failing to realize that the two premises are mutually exclusive and that a forgery cannot be valid. "Not believing in the consent of my father and mother, knowing all too well my own non-approval, at the same time I believed completely that this paper deprived me of both my sister and Sergeevka; besides the bitter insult of such losses, I was irritated and stung to the depths of my heart by such a base deception" (1:366).

Trapped by this absurd and painful dilemma, Sergei identifies his own will with absolute justice, and attempts (with only partial success) to effect by himself the same supposedly divine punishment that Volkov had met with previously. "In order not to put off my vengeance for long, I ran out of the room in a rage, dashed into the cabinetmaker's workroom, grabbed a wooden mallet, ran back to the drawing room, and, approaching quite close, let the mallet fly straight at Volkov" (1:367). Sergei of course is punished by his parents for his aggression, but he refuses (for the first time) to submit, preferring further punishment to asking Volkov's pardon, since he alone is responsible in Sergei's eyes for the entire sequence of events. Sergei sees his act as merely the expression of inevitable justice, with himself the instrument (1:367). In keeping with his new conception of transcendent morality, Sergei steadfastly adheres to his principles rather than compromise them for the sake of social harmony, which would have been unthinkable in the earlier days, when he submitted to adult authority and love was the highest norm. He is ostracized, made to stand in a corner in an empty room until he asks Volkov's pardon. Sergei's evaluation of himself at this point clearly indicates the moral system he now subscribes to. "I imagined myself some hero, some martyr, of which I had read and heard, suffering for the truth, for justice" (1:368).

Only after falling sick and recovering does Sergei modify his moral absolutism and seek mutual pardon of his tormentors (1:370). The illness, induced by the long hours of standing, suggests a martyr's death in defense of principle, but his new willingness to apologize after his recovery indicates movement away from his extreme position and a partial recognition of the importance of equitable relations. Throughout his struggle with his uncles and Volkov, Sergei is indeed in earnest, acting in accord with the absolute moral norm he has fashioned for himself; the adults with whom he is in conflict, and the narrator as well, view Sergei's terror with considerable irony, coming to realize the serious and rigid moral foundation of Sergei's actions only after he falls ill. The circumstances precipitating Sergei's illness may be ridiculous from the adult point of view, but only because the specific circumstances obscure by their pettiness the serious principles that lie behind them.

Sergei's final moral perceptions in this chapter develop further his incipient sense of equity. He notices that he consistently receives higher marks from Matvei Vassilievich, his writing teacher, than does the poor and walleyed Andriusha. Although he does not realize that the teacher's true purpose is to flatter his parents, Sergei judges his actions to be inherently unfair (ne-spravedlivo) (1:371). Finally, he observes the same Matvei Vassilievich, who is also the teacher in the one public school in the city, ordering students birched for misconduct and incorrect answers. In a complete reversal of his earlier acceptance of adult moral authority and of expiatory punishment (especially during his phase of moral absolutism), Sergei is not only horrified by the spectacle of corporal punishment (which, as is clearly pointed out in the text, injures no one, rolling off the students' backs like water), but also fails to see any merit in his mother's rationalizations of Matvei Vassilievich's conduct. Instead, Sergei develops "such an aversion to Matvei Vassilievich that after a month he had to be dismissed" (1:374). Thus Sergei's moral development, which began in total subjection to outside authorities and proceeded through a stage of rigorous application of norms derived from a transcendent, universal but logical principle, has reached in a relatively short period a stage in which justice has been so internalized and modified by a sense of equity that not only does he feel that the punishment should fit the crime but that the very necessity of external punishment is uncertain.

The next significant incidents, recorded in the chapter entitled "Ufa," coincide with the birth of Sergei's younger brother. Moral questions reappear for Sergei on a somewhat more refined level than was maintained in the conflict with his uncles, when there was a close connection between moral issues and physical reality. Now the problem revolves around the matter of truth itself, rather than right or wrong, and there is little or no immediate connection between acts and consequences in the physical world. The correct and legitimate use of language is the new focus of concern.

This aspect of ethical behavior is introduced at the beginning of the chapter, when Sergei's parents request him to write to Praskov'ia Ivanovna that he loves her and wants to visit her, although he has never seen her and is somewhat apprehensive of her after hearing about her at Parashino. He questions his parents' insistence on the letter: "I could not love, and did not wish to see, Praskov'ia Ivanovna, because I didn't know her, and realizing that I was writing a lie, something always condemned by us, I openly asked: 'Why am I being forced to say what isn't true?'" (1:428–429). But he is forced to write, on the grounds that he will come to love Praskov'ia Ivanovna when he meets her and that she will help Sergei and his family; doubtless his parents are considering their position as Praskov'ia Ivanovna's probable heirs (1:429). For Sergei, however, the truth is not subject to modification. His parents' arguments are incomprehensible and he submits to them only unwillingly. For him at this point the fact of a lie outweighs any harmless, beneficial, or even purely altruistic purpose in lying, and indeed he has begun to notice, and presumably to resent, the fact that his parents at times lie to him out of altruism. "I had already more than once noticed that people would tell a lie in order to calm me" (1:430).

Sergei's increased ability to discern reality and to make inferences even in the face of elaborate adult efforts to convince him of the contrary emerges with particular clarity during his mother's confinement. His increased powers of observation and of inference allow him to see through the protective prevarications which seek to keep from him the fact that his mother is in reality seriously ill, even near death. The key terms for Sergei's ability to perceive the actual situation are *zametit'* and *gadat'* ("notice" and "guess"). The efforts by adults (whom at one time Sergei would have believed simply because they were adults) to convince him of the contrary meet with doubt and ultimately with rejection and rebellion, although this is directed toward servants, perhaps both because of the ineptness of their efforts at deception and because of their relatively weaker authority. Sergei openly confronts his would-be deceivers, clearly preferring the truth and knowledge, even if painful, to ignorance imposed through lies:

> Evseich wasn't with us, but he soon came, and Parasha met him with the question: "Well, is the mistress better?"—
> "Better"—answered Evseich, but with an uncertain voice. I

> noticed this, but calmed down a bit. . . . Doubt began to
> creep into my mind. I looked fixedly into Evseich's and Para-
> sha's eyes and said firmly, "You're not telling the truth."
> They became confused, glanced at one another and did not
> soon answer. I noticed all this and after that no longer listened
> to any assurances or consolations. (1:434)

Given the situation of his mother's closeness to death, Sergei's desire to know the truth contrasts sharply with his desire to avoid the facts on the occasion of his grandfather's death. His desire to know the truth at any cost to himself presupposes the accommodation with the facts of human existence he has achieved earlier, indicating that various levels of his development are interdependent.

Just as, in his conflict with his uncles, he modified his insistence on rigid adherence to principles and appropriate punishment for their violation, Sergei's enunciation of the principle of the truth above all else soon undergoes modification in the direction of the maintenance of social harmony. In effect, he accepts a benevolent double standard; he demands full truth for himself, but agrees to conceal inadvertent words of Parasha's that might cause her difficulties, and, more importantly, he conceals his real emotions in the presence of his mother for the sake of her health (1:437). After the achievement of this flexible and decidedly adult modus operandi, the further development of Sergei's moral personality for the rest of the text consists mainly in the increasingly effective application of his principles to social reality.

One final incident reveals Sergei's ethical development. In the chapter "First Spring in the Country" Sergei is confronted with a complex situation in which the principle of altruism at which he had arrived at the time of his mother's confinement must be applied; for the first time, he must weigh a number of factors in reaching a decision as to what course of action to take. In the course of doing so he affirms the ethic of equity (not mere equality) and compassion, toward which his moral growth has been tending. Sergei, out of curiosity, enters his aunt Tat'iana Stepanovna's storehouse, in which she has secretly been hoarding goods of various sorts, even sugar, in lieu of the dowry she fears she will never receive. First Matresha, whose duty it is to guard the storehouse, entreats Sergei not to tell his aunt that he had been there; then Parasha, moved to rash words at learning of

Tat'iana Stepanovna's hoarding, begs Sergei to swear he will not tell his mother what she has said. He gives his oath, although he has little idea of what this signifies (1:524). Finally, Sergei's mother enjoins him not to tell his aunt of his adventure lest Matresha be punished, which possibility had not occurred to him when Matresha implored his silence. Sergei has, however, already concealed Parasha's statements about Tat'iana Stepanovna from his mother, the first time he has intentionally deceived her, and finally arrives at a resolution which takes full account of the probable consequences for others of an act which would be required by a strict adherence to the truth.

> I felt somehow uneasy the whole day; I didn't even go near my aunt, and spent little time with my mother, but walked with my sister or read the whole time. Toward evening, however, I thought up the following justification for myself: Since Mother herself had told me that I must conceal from Auntie the fact that I had gone into her storehouse lest she beat Matresha, then I must conceal Parasha's words from Mother, lest she send her away to Old Bagrovo. I became calm and went to bed happy. (1:525)

In his elaboration of a norm of equity, Sergei for the first time not only conceals a material fact from his mother, previously his primary source of morality, but on the very authority of that source infers an obligation ("ia dolzhen") to deceive her. Thus Sergei places himself in a world of moral adults, for whom independent altruism functions as the ultimate norm.

With Sergei's arrival at an adult moral principle, his basic development is complete, but the final stage of his growth in the moral sphere and in other areas is intertwined in the latter part of *Years of Childhood* with a further theme which, while not of the significance of the three areas already discussed, serves to open the ending of *Years of Childhood*, suggesting potential lines of expansion beyond the points of relative maturity Sergei has attained on the perceptual, social, and ethical levels.

This theme centers around the rather enigmatic figure of Praskov'ia Ivanovna, by whom Sergei has been puzzled at least since his first visit to Parashino, and her residence at her estate of Churasovo, which Sergei's family visits twice after their move to Bagrovo. Although her precise significance is somewhat obscure, Praskov'ia Ivanovna and her estate seem to provide a bridge from the world of childhood in which Sergei has heretofore lived, whether in Ufa or at Bagrovo, to a larger world outside, to which he is ready to make the transition at the close of the text. As is often the case in *Years of Childhood* and in *Reminiscences*, Sergei's experiences at Churasovo tend to demythologize a reality that seems at first to depend in large measure on literary stereotypes; indeed, in some respects the Churasovo chapters of *Years of Childhood* recall the overall structure of *Reminiscences*, for here too a mode of perception which derives in large measure from fairy tale is overcome and abandoned. Such incidents as Sergei's first experience in the gymnasium in *Reminiscences* and his first stay at Bagrovo in *Years of Childhood* are perceived by him in the categories of faëry, but his use of literary patterns to structure reality in these instances are in fact manifestations of a desire to escape that reality, in other words, to exploit aesthetic models as solutions to psychological stress.

In the chapters set in Churasovo there appears to be much less psychological need to resort to literary models to deal with stress, and there is a tendency toward the wholesale elimination of the aesthetic as a mode for perceiving reality. Aksakov seems to be insisting on the necessity for the adult to effect the disjunction of art and life. Only the child confuses the two, and given Aksakov's acceptance of the inevitability of change and growth, to retain such a fusion of the two categories is to remain immature. In this regard it may be worth considering Aksakov's own separation of practical life and his artistic pursuits, all of them clearly delineated from ordinary activity: fishing, hunting, acting, card-playing. The last phase of childhood is the abandonment of the stories of childhood (except in memory, as Aksakov points out in *Reminiscences*) and acceptance of the mundane quality of adult human life.

Fairy tales often deal with the same processes of maturation that engage Aksakov on those occasions when he resorts to their plots: chapter 3 of *Family Chronicle*, the first half of *Reminiscences*, and the Churasovo chapters of *Years of Childhood*. He presents the fairy tale in an undisplaced form in *Years of Childhood*, introducing the figure of a traditional teller of such tales in the chapter "First Spring in the Country." "The Little Crimson Flower" ("Alen'kii tsvetochek"), appended to *Years of Childhood*, is a Russian version of "Beauty and the Beast," but despite its fabulous quality, it may be read as a concentration of the central theme of *Years of Childhood*, the theme of maturation. Presented as something originating in the country and preserved by Bagrov's memory, this tale and many others find their source in childhood, memory being the means of access, as *Reminiscences* puts it. It is thus an analogue in genre to the pastoral provided by rural environment or by the memory of childhood. A characteristic exercise in an established genre, "The Little Crimson Flower" permits Aksakov to present directly a form he can only allude to elsewhere. While he presents the tale as a reproduction of a traditional version, as all tellers do, a comparison of Aksakov's version with a true folk version indicates how much of Aksakov's art lies in his ability to expand and embellish a narrative kernel into a tale ten times the length of the actual folk versions.[8]

"The Little Crimson Flower," which is set in a distant enchanted palace, a place of pleasant but enforced confinement that is presided over by an ambiguous being, constitutes a fairly direct allegory of Sergei's experiences at Churasovo, although of course the happy fairy-tale resolution is lacking. The luxurious manor house at Churasovo, with its murals, chandeliers, paintings, and mirrors, seems to Sergei on his first trip there like something out of the tales of Sheherazade (1:469). At first Sergei naïvely confuses the artifice of this décor with the objects represented and thinks he is perceiving yet another new world of "forests, flowers, and fruits unfamiliar to me, birds, beasts, and people unknown to me" (1:465). In fact, this painted world is little more than an inept parody of nature, or an imitation of the luxury of the palaces of the capital, an expression of the whimsy of provincial wealth not far above the work of a shop-sign painter and capable only of impressing a child, according to the adult narrator's comment (1:468). The lifelessness of the paintings suggests the sterility, artificiality, and ambiguity that pervade the fairy-tale world of Churasovo and are particularly apparent in its mistress, Praskov'ia Ivanovna.

Praskov'ia Ivanovna is a sort of benevolent witch whose house, with guests constantly coming and going, is a wound clock (1:481). She tells her guests, in true fairy-tale fashion, "'Ask, order—everything will be done'" (1:468), but at the same time a note of sterility and even of oppression persists. Herself a child-

8. See A. N. Afanas'ev, "Zakliatyi tsarevich" ["The Bewitched Tsarevich"], 2:358–359.

less widow, Praskov'ia Ivanovna dislikes small children and segregates Sergei and his sister from the life of the rest of the house; Sergei learns that she has been a somewhat harsh step-mother to a destitute and orphaned cousin, Aleksandra Ivanovna, who now acts as Praskov'ia Ivanovna's housekeeper and facto-tum. Her household, ostensibly a stately pleasure dome, is rife with parasitic servants who indulge in every misconduct behind their mistress's back, to the horror of the Bagrov servants and the puzzlement of Sergei, who has never seen such goings-on.

The ambiguity of Praskov'ia Ivanovna, who greets Sofia Niko-lavna warmly but slights her children, constitutes the central problem for Sergei during his first stay at Churasovo. To his earlier notions of Praskov'ia Ivanovna as an enormous, vague, and perhaps hostile being are added his own experience of her and the conflicting opinions of his mother and Aleksandra Iva-novna, which in combination leave Sergei in a quandary as to Praskov'ia Ivanovna's moral quality: "Is Praskov'ia Ivanovna good or not altogether good?" (1:477). The ambiguity of her be-havior is by no means resolved by a lengthy description of her, not from the point of view of a child, but directly from the primary level of narration (1:478–481), where attention is given both to her faults and to her virtues.

In the context of Churasovo, with its artificiality and air of enforced gaiety, a child is seen only as an object of condescen-sion and a source of amusement, a situation particularly galling to Sergei, who resents every attempt, even by his parents, to deny him equal status on the grounds of his still being a child of seven. "I felt that they weren't interested in me, but were only enjoying themselves; I didn't like that and therefore my answers were sometimes impolitely sharp and unsuited to my age and characteristics. Mother reproached me for this when we were alone; I answered that it was annoying when people put my words to ridicule and even spoke with me only to have a laugh" (1:482). Finally, Churasovo comes to seem a trap to Sergei, de-priving him of his physical freedom and preventing unfettered discussion with his mother of the many questions in his mind centering on Praskov'ia Ivanovna. He fails to reconcile imposed opinion and personal observation. "I did not understand Pra-skov'ia Ivanovna; I took people's word for it that she was good, but I was constantly dissatisfied with her attitude toward me, my little sister and my little brother, whom she once had nearly ordered spanked for crying too loudly; it was a good thing that Mother didn't obey" (1:484–485). Sergei's attitude toward her still retains his earlier fear of her as some sort of omnipotent, mythical being; a further trip to Churasovo will be required for Sergei to overcome the fairy-tale structure of his perceptions of a social reality completely different from his prior experience.

On that second trip, "A Summer Journey to Churasovo" ("Let-niaia poezdka v Churasovo"), everything which had on the first visit seemed marvelous, if ambiguous, has now lost even its power to enchant, a fact which is signaled by a stop on the way to Churasovo at the estate of a certain Durasov, whose name suggests both *Churasovo* and *fool* (*dura, durak*). In a recapitulation of the larger movement of the journey, Sergei is torn from a planned fishing expedition so that his parents may visit Durasov. The mansion on Durasov's estate of Nikol'skoe makes Sergei think of knightly castles, English manors, and an enchanted palace of Sheherazade (1:536–537), all familiar to him from his reading. Sergei is still capable of amazement, although Nikol'skoe, for all its sumptuousness, is an ostentatious sham, its owner bolstering his own status by aping the latest European fashion in everything from chamber music to prize English pigs. In several physical particulars, such as its elaborate gardens, Nikol'skoe recalls and surpasses Churasovo, while the exaggerated beneficence of Durasov also parodies Praskov'ia Ivanovna's hospitality. His laughter at Sergei's unconcealed amazement recalls the adults' use of Sergei for entertainment on his first visit to Churasovo.

With Churasovo's power to impress and its fairy-tale qualities destroyed by the stop at the even more grandiose Nikol'skoe, Churasovo becomes, despite Sergei's warmer feeling for Praskov'ia Ivanovna as a person (1:546), more openly a prison, its mistress refusing to let her guests return to Bagrovo. They, not wishing to offend their future legatrix, submit to her wishes. "With each day this city life in the country bored me more and more; even Mother wanted sooner to return to Bagrovo, though she disliked it, because my little brother, who had had his second birthday, had stayed there. Father was very sad and even wept" (1:552). Deliverance comes only through news that Aleksei Stepanovich's mother, Arina Vasil'evna, is seriously ill (1:553). The family leaves Churasovo on the funereal journey that ends with Sergei's final experience with death.

With the ceremonies following his grandmother's death, Sergei at last is able to perceive the essence of Bagrovo, much as he had begun to perceive the essence of Churasovo on his second visit there; in both cases it is apparent that the places of his childhood are no longer adequate, that further growth requires a new locus. For the first time Sergei realizes fully the nature and extent of the conflict between his mother and the Bagrov women; he had often been exposed to manifestations of this hostility in the past, but without being able to comprehend its language, so to speak. Only after witnessing his mother's offer of an adequate dowry to Tat'iana Stepanovna, the youngest Bagrov daughter and thus the least well-provided for, does Sergei recognize the moral fortitude of his mother's constant refusal to match the behavior of her female in-laws:

> There followed new and very warm thanks on Tat'iana Stepa-
> novna's part. Only then was the position in which my
> mother lived in the family of my father fully explained for me.
> Recalling everything I had heard at various times from
> Parasha and words of my mother's that had slipped out during
> heated conversations with my father, I formed for myself
> a fairly clear understanding of the qualities of the people with
> whom she was living. One can imagine what a lofty being
> my mother appeared to me to be! (1:572)

The social realities of Bagrovo have now been unraveled, and the estate in large measure already relegated to the past, as suggested by Arina Vasil'evna's death. The only possible development is now outward.

Years of Childhood ends, more or less as it began, with a journey, this time a double journey, first to Churasovo and then to the great world beyond, of which Churasovo itself has now become an inadequate emblem. The fact that Churasovo has now been reduced to the prosaic is suggested on the way there, when the Bagrovs find Nikol'skoe closed and its eccentric master Durasov departed, with only the memory of his English pigs remaining as the subject of rather mocking anecdotes by his peasants. When Sergei realizes that serfs do not necessarily consider their masters paragons of good sense, he has had another insight into the world as it in fact is (1:578). Churasovo too is now merely a place like others, with Praskov'ia Ivanovna less mysterious, but also rather kinder and less despotic in Sergei's eyes, although he perceives considerably less good will toward him and his family on the part of Praskov'ia Ivanovna's companions and servants.

When Sergei imparts this perception to his mother, she tells him this is nonsense, and for the first time he feels that Sofia Niko-lavna herself is concealing the truth from him (1:580).

With this loosening of the tie between mother and son, the family unit binding Sergei, his parents, and his little sister and brother is for the first time broken up, and motifs of separation conclude the text. At the suggestion of Praskov'ia Ivanovna, who previously refused to let her relatives leave, Sofia Nikolavna and Aleksei Stepanovich, along with Sergei, set out for Kazan, leav-ing behind Sergei's sister and infant brother. These separations, though temporary, signal the close of the text and the end of childhood, as does the departure for the city of Kazan. The sep-aration from his sister, his constant companion and the symbol of his own childhood, is clearly a traumatic closing of an era for Sergei. For the first time, at the very close of the text, he briefly engages in nostalgic memory, the dominant characteristic of the adult narrator of the entire text, with whom in a sense Sergei has now become identical, after passing through all the stages of unreflective childhood:

> Instead of joy that I was leaving Churasovo if only for a while
> and would see a new rich city of which I had heard a great
> deal, I felt that my heart was breaking from sorrow. My dear
> little sister, all in tears, with reddened eyes, pining for
> her brother and nurse, but silently submitting to her fate, was
> constantly in my imagination, and I myself cried quietly
> for a long time, not paying heed to what was happening
> around me, and contrary to my habit, not dreaming about what
> waited ahead for me. (1:582)

At the moment of this memory, childhood is indeed over, and adult life, forever haunted by the echoes of the tales of child-hood, has begun. As ever in Aksakov's works, intimations of movement and growth counterbalance this retrospective finale; the very act of remembering takes place in a moving carriage, and the physical motion parallels the movement of the central personality into a new level of existence, as yet only pure poten-tial. "But ahead awaited me the start of the most important event of my life . . ." (1:582). The concluding interpunction leaves the future open, to be filled, in a sense, by the already-written *Remi-niscences,* but within the context of *Years of Childhood* itself implying the world that awaits every individual beyond the boundary of his own family and past the years of his own childhood. Aksakov reinforces both the sense of childhood completed and the world beyond its limits by intruding in his own words, after Bagrov's final words, "Here young Bagrov's account of his childhood ends. He maintains that further stories belong not to his childhood, but already to his boyhood. S. A." (1:582).

Thus with a concluding reassertion of the distinction between the narrator of *Years of Childhood* and his own ostensibly modest role, Aksakov ends his longest and most intimate work. With the reconstruction of early childhood, indeed of his own long-past period of immaturity and growth, Aksakov brought to a close a trilogy which in scope and artistic accomplishment remains one of the masterpieces of Russian prose.

8

Farewell to Arcadia: Final Works

In the year and one-half between the publication of *Years of Childhood* in late 1857 and his death in April of 1859, Aksakov published a volume entitled *Various Works* (*Raznye sochineniia*), containing his *Literary and Theatrical Memoirs*, dealing with the 1820s, and several shorter pieces of various dates ("The Blizzard," "Biography of Zagoskin," "A Few Words about M. S. Shchepkin"). He also completed two works that serve as fitting conclusions to his late-blooming literary career. The first and longer of these, "Butterfly Collecting" ("Sobiranie babochek"), 1858, recounts Aksakov's brief infatuation, during his last year at the University of Kazan, with the collecting of butterflies (thus anticipating Nabokov in the matter of lepidoptery in Russian literature by some sixty years). Full of detail on the nomenclature, appearance, habitats, and habits of various butterflies and moths, on the manner in which they are stalked and captured and on the methods of mounting and displaying such trophies, "Butterfly Collecting" clearly is informed by the same attitude toward nature and the ethic of the hunt that marks Aksakov's earlier works. At the same time, the piece is a memoir, as its subtitle "A Story from Student Life" ("Rasskaz iz studentskoi zhizni") suggests. It is the final memoir dealing with Aksakov's school days, and therefore has a clear narrative structure and theme, the final dalliance with the things of a child. This note of personal significance was generally lacking in earlier works on hunting, as was any sustained narrative. This recombination of Aksakov's own genres endows "Butterfly Collecting" with a more light-hearted attitude toward its particular form of the hunt, but at the same time imbues it with a sense of personal nostalgia. In

the final analysis, the permanent value of this episode in Aksakov's life as a hunter rests on the fact that

> there has remained with me for my whole life the joyous
> memory of this time, of many happy, blessed hours. My hunt-
> ing for butterflies took place under the open sky and was
> surrounded by the various phenomena, beauties, wonders of
> nature. . . . All my attention, it seemed, was directed to
> my valuable quarry; but nature, imperceptibly to me, was
> illuminating my spirit with its eternal beauties, and such
> impressions, arising at a later time brightly and clearly, are
> grace-giving, and remembering them summons forth a joyous
> feeling from the depths of man's soul. (2:221)

Here, perhaps more explicitly than in any previous work, Aksakov equates nature and the memory of childhood as sources of
transcendent value—the quasi-religious dimension of both is
suggested by the term grace-giving (blagodatnyi)—in the world
of adulthood, with its risk of alienation from both the environment and the self.

Written five months before his death, Aksakov's final work,
"Sketch of a Winter's Day" ("Ocherk zimnego dnia"), fuses, like
"Butterfly Collecting," a memory-piece and the hunt. It particularly emphasizes the aesthetic element in man's relation with
nature and in the remembrance and artistic recreation of that
relation. Unlike "Butterfly Collecting," "Sketch of a Winter's
Day," as its title suggests, deals not with a general topic or with a
distinct phase in Aksakov's past, but with one specific hunt, or
rather with the circumstances leading up to it. In fact, the hunt
itself is not described; true to its designation as an ocherk,
"Sketch of a Winter's Day" focuses on a single brief interval of
time, presented in detail, rather than on an action. Although
little happens in the sketch and it is outwardly nothing more
remarkable than a lengthy weather report, Aksakov transforms
the simplest material into a subtle summation of his art.

The sketch deals with a few days during the winter of 1813,
opening with a period of extreme cold in which even the mer-
cury in a thermometer congeals. As one would expect in Aksakov, the moment of intense cold is also a moment of death; the
ground, bare of snow, freezes to unusual depths, the wind dies
down completely, both people and livestock fall sick. In its description of nature immobilized in the dead calm of winter,
"Sketch of a Winter's Day" distantly echoes passages in "The

Blizzard," written some twenty-four years earlier, providing a certain apt symmetry in Aksakov's career as a prose writer. However, the overt, even flagrant metaphors and obvious poeticism of "The Blizzard" are eliminated, distilled into a subtle poetry of precise description, as a brief comparison reveals:[1]

> The sun was sinking to the West, and, raking its slanted rays over the boundless masses of snow, clothed them with a jewellike crust, and the grove, deformed by the frost clinging to it, from a distance presented, in its costume of ice and snow, wondrous and various obelisks, also sprinkled with a diamond glitter. Everything was magnificent. ("The Blizzard," 2:408)

> The sight of nature in winter was magnificent. The cold had drawn the moisture out of trunks and branches, and the shrubs and trees, even reeds and tall grass were covered with a down of sparkling frost, over which the rays of the sun slipped harmlessly, only bestrewing them with the gold sparkle of flames of diamond. ("Sketch of a Winter's Day," 2:464)

This interval of suspended life, clearly an aberrant situation for Aksakov, is broken by the start of motion, of a sequence of events that constitute the narrative proper: first the wind begins to blow, clouds cover the sky, and finally snow begins to fall. Only at this point does Aksakov himself (twenty-one at the time) appear. He is himself at a specific moment in his life, not the rather schematic, generalized hunter in earlier works; even more than the earlier hunter or fisherman, Aksakov is here an entranced observer of nature, specifically of the falling snow. He goes out into the fields "in order to enjoy this picture fully" (2:464). As with earlier picture metaphors (in *Notes on Fishing*), the emphasis is on erasing the boundary between observer and observed, removing the frame and experiencing nature from within. One could hardly feel more at the center of natural events and engulfed by them than in the midst of a snowstorm. In a recapitulation of many of Aksakov's privileged moments in na-

---

1. The earlier story was republished by Aksakov in 1858 in *Various Works*, so that "The Blizzard" would have been relatively fresh in his mind when he composed "Sketch of a Winter's Day." In his introduction to "The Blizzard" in *Various Works*, Aksakov gives as one of his reasons for publishing it again the fact that "some of my readers might be interested in finding out how the same person wrote twenty-three years before the appearance of *Family Chronicle* and *Reminiscences*" (2:404).

ture, boundaries disappear and the absence of sound intensifies the visual impression; key words such as *marvelous* and *stillness* figure in the description: "A marvelous spectacle presented itself to my eyes: the entire boundless expanse around me presented the sight of a stream of snow, as if the heavens had been sundered and had strewn a snowy down and had filled the entire air with movement and an amazing stillness. The long winter twilight set in; the falling snow began to cover everything and veiled the earth in a white murk" (2:464).

Even with the onset of evening, Aksakov still avoids entering the house, walking about the orchard instead, to watch "objects fuse and sink in the darkening air" (2:465). Finally forced inside, he gazes out the window until it is impossible to distinguish the falling snowflakes. This rapt contemplation of and merger with nature runs through all of Aksakov's works (we might recall Aleksei Stepanovich in the fourth chapter of *Family Chronicle* or Sergei's frequent moments at the window in *Years of Childhood*) but perhaps reaches its peak of intensity in "Sketch of a Winter's Day." It is also worth noting that the correlation of snow and death is lacking here (the moment of dangerously dead calm precedes the snow); as it did in Sergei's perception of the beauty of the snowy landscape after his grandfather's death, the aesthetic rather than psychological element predominates. Aksakov's willing and delighted self-abandonment in what had previously been his prime metaphor for death may suggest the author's acceptance of his own approaching end. The spell is finally broken by a shift from rapt observation to intended action as Aksakov the hunter takes over and considers the opportunities for tracking game that the new snow will provide; indeed, in a demonstration of hunterly foresight, preparations have already been made for the next day's hunt. Still, awakening before the late winter dawn, Aksakov awaits daybreak and observes, almost as if he were Monet, the subtle gradual changes in the quality and intensity of the light, viewing them with the same absorption he had experienced in the snowstorm on the previous day. Again the poetry of silent contemplation asserts itself. "How fine, how sweet it was in my soul! Calm, quiet, and light. Some obscure, warm daydreams, full of languor, filled my soul" (2:465). However, the light is finally bright enough to allow tracking game, and again the active phase of the man-nature relationship takes over: "'The horses are ready; time to go, sir,' rang out the

voice of Grigorii Vasil'ev, my hunting companion and as passionate a hunter as I. That voice returned me to reality. My day-
dream dissolved. Hares' tracks started flickering before my eyes. I
quickly took down from the wall my favorite gun, my trusty
Spanish hunting piece . . ." (2:466). "Sketch of a Winter's Day"
thus offers a brief but intense recapitulation of the dual-faceted
relation that obtains between man and nature throughout Aksakov's works: intense but passive contemplation of nature as a
totality, alternating with the attempt to act, to intervene and master at least one distinct element of nature.

With the lifting of the gun and the full assumption of the
active role of the hunter, the intense aesthetic moment ends and
the text breaks off. (The interpunction is Aksakov's.) In its conclusion as in its theme and structure, "Sketch of a Winter's
Day" repeats, within its lyric and reduced compass, a pattern
characteristic of Aksakov's works generally. Aksakov's text once
again ends with a beginning to which every event of the preceding narrative has been tending and whose value has been increased in proportion to the degree of retardation. Although the
specific action being embarked on is hunting, the time of day,
the setting out on the hunt, and the demonstrative interruption
of the text at the moment of total potentiality, (recalling in its
way Pushkin's line "Whither then shall we sail . . ."), forms a
fitting conclusion to Aksakov's literary activity. "Sketch of a
Winter's Day" ends, as do so many of Aksakov's works, with
a beginning; the avoidance of closure may indeed constitute the
controlling Aksakovian device.[2]

From this insistence on the endless continuity and continuation of both life and narrative flows Aksakov's compensatory
stress on beginnings and his pervasive interest in process. In the
world of his narrative, the inception of action or being and the
initiation of individuals acquire an importance and function
analogous to that of climax and dénouement in more usual literary texts; as I have noted, apparent endings are illusory and
constantly imply new or different lives and narratives (the frequent final departures, the inscribing of the name Sergei). At
the same time, all of these beginnings, and the narratives which

2. Barbara Herrnstein Smith, *Poetic Closure: A Study of How Poems End*, pp.
117–121, briefly discusses the role of endings in fiction and drama. She suggests
that open-endedness may have "the corollary effect of leaving the boundary between art and reality indistinct," p. 120 (n. 15).

unfold (or could unfold, in cases where they conclude the narrative and Aksakov does not develop their potential) are of necessity viewed retrospectively, preserved by memory and presented by art. Only from the standpoint of the present can the significant initiation, birth, or departure in the past be accurately assessed, its full consequences recognized. This tension between looking backward and looking forward, between retrospection and anticipation, memory and hope, is perhaps resolved for Aksakov specifically through his art, which creates a secondary reality that draws on past experience yet renders that experience immediate through the atemporal permanence of art.

Thus, in its use of memory, its divergent but complementary responses to nature, and its structural openness reflecting a basic openness to life, "Sketch of a Winter's Day" forms, for all its modest brevity, the quintessential Aksakovian text, orchestrating the ordinary and specific into an intensely lyric pattern of universal significance. In its subtle refinement of Aksakov's deepest insights, "Sketch of a Winter's Day" brings his literary career to a fitting close.

If we consider Aksakov's works as a totality, we can sense a certain coherence, a sensibility, rooted in Aksakov's personality, that informs them all. It is difficult and perhaps reductive to affix a label to this unifying quality, since it obviously does grow out of Aksakov's own experience and expresses his uniqueness as a writer, but the term *pastoral*, to which we have had recourse on numerous occasions, may be the most all-encompassing, if by the same token somewhat vague. If we understand by pastoral not only a form of poetry or literature that stresses rural ease over urban complexity, but a system of values that favors simplicity and wholeness over complexity and fragmentation, then Aksakov's works can all be considered pastoral in some sense. More importantly, in the context of Russian literature and culture of the mid-nineteenth century and later, they often serve as a radical or paradigmatic statement of one pole of the response to Russia's historical situation as that impinged on the individual.

This is perhaps most overt in the literary memoirs and in *Family Chronicle*. The memoirs share with Aksakov's other works a nostalgia for a simpler time when motives were purer and actions, though at times comical, were more sincere. This nostalgia of cultural experience contrasts sharply with many cultural attitudes of the 1840s and 1850s. The late classical, verse-oriented culture of Derzhavin and Shishkov and the literary dabbling of the 1820s which Aksakov describes in his various memoirs were forms of self-expression of a gentry secure in its sense of self. Twenty years later, such self-contained and self-satisfied attitudes were the object of rejection and ridicule by various camps. Innocently asocial, frivolous, and studiedly elegant art was hopelessly outmoded in the socially aware, brave new world of the literature of the 1840s, with its emphasis on realism as method, national expression and social criticism as the message (at least as far as the dominant critics, such as Belinskii, viewed literature), and new journals of relatively broad circulation as a medium.

In addition, neither Westerners nor Slavophiles could be entirely happy with memoirs dealing sympathetically with Derzhavin or Shishkov, who were typical of a culture closely linked with a state apparatus opposed by both groups, though from different perspectives—the appearance of these pieces in Pogodin's *Muscovite*, with its official nationalist slant, was hardly inappropriate. As for the *Literary and Theatrical Memoirs*, dealing with the 1820s, they present, in pointed contrast to the times in which they appeared, a world of literary journalism in which, if controversy did arise, it was more of a squabble within a fraternity over the rules of the game than pitched debates over political and philosophical matters of earth-shaking importance. Aksakov does not necessarily favor the old way over the new, but clearly presents the alternative of an earlier, less complex day.

Family Chronicle can be read as a statement of the autonomy of the Russian gentry, appearing virtually on the eve of its decline as the dominant class in Russian society or in Russian culture. In its assertion of the value of the gentry, the novel had a certain congruence with Slavophile attitudes, though it could by no means be considered an unqualified endorsement or presentation of them. Its significance as a work of imaginative literature, with a structural complexity outweighing any potential political or social import, led to its immediate acceptance not only by Russian critics of every stripe but also and more importantly by Russian readers, who were in general more interested in good reading than in the often rather parochial debates of the ideologues who were coming to dominate the main journals published in the capitals.

As a work of literature, *Family Chronicle*, though a work of a man in his sixties, fit neatly with the latest literary currents. The 1840s and 1850s were the formative years, both in doctrine and practice, of Russian realism, with prose forms dominating. *Family Chronicle*'s copious and meticulous attention to the minute, physical details of a specific way of life provided a demonstration of the possibilities of realist prose that was matched only by Tolstoi at the time. In keeping with the empirical, even statistical, tendency underlying realism, Aksakov, like Tolstoi and to some extent Turgenev, depicted neither the heroic nor the grotesque, but rather the mean of ordinary life in such a way that it becomes an aesthetic form. This canonization of ordinary life has been significant in Russian literature down to the present, as *Doctor Zhivago* attests, but found its fullest expression in the Russian family novel of the 1860s and 1870s, with its affirmation of the coherent society of the family, specifically the gentry family. It serves as a counterweight both to the isolation of the individual, who, no matter how heroic, runs the risk of becoming superfluous, and to the annihilating demands of the larger society, particularly the state.

Family Chronicle in certain respects served as a model, a "prehistory" and "golden age," in terms of both content and form, to the family novels of Turgenev, Goncharov, and especially Tolstoi, whose *Family Happiness, War and Peace,* and *Anna Karenina* all confirm the centrality of the patriarchal, harmonious gentry family in creating value in existence. Aksakov's note of nostalgia for the world of the eighteenth century provincial gentry well suited the sense of loss of the old ways among genteel readers buffeted by emancipation and by the growing rate of social change. In many respects a myth (a fact of which Aksakov seemed more cognizant than did some younger contemporaries, such as Tolstoi), the family novel, with its emphasis on organic growth, continuity of cause and effect, and meaningful form, both in life and literature, provided a certain aesthetic refuge only too obviously imperiled or lacking altogether in real life. Even Dostoevskii, by showing the consequences of the breaches in the integrity of the family community occasioned by moral or ideological error, affirms the tradition; *The Brothers Karamazov* is an inverse family novel rather than an antinovel. Only twenty years after *Family Chronicle*, the bitter, radical satirist Saltykov-Shchedrin launched a frontal attack on the premises and form of the family novel, turning them upside down in *The Golovlev Family*, which depicts a gentry family on its decaying estate as a sterile, death-oriented, self-devouring matriarchy. In various structural features and specific details, Saltykov-Shchedrin clearly has *Family Chronicle* in mind as the paradigmatic text of the pastoral of the family novel.

Aksakov's works on childhood, like Tolstoi's trilogy, have a more universal or atemporal appeal, in that they are not rooted in a social or historical pastoral of a certain way of life, but draw on the personal past, with which any reader can potentially identify. On the level of realism, such works were investigations into aspects of perception and development of the psyche that had previously been unrecognized. The apparent freedom from overt ideological freight in such works of course conceals a more subtle implication consonant both with pastoral and with realism. *Years of Childhood*, and to a lesser extent *Reminiscences*, affirm again the value of ordinary experience, no matter how minute, mundane, or insignificant it may appear to the outside observer. Such an aesthetic stance assumes the priority of the individual as a source of meaning, as well as the essential equivalence and equality of individuals. The pastoral of childhood is however a transitory stage, not because of history but because of the development of the individual. It is recognizable only when it is past, when a more complex personality, rendered self-conscious through its contact with and partial enslavement by time and society, can view through memory a freedom irrevocably lost to it.

The implicit contradictions of both social and personal pastoral lead to the world of absolute pastoral Aksakov presents in the books on hunting in its various forms. Here unconditional freedom, along with complete responsibility for one's own actions, immediately confirmed by success or failure, reigns supreme. Society is obliterated (at least temporarily) and the requirements of nature ignore all individual features except skill. Individuals are replaced by the hunter, who exists outside time and social bonds. This total immersion in the immediacy of the experience of nature, while suppressing the individual as a social phenomenon, effectively reintegrates man into nature, providing the restored wholeness Aksakov's younger contemporaries sought in vain in some social structure, whether past or potential. The radical core of anarchism (of an aesthetic, not a political sort) in Aksakov is most clearly revealed in the hunting works, although it is present, in attenuated forms, in virtually all his works. Aksakov, first and most overtly in Russian literature, articulates this desire for withdrawal as a solution or alternative to the contradictions imposed both by biological experience and by social context.

The lure of such an option has always been strong in the Russian tradition, beginning with medieval monks setting out alone into the wilderness and continuing down to the present, with figures such as Solzhenitsyn proposing an anachronistic Russia withdrawing to a Siberian fastness. While such actions or appeals need not concern us here, they do point to an extreme alienation based on what are perceived to be (often rightly, perhaps) excessive demands on the individual from the social sphere. Similar patterns of withdrawal (ukhod), of opting out in search of a more valid pattern of existence or source of meaning, can be found in writers from Tolstoi (who shifts his ideal from the gentry family to the peasant household as the limitations of the former became apparent) to Pasternak and Solzhenitsyn (note Nerzhin's choice of Siberia and silence in The First Circle). All of these authors are of course, in their various ways, motivated by social and moral concerns that are in large measure alien to Aksakov. However, there is in each of them the frequent implication that such withdrawals are not only moral but also aesthetic acts, retreats by central characters into simpler and truer forms, into an existence of aesthetic wholeness that is precluded by their current situation and that cannot really be described in ordinary fiction. Such a withdrawal often forms a conclusion. In Pasternak it is most obviously aesthetic, and it is interesting to note that a key symbolic situation in Doctor Zhivago, that of the protagonist's contemplating and merging with nature while at a window, echoes and deepens the use of windows as a membrane between the human and natural realms found in Years of Childhood and elsewhere in Aksakov.

Although the authors mentioned, along with others, represent a strain in Russian culture operating as a component in works of great complexity, the more obvious pastoral has also found expression in writers such as Mikhail Prishvin and Vladimir Soloukhin (who deliberately alludes to Aksakov in some works).[3] The movement of the last decade and a half known as "village

3. Prishvin is also reminiscent of Aksakov in the problems of classification by genre that his works have presented. See Ray J. Parrott, Jr., "Questions of Art,

prose," embracing such writers of great talent as Vasilii Shuk-shin, Viktor Astaf'ev, and Valentin Rasputin, attests to the con-tinued, even renewed viability of pastoral in the present day. Their works have aroused criticism and controversy in the Soviet Union precisely because they are perceived as turning away from the demands of contemporary society and the literary forms felt to embody and serve them. The only pastoral world now is that of the village, but the assertion of the value of the ordinary, the sacralization of nature and of tradition (even as it dies), the so-phisticated simplification of form characteristic of pastoral, evinces the continued importance of a pastoral orientation in Russian literature and for Russian culture more broadly. As the first and fullest expression of this aspect of the Russian, and more broadly the modern, sensibility, the works of Sergei Timo-feevich Aksakov remain central to the intense search for value that informs literature in Russia and renders it vital far beyond its immediate boundaries.

Fact, and Genre in Mikhail Prishvin," pp. 465–477. Deliberately echoing Ak-sakov, to whom he alludes, Soloukhin has written a book on mushroom hunting entitled *The Third Hunt* (*Tret'ia okhota*). Soloukhin also refers to Aksakov in various other works.

Bibliography

I. AKSAKOV'S WORKS

There is no complete edition of all of Aksakov's works. However, all of his major works appear in each of the following editions.

Aksakov, Sergei Timofeevich. *Polnoe sobranie sochinenii S. T. Aksakova.* 6 vols. St. Petersburg: Martynov, 1886.
———. *Sobranie sochinenii.* 4 vols. Moscow: GIKhL, 1955–1956.
———. *Sobranie sochinenii.* 5 vols. Moscow: Pravda, 1966.

I have used the 1955–1956 edition for most references. Aksakov's three major works have been translated into English. The trilogy was translated by J. D. Duff, under the titles *A Russian Gentleman* (*Semeinaia khronika*) (London: E. Arnold; New York: Longmans, Green, 1917); *Years of Childhood* (*Detskie gody Bagrova-vnuka*) (London: E. Arnold; New York: Longmans, Green, 1916); and *A Russian Schoolboy* (*Vospominaniia*), which also includes a translation of "Butterfly Collecting" (London: E. Arnold; New York: Longmans, Green, 1917). *Family Chronicle*, along with excerpts from *Years of Childhood* and *Reminiscences*, has also been translated by M. C. Beverley (London: Routledge; New York: E. P. Dutton, 1924), and *Years of Childhood* has been translated by Alec Brown (New York: Random House, 1960). The Duff translations were republished by Oxford University Press in 1923 (*Years of Childhood*) and 1924 (*A Russian Gentleman* and *A Russian Schoolboy*), with various subsequent editions. They have also been reissued in paperback by Hyperion Press of Westport, Conn. (1977). The Beverley translation of *Family Chronicle* was reissued in paperback by Dutton in 1961.

II. MANUSCRIPTS AND UNPUBLISHED LETTERS

Letters, manuscripts, and other archival material cited are preserved for the most part in the Aksakov *fondy* (files) and other *fondy* of the following archives in the Soviet Union:

Central Government Archives of Literature and Art, Moscow (Tsentral'nyi gosudarstvennyi arkhiv literatury i iskusstva). Abbreviation: TsGALI.

Institute of Russian Literature and Art, Pushkin House, Leningrad (Institut russkoi literatury i iskusstva, Pushkinskii dom). Abbreviation: PD.

Manuscript Division of the Lenin Library, Moscow (Biblioteka imeni Lenina, rukopisnyi otdel). Abbreviation: LL.

III. PUBLISHED SOURCES

There has been no systematic publication of Aksakov's letters. The following bibliography lists only the more significant publications of letters; for a more complete bibliography of individual letters and fragments, see K. D. Muratova, *Istoriia russkoi literatury XIX veka, bibliograficheskii ukazatel'* (Moscow and Leningrad: AN SSSR, 1962).

Afanas'ev, A. N. "Zakliatyi tsarevich." In A. N. Afanas'ev, *Narodnye russkie skazki.* 3 vols. Edited by V. Ia. Propp. Moscow: GIKhL, 1957.

Aksakov, Ivan Sergeevich. *I. S. Aksakov v ego pis'makh.* Vols. 1–3, Moscow, 1888–1892; vol. 4, St. Petersburg, 1896. Vols. 1 and 2 contain excerpts from Sergei Timofeevich's letters to his son.

———. "Ocherk semeinogo byta Aksakovykh." *I. S. Aksakov v ego pis'makh.* 1:11–24.

Aksakov, Konstantin Sergeevich. "On the Internal State of Russia." Translated by Valentine Snow. In *Russian Intellectual History: An Anthology,* edited by Marc Raeff. New York: Harcourt, Brace and World, 1966.

Aksakova, Vera Sergeevna. *Dnevnik Very Sergeevny Aksakovoi (1854–5).* Edited by N. V. Golitsyn and P. E. Shchegolev. St. Petersburg: Ogni, 1913.

Annenkov, P. V. "S. T. Aksakov i ego *Semeinaia khronika.*" In *Vospominaniia i kriticheskie ocherki: Sobranie statei i zametok 1849–1868 godov.* 2 vols. (St. Petersburg, 1879), 2:109–132.

———. *Zamechatel'noe desiatiletie.* In *Literaturnye vospominaniia,* edited by B. M. Eikhenbaum. Leningrad: Academia, 1928.

Arkhangel'skii, A. S. "S. T. Aksakov: Detstvo i studenchestvo." *Russkoe obozrenie* 34 (July 1895): 37–56; 34 (August 1895): 498–513; 35 (Sept. 1895): 63–92.

Aronson, M., and S. Reiser. *Literaturnye kruzhki i salony.* Edited by B. M. Eikhenbaum. Leningrad: Priboi, 1929.

Bialyi, G. A. "Aksakov." *Istoriia russkoi literatury,* vol. 7. Edited by B. P. Gorodetskii. Moscow and Leningrad: Akademiia nauk SSSR, Institut russkoi literatury, 1955, pp. 571–595.

Brodskii, L. N., ed. *Literaturnye salony i kruzhki: Pervaia polovina XIX veka.* Moscow and Leningrad: Academia, 1930.

Chicherin, A. V. "Russkoe slovo Sergeia Aksakova." *Russkaia literatura,* 1976, no. 2, pp. 120–126.

Danilov, V. V. "S. T. Aksakov, S. N. Glinka i V. V. Izmailov v Moskovskom tsenzurnom komitete." *Izvestiia po russkomu iazyku i slovesnosti*, 1928, vol. 1, book 2, pp. 507–524.

Dmitriev, M. A. *Melochi iz zapasa moei pamiati.* Moscow, 1869.

Dobroliubov, N. A. "Derevenskaia zhizn' pomeshchika v starye gody." In *Sobranie sochinenii.* 9 vols. Moscow: GIKhL, 1962, 2:290–326.

Dunin, A. A. "Materialy po istorii russkoi literatury i kul'tury: I. S. Aksakov v Iaroslavle." *Russkaia mysl'*, 1915, no. 8, pp. 107–131.

Durylin, S. "Gogol' i Aksakovy (s tremia neizdannymi zapiskami Gogolia)." *Zven'ia* 3–4. Moscow and Leningrad: Academia, 1934, pp. 325–364.

Eliade, Mircea. *Images and Symbols.* Translated by Philip Mairet. New York: Sheed and Ward, 1969.

————. *Patterns in Comparative Religion.* Translated by Rosemary Sheed. Cleveland: World Publishing Co., 1963.

Freeborn, Richard. *The Rise of the Russian Novel.* Cambridge: Cambridge University Press, 1973.

Frye, Northrop. *Anatomy of Criticism.* New York: Atheneum, 1968.

Gray, Camilla. *The Russian Experiment in Art, 1863–1922.* New York: Abrams, 1971.

Karamzin, N. M. "Rytsar' nashego vremeni." In *Izbrannye sochineniia* 2 vols. Moscow and Leningrad: Khudozhestvennaia literatura, 1964, 1:755–782.

Khomiakov, A. S. "Sergei Timofeevich Aksakov." In *Polnoe sobranie sochinenii.* Moscow, 1900, 3:370–375.

Kriazheva, V. P. "Iz istorii ideino-tvorcheskikh sviazei S. T. Aksakova s N. V. Gogolem." *Uchenye zapiski Leningradskogo gosudarstvennogo pedagogicheskogo instituta im. Gertsena* 245 (1963): 217–235.

————. "K voprosu ob esteticheskikh vzgliadakh S. T. Aksakova." *Uchenye zapiski Leningradskogo gosudarstvennogo pedagogicheskogo instituta im. Gertsena* 273 (1965): 32–49.

Kruti, I. "S. T. Aksakov v istorii russkoi teatral'noi kritiki." *Teatr: Sbornik statei i materialov.* Moscow: VTO, 1945, pp. 183–199.

Kuleshov, V. I. *Slavianofily i russkaia literatura.* Moscow: Khudozhestvennaia literatura, 1976.

Likhachev, D. S. *Poetika drevnerusskoi literatury.* Leningrad: Nauka, 1967.

Lomunov, K. N., S. S. Dmitriev, and A. S. Kurilov, eds. *Literaturnye vzgliady i tvorchestvo slavianofilov: 1830–1850–ye gody.* Moscow: Nauka, 1978.

Lotman, Iu. M. *Struktura khudozhestvennogo teksta.* Moscow: Iskusstvo, 1970.

Luzhin, N. L. "K voprosu o vzaimootnosheniiakh L. N. Tolstogo i S. T.

Aksakova." *Izvestiia Akademii nauk SSSR, otdelenie literatury i iazyka*, 15, no. 2 (March–April 1956): 161–165.

Lynen, John F. *The Pastoral Art of Robert Frost.* Yale Studies in English, no. 147. New Haven: Yale University Press, 1960.

Maikov, L. N., ed. "Pis'ma S. T., K. S., i I. S. Aksakovykh k I. S. Turgenevu," *Russkoe obozrenie*, 1894, no. 8, pp. 460–484; no. 9, pp. 5–38; no. 10, pp. 478–501; no. 11, pp. 7–30; and no. 12, pp. 591–601.

Maikov, Valerian. *N. V. Gogol' i S. T. Aksakov. K istorii literaturnykh vliianii.* St. Petersburg, 1892.

Markov, Vladimir. "The Poetry of Russian Prose-Writers." *California Slavic Studies* 1 (1960): 73–109.

Mashinskii, S. I. "Iz istorii tsenzorskoi deiatel'nosti S. T. Aksakova (po novym materialam)." *Izvestiia Akademii nauk SSSR, otdelenie literatury i iazyka*, 18, no. 3 (May–June 1959): 238–252.

———. "Novye materialy o S. T. Aksakove." *Izvestiia Akademii nauk SSSR, otdelenie literatury i iazyka*, 14, no. 3 (May–June 1955): 239–254.

———. *S. T. Aksakov: Zhizn' i tvorchestvo.* Moscow: GIKhL, 1961.

———. *S. T. Aksakov: Zhizn' i tvorchestvo.* 2d, expanded ed. Moscow: Khudozhestvennaia literatura, 1973.

Miliukov, Pavel M. "S. T. Aksakov." In Pavel M. Miliukov, *Iz istorii russkoi intelligentsii.* 2d ed. St. Petersburg, 1903, pp. 52–72.

Nabokov, Vladimir. *Speak, Memory.* Rev. ed. New York: Putnam's, 1966.

Nelson, Lowry, Jr. "Night Thoughts on the Gothic Novel." *Yale Review*, n.s. 2, no. 2 (Winter 1963): 236–257.

Ortega y Gasset, José. *Meditations on Hunting.* Translated by Howard B. Wescott. New York: Scribners, 1972.

Ostrogorskii, Viktor. *Sergei Timofeevich Aksakov: Kritiko-biograficheskii ocherk.* St. Petersburg: Martynov, 1901.

Panaeva, Avdot'ia. *Vospominaniia.* 4th ed. Edited by Kornei Chukovskii. Moscow and Leningrad: Academia, 1933.

Parrott, Ray J., Jr. "Questions of Art, Fact, and Genre in Mikhail Prishvin." *Slavic Review* 36, no. 3 (September 1977): 465–477.

Pavlov, M. N., ed. "Iz semeinoi perepiski starikov Aksakovykh." *Russkii arkhiv*, 1894, no. 3, pp. 99–136. Letters of Aksakov's parents.

———. "S. T. Aksakov kak tsenzor." *Russkii arkhiv*, 1898, no. 5, pp. 81–96.

Piaget, Jean. *The Moral Judgment of the Child.* Translated by Marjorie Gabain. New York: Macmillan, Free Press, 1965.

Ponomarev, S. "Iz pisem k M. A. Maksimovichu: Pis'ma S. T. Aksakova." *Kievskaia starina*, 1883, no. 4, pp. 829–840.

Pritchett, V. S. "A Russian Cinderella." In *The Living Novel and*

Later Appreciations. New York: Random House, 1964, pp. 413–419.

Propp, V. Ia. "Ritual'nyi smekh v fol'klore: Po povodu skazki o Nesmeiane." In *Fol'klor i deistvitel'nost'.* Moscow: Nauka, 1976, pp. 174–204.

Radcliffe, Ann. *The Mysteries of Udolpho.* Edited and with an introduction by Bonamy Dobrée. New York: Oxford University Press, 1966.

Rosenmeyer, Thomas G. *The Green Cabinet: Theocritus and the European Pastoral Lyric.* Berkeley and Los Angeles: University of California Press, 1969; paperback ed. 1973.

Shenrok, V. I. "S. T. Aksakov i ego sem'ia." *Zhurnal Ministervstva narodnogo prosveshcheniia,* 1904, no. 10, pp. 355–418; no. 11, pp. 245–271; no. 12, pp. 229–290.

Shishkov, A. S. *Rassuzhdenie o starom i novom sloge rossiiskogo iazyka.* St. Petersburg, 1803.

———. *Razgovory o slovesnosti.* St. Petersburg, 1811.

Shubert, A. I. *Moia zhizn'.* Edited by A. Derman. Leningrad: Academia, 1929.

Smirnov, V. D. *Aksakovy, ikh zhizn' i literaturnaia deiatel'nost': Biograficheskii ocherk.* St. Petersburg, 1895.

Smith, Barbara Hernnstein. *Poetic Closure: A Study of How Poems End.* Chicago: University of Chicago Press, 1968.

Soloukhin, Vladimir. *Tret'ia okhota.* Moscow: Sovetskaia Rossiia, 1968.

———. "Volshebnaia palochka Aksakova." In *S liricheskikh pozitsii.* Moscow: Sovetskii pisatel', 1965, pp. 58–65.

Stanzel, Franz. *Narrative Situations in the Novel.* Translated by James P. Pusack. Bloomington: Indiana University Press, 1971.

Talbot-Rice, Tamara. *A Concise History of Russian Art.* New York: Praeger, 1963.

Todorov, Tsvetan. "Narrative Men." In *The Poetics of Prose,* translated by Richard Howard. Ithaca, N.Y.: Cornell University Press, 1977.

Tolstoi, L. N. *Polnoe sobranie sochinenii.* Jubilee edition. Moscow: GIZ-Goslitizdat, 1928–1959.

Trutovskii, K. A. "Vospominaniia o S. T. Aksakove." *Russkii khudozhestvennyi arkhiv,* 1892, no. 2, pp. 49–56; nos. 3–4, pp. 129–135.

Tseitlin, A. S. *Stanovlenie realizma v russkoi literatury: Russkii fiziologicheskii ocherk.* Moscow: Nauka, 1965.

Walicki, Andrzej. *The Slavophile Controversy: History of a Conservative Utopia in Nineteenth-Century Russian Thought.* Translated by Hilda Andrews-Rusiecka. Oxford: At the Clarendon Press, 1975.

Index

Studies of the Russian Institute

Abram Bergson. *Soviet National Income in 1937.* 1953.

Ernest J. Simmons, Jr., ed. *Through the Glass of Soviet Literature: Views of Russian Society.* 1953.

Thad Paul Alton. *Polish Postwar Economy.* 1954.

David Granick. *Management of the Industrial Firm in the USSR: A Study in Soviet Economic Planning.* 1954.

Allen S. Whiting. *Soviet Policies in China, 1917–1924.* 1954.

George S. N. Luckyj. *Literary Politics in the Soviet Ukraine, 1917–1934.* 1956.

Michael Boro Petrovich. *The Emergence of Russian Panslavism, 1856–1870.* 1956.

Thomas Taylor Hammond. *Lenin on Trade Unions and Revolution, 1893–1917.* 1956.

David Marshall Lang. *The Last Years of the Georgian Monarchy, 1658–1832.* 1957.

James William Morley. *The Japanese Thrust into Siberia, 1918.* 1957.

Alexander G. Park. *Bolshevism in Turkestan, 1917–1927.* 1957.

Herbert Marcuse. *Soviet Marxism: A Critical Analysis.* 1958.

Charles B. McLane. *Soviet Policy and the Chinese Communists, 1931–1946.* 1958.

Oliver H. Radkey. *The Agrarian Foes of Bolshevism: Promise and Defeat of the Russian Socialist Revolutionaries, February to October, 1917.* 1958.

Ralph Talcott Fisher, Jr. *Pattern for Soviet Youth: A Study of the Congresses of the Komsomol, 1918–1954.* 1959.

Alfred Erich Senn. *The Emergence of Modern Lithuania.* 1959.

Elliot R. Goodman. *The Soviet Design for a World State.* 1960.

John N. Hazard. *Settling Disputes in Soviet Society: The Formative Years of Legal Institutions.* 1960.

David Joravsky. *Soviet Marxism and Natural Science, 1917–1932.* 1961.

Maurice Friedberg. *Russian Classics in Soviet Jackets.* 1962.

Alfred J. Rieber. *Stalin and the French Communist Party, 1941–1947.* 1962.

Theodore K. von Laue. *Sergei Witte and the Industrialization of Russia.* 1962.

John A. Armstrong. *Ukrainian Nationalism.* 1963.

Oliver H. Radkey. *The Sickle under the Hammer: The Russian Socialist Revolutionaries in the Early Months of Soviet Rule.* 1963.

Kermit E. McKenzie. *Comintern and World Revolution, 1928–1943: The Shaping of Doctrine.* 1964.

Harvey L. Dyck. *Weimar Germany and Soviet Russia, 1926–1933: A Study in Diplomatic Instability.* 1966.

(Above titles published by Columbia University Press.)

Harold J. Noah. *Financing Soviet Schools*. New York: Columbia University Teachers College, 1966.

John M. Thompson. *Russia, Bolshevism, and the Versailles Peace*. Princeton: Princeton Univ. Press, 1966.

Paul Avrich. *The Russian Anarchists*. Princeton: Princeton Univ. Press, 1967.

Loren R. Graham. *The Soviet Academy of Sciences and the Communist Party, 1927–1932*. Princeton: Princeton Univ. Press, 1967.

Robert A. Maguire. *Red Virgin Soil: Soviet Literature in the 1920's*. Princeton: Princeton Univ. Press, 1968.

T. H. Rigby. *Communist Party Membership in the U.S.S.R, 1917–1967*. Princeton: Princeton Univ. Press, 1968.

Richard T. de George. *Soviet Ethics and Morality*. Ann Arbor: Univ. of Michigan Press, 1969.

Jonathan Frankel. *Vladimir Akimov on the Dilemmas of Russian Marxism, 1895–1903*. Cambridge: Cambridge Univ. Press, 1969.

William Zimmerman. *Soviet Perspectives on International Relations, 1956–1967*. Princeton: Princeton Univ. Press, 1969.

Paul Avrich. *Kronstadt, 1921*. Princeton: Princeton Univ. Press, 1970.

Ezra Mendelsohn. *Class Struggle in the Pale: The Formative Years of the Jewish Workers' Movement in Tsarist Russia*. Cambridge: Cambridge Univ. Press, 1970.

Edward J. Brown. *The Proletarian Episode in Russian Literature*. New York: Columbia Univ. Press, 1971.

Reginald E. Zelnik. *Labor and Society in Tsarist Russia: The Factory Workers of St. Petersburg, 1855–1870*. Stanford: Stanford Univ. Press, 1971.

Patricia K. Grimsted. *Archives and Manuscript Repositories in the USSR: Moscow and Leningrad*. Princeton: Princeton Univ. Press, 1972.

Ronald G. Suny. *The Baku Commune, 1917–1918*. Princeton: Princeton Univ. Press, 1972.

Edward J. Brown. *Mayakovsky: A Poet in the Revolution*. Princeton: Princeton Univ. Press, 1973.

Milton Ehre. *Oblomov and his Creator: The Life and Art of Ivan Goncharov*. Princeton: Princeton Univ. Press, 1973.

Henry Krisch. *German Politics under Soviet Occupation*. New York: Columbia Univ. Press, 1974.

Henry W. Morton and Rudolf L. Tökés, eds. *Soviet Politics and Society in the 1970's*. New York: Free Press, 1974.

William G. Rosenberg. *Liberals in the Russian Revolution*. Princeton: Princeton Univ. Press, 1974.

Richard G. Robbins, Jr. *Famine in Russia, 1891–1892*. New York: Columbia Univ. Press, 1975.

Vera Dunham. *In Stalin's Time: Middleclass Values in Soviet Fiction*. Cambridge: Cambridge Univ. Press, 1976.

Walter Sablinsky. *The Road to Bloody Sunday*. Princeton: Princeton Univ. Press, 1976.

William Mills Todd III. *The Familiar Letter as a Literary Genre in the Age of Pushkin*. Princeton: Princeton Univ. Press, 1976.

Elizabeth Valkenier. *Russian Realist Art. The State and Society: The Peredvizhniki and Their Tradition*. Ann Arbor: Ardis, 1977.

Susan Solomon. *The Soviet Agrarian Debate.* Boulder, Colo.: Westview, 1978.

Sheila Fitzpatrick, ed. *Cultural Revolution in Russia, 1928–1931.* Bloomington: Univ. of Indiana Press, 1978.

Peter Solomon. *Soviet Criminologists and Criminal Policy: Specialists in Policy-Making.* New York: Columbia Univ. Press, 1978.

Kendall E. Bailes. *Technology and Society under Lenin and Stalin: Origins of the Soviet Technical Intelligentsia, 1917–1941.* Princeton: Princeton Univ. Press, 1978.

Leopold H. Haimson, ed. *The Politics of Rural Russia, 1905–1914.* Bloomington: Univ. of Indiana Press, 1979.

Theodore H. Friedgut. *Political Participation in the USSR.* Princeton: Princeton Univ. Press, 1979.

Sheila Fitzpatrick. *Education and Social Mobility in the Soviet Union, 1921–1934.* Cambridge: Cambridge Univ. Press, 1979.

Wesley Andrew Fisher. *The Soviet Marriage Market: Mate-Selection in Russia and the USSR.* New York: Praeger, 1980.

Jonathan Frankel. *Prophecy and Politics: Socialism, Nationalism, and the Russian Jews, 1862–1917.* Cambridge: Cambridge Univ. Press, 1981.

Robin Feuer Miller. *Dostoevsky and The Idiot: Author, Narrator, and Reader.* Cambridge, Mass.: Harvard Univ. Press, 1981.

Diane Koenker. *Moscow Workers and the 1917 Revolution.* Princeton: Princeton Univ. Press, 1981.

Patricia K. Grimsted. *Archives and Manuscript Repositories in the USSR: Estonia, Latvia, Lithuania, and Belorussia.* Princeton: Princeton Univ. Press, 1981.

Ezra Mendelsohn. *Zionism in Poland: The Formative Years, 1915–1926.* New Haven: Yale Univ. Press, 1982.

Hannes Adomeit. *Soviet Risk-Taking and Crisis Behavior.* Winchester, Mass.: George Allen & Unwin, 1982.

Seweryn Bialer and Thane Gustafson, eds. *Russia at the Crossroads: The 26th Congress of the CPSU.* Winchester, Mass.: George Allen & Unwin, 1982.